MOCKINGBIRD AT THE MOVIES

Edited by C. J. Green
with David Peterson

Mockingbird Ministries
Charlottesville, VA

Mockingbird Ministries
100 West Jefferson Street
Charlottesville, VA 22902
www.mbird.com

Cover design by Tom Martin. Published 2015 by Mockingbird Ministries.

ISBN-13: 978-0-9907927-5-8
ISBN-10: 0-9907927-5-7

ACKNOWLEDGEMENTS

Many thanks to all the writers who contributed to this publication, for bringing invaluable light and grace to the printed page. A huge thank you to David Peterson for his edits during the book's early drafts. Thanks to Ken Wilson, Ethan Richardson, and Luke Wilson for copyediting; David Zahl for oversights and insights; Tom Martin for yet another fantastic cover; Will McDavid for formatting wisdom; Maddy Partridge for emotional balance; and Christ Church, Charlottesville for shelter. Most of all, thanks to the wider Mockingbird community, all of our readers and donors: for their prayers and support, we are unendingly grateful.

CONTENTS

INTRODUCTION

It was an ill-defined notion but there nevertheless—my vague childhood idea that 'Hollywood' had it in for me. As if it were a secret society that gathered around candlelit conference tables discussing how it could sneak more sex, drugs, and sin into movies in order to catch innocent minds like my own unawares. As a kid, I'd hear people, especially with Christian tendencies, scoff about gratuitous violence and say, "Classic Hollywood." But that a great many movies might be inappropriate for children doesn't discount the fact that the fear of movies often goes to battle with the lived experience of them: the comfort of a glamorous rom-com, or the catharsis of a well-crafted tear-jerker, or the way that a foulmouthed comedy makes your stomach hurt from laughing.

This little book, however, attempts not to point out the 'intersection' of Christianity and film, as though they were two distinct entities, but more to say that the Gospel seems to breathe out of those things that affect us the most, film included. This is what French philosopher Simone Weil meant when she wrote, "The world is the closed door. It is a barrier. And at the same time it is the way through...Every separation is a link." The questionable output of Hollywood might seem a far cry from the Gospel of Christ, but we find, in the end, that they aren't as incompatible as they might at first seem.

The first movie that made me cry was the full-length *Pokémon* movie. As the protagonist, Ash, dove in front of a magical ice blast in order to stop the climactic final battle, he turned to stone before my very eyes. I was just five years old and completely beside myself. Only when Ash had been showered in the tears of all of his Pokémon was he thawed out to life, and as he was raised I realized that I would have to see this again, and again, and again, if only just to feel what I felt that first time through.

Sometimes we watch movies just to feel something—to cry or laugh or shrink back into the couch, listening to our pulses speed up as the private eye descends the creaky staircase into the serial killer's basement. Movies themselves are like private eyes, sneaking into the basement of our own subconscious, shining a flashlight in the dark. They serve as an external force poking at an internal sleeper, waking him up and bringing him to the surface in some sort of emotional outburst. This is something we at Mockingbird refer to as 'abreaction'—even if a movie doesn't read like a Bible study, it nevertheless takes a heavy dose of truth to wake the dead. A good movie makes you want to talk about it, or watch it again, or force someone else to watch it with you while you watch them, hoping they have the same experience you did the first go-round.

As a ministry, Mockingbird seeks to point out the natural links between the Gospel message and the doldrums of daily life, in which movies often play a significant role: NPR reported in 2013 that Americans spent over twenty billion dollars on movies, and my own mother reported that in 1978 she watched *Grease* seven times back-to-back. We live in an increasingly visual society, where pictures on social media denote how we feel, where we can order pizza with emojis. But something about the 'motion picture' remains particularly special, because it's not just the visuals—it's the acting and the music and the stories. And often the stories work like doors, opening up and leading us into a world of sacrifice, or freedom, or deep human suffering. They can be arrows pointing us to what matters most. And, in a world where the Christian faith can feel like an extracurricular, the ministry of everyday life cannot risk ignoring these silver signposts.

Mockingbird at the Movies brings together the many voices of Mockingbird's contributing writers, from all tastes, backgrounds, and perspectives. We've got essays from film experts, casual fans, pastors, theologians, and even a few critics. But what you hold in your hands is not necessarily a book of 'reviews.' Obviously we love the movies we've written about, and hope you do too, but with this project we've decided to dish out less opinions than observations, explaining why these are the movies that have stayed with us, in hopes that they stay with you as well. If one essay doesn't strike your fancy, move on to the next, because no two are the same. Several of them first appeared on our website, and many, including a wide-ranging selection of annotated lists, are brand new.

By no means should this little book be considered a comprehensive look at cinematic spirituality. We tried to collect a broad smattering of titles from a wide range of genres, both new and old, familiar and strange, scary and funny and moving—but the case is far from closed. The Spirit of God continues stretching toward us, using everything in his way—from fantasy movies to cult classics to Oscar-winning dramadies—to keep us from forgetting the good news of God's indiscriminate compassion for humankind. Our hope is that these essays, much like Pokémon tears, will help turn stone to flesh or, at the very least, serve as a healthy reminder to pop in a movie every once in a while, turn down the lights, and kick up your feet.

— C. J. Green, Editor

ROUGHING UP WES ANDERSON

by

David Zahl

It is easy to forget that all of Wes Anderson's films have happy endings. Sadness and loss pervade much of his work, as does a sardonic sense of humor that frequently goes along with a downcast view of the world. Plus, the urban aesthetes who comprise the most loyal portion of his audience tend to be a cynical lot, so you could excuse casual observers for extrapolating a certain darkness. Yet they would be mistaken. He always leaves viewers on an upbeat note.

This does not mean that his work steers clear of ugliness or tragedy. Dramatic upheavals are common. But in his filmic universe, catastrophe serves a redemptive purpose. More than that, it signals the hand of God.

The very mention of a religious dimension to Wes Anderson's films may sound surprising, even bizarre. It is certainly not what he is known for. Critics praise his visual imagination, his attention to detail, his pet themes, and oft-imitated (but never replicated) whimsy. They do not, as a group, gravitate toward spiritual language when discussing his movies. If anything, Wes has been criticized for the emotional distance of his dollhouse-like visions. The net effect of the fanciful scenery and mannered dialogue is to keep the viewer from fully entering into the picture, heart-wise, to say nothing of the spirit. Everything is so gloriously precise; it seems there is no room in a Wes Anderson film for any deity other than Wes Anderson.

While such a view may not be entirely unfounded, it does not account for the stories themselves, in particular the trilogy of *The Darjeeling Limited*, *Moonrise Kingdom*, and *The Grand Budapest Hotel*. What emerges is something more akin to the fake Italian talk show interview with Wes that's included on the Criterion edition of *The Life Aquatic*.[1] Following a series of increasingly awkward exchanges, the befuddled host asks the director point-blank if he believes in God. Wes answers, "Eh, I think so. Yeah. I mean, roughly."

By "roughly" he no doubt meant "approximately." Yet given the films in question he might as well have been using it in the physical sense. In Anderson's films, God intervenes upon hapless human beings with force, often in the guise of something cataclysmic and unpleasant—a divine interruption as opposed to something engineered by one of the protagonists. However precious his sensibility may be in other ways—that is, the opposite of gothic—Wes demonstrates time and again an implicit grasp of what novelist Flannery

1. *Monda Monda!* is the title given to this overseas Merv Griffin send-up, a worthy follow-up to *The Peter Bradley Show* feature on *The Royal Tenenbaums* DVD, which parodied Charlie Rose to hilarious effect.

O'Connor once described in relation to her own work:

> I suppose the reasons for the use of so much violence in modern fiction will differ with each writer who uses it, but in my own stories I have found that violence is strangely capable of returning my characters to reality and preparing them to accept their moment of grace. Their heads are so hard that almost nothing else will do the work. This idea, that reality is something to which we must be returned at considerable cost, is one which is seldom understood by the casual reader, but it is one which is implicit in the Christian view of the world.[2]

Where Flannery speaks of hard-headedness, Wes' characters tend to be softer, not so much calloused by suffering and indignity as consumed with charming minutiae and narcissistic navel-gazing. But the inwardness proves intractable and warrants just as much of an abrupt, outside interruption. In *The Royal Tenenbaums*, it takes the form of a maniacal car crash; in *The Life Aquatic*, a pirate attack; in *Fantastic Mr. Fox*, an uprooting; and so on.

Nowhere does Wes reflect Flannery's perspective more blatantly than in *The Darjeeling Limited* (2007). The film tells the story of three privileged brothers, the Whitmans, and their sub-continental 'spiritual journey'—by rail—following the sudden death of their father and prolonged absence of their mother. As we find out, each sibling has been distracting himself from the pain in his own self-destructive fashion: Francis (Owen Wilson) through suicidal recklessness, Peter (Adrien Brody) through emotional isolation, Jack (Jason Schwartzman) through co-dependency, and all of them through substance abuse. Together they comprise a lovable if dysfunctional set of siblings, arrested in their development to a comical degree, yet doing the best they can with the hand they have been dealt. That is to say, they are looking for healing. Sort of.

---

2. O'Connor, Flannery. "On Her Own Work," collected in *Mystery and Manners*.

Unfortunately, the Whitman brothers sabotage the purpose of their trip for themselves, wreaking so much havoc that they are booted from their train in the middle of the Indian countryside. Standing on the railway platform, they receive a telegram from their estranged mother (living in India herself), entreating them to stay away from the convent where she has taken up residence. Her message leaves them even more demoralized and defeated than before.

The next morning, making their way back to civilization alongside a roaring river, they spy three little boys—brothers perhaps—precariously traversing the busiest part of the rapids, groceries in tow. When the boys' makeshift ferry capsizes, all three Whitmans spring into action and attempt to save their younger Indian counterparts. They are only partly successful; one of the boys dies. The two surviving children bring the dumbstruck Whitmans back to their village where the camera lingers silently on several scenes of grief, shifting the tone of the film dramatically.

We watch as a day or so later the Whitmans board a bus, bound for the city. A fellow passenger asks what brought them to such a remote place. Francis answers, "Well, originally, I guess we came here on a spiritual journey. But that didn't really pan out." At that moment, one of the other children hops on board and invites them to the boy's funeral. They accept without hesitation.

The next scene is masterful. As The Kinks' "Strangers" plays, Wes conducts a slow-motion montage of the burial. The sun is shining though, and everyone is wearing white. The father anoints his deceased son's body with oil, and places him on a bier. After the fire dies down, the mourners wash themselves in the river, Whitmans included. Wes doesn't dwell on the baptismal imagery, but it's there for all to see. They are not the same afterward, at least not wholly. They are more patient with one another, less petty, lighter somehow.

The accident represents the hinge upon which not only the film turns, but the Whitmans themselves. The death of the boy brings them into contact with their own grief, and suddenly all of their attempts to circumvent their pain, including the spiritual ones, dissolve into thin air. At last their chattering stops, and the brothers take notice of their neighbors, perhaps for the first time. Their spiritual journey begins where they think it ends.

No one knows exactly what Wes and his co-writers were trying to say in the film, if anything. But the tale they decided to tell bears out an inconvenient truth: You cannot contrive a spiritual experience. In fact, the attempt tends to backfire. Breakthroughs of the kind that the Whitmans undergo cannot be planned with laminated itineraries. Instead, spiritual experiences happen to a person, and often through what that looks like a disaster.

Perhaps this is part of what Martin Luther meant in Thesis 21 of his Heidelberg Disputation, when he formulated:

> Only through suffering and the Cross can a sinner come to know God. Suffering is the only clear indication of God's operation on the sinner. Knowledge of God comes when God happens to us, when God does himself to us. We are crucified with Christ (Gal 2:19).

The Darjeeling Limited does not settle for merely lampooning Western attempts at commodifying Eastern spirituality. Instead, it gives us a glimpse of genuine spirituality, the sort which, fortunately for us, cannot be divorced from a theology of the cross. This is good news for the Whitmans, and it is good news for us. Despite our ingenuity with self-medication and denial, God is merciful enough to cut through our defenses, often when we least expect it.

It would be five years until Wes made his next live-action film, but when *Moonrise Kingdom* appeared in 2012, it derived much of its power from a similar dynamic.[3]

Moonrise Kingdom depicts the life of a fictional New England island named New Penzance during the summer of 1965, in the days leading up to "the region's worst meteorological disaster in the second half of the twentieth century." As with all Anderson films, it is filled to the brim with quirky detail, understated running jokes, eccentric characters, terrific music, and gorgeous set pieces. Thematically, his hallmarks are on full display: precocious children, melancholy adults, and joyful mischief. *Moonrise* may not usurp *Tenenbaums* as the most beloved of his films, or *Rushmore* as the giddiest, *Zissou* as the most idiosyncratic, or *Darjeeling* as the most profound, but it nonetheless represents the zenith of Wes' peculiar vision. In fact, it may be the most generous expression of it yet.

At the heart of *Moonrise Kingdom* lies the romance between two twelve-year-olds, Sam Shakusky and Suzy Bishop. Both are outcasts, orphan Sam being the round peg in New Penzance's square-holed Khaki Scout troupe, and Suzy the temperamental introvert in a family of mild-mannered boys and attorney parents. The two meet backstage at a Vacation Bible School production of "Noye's Fludde" and become fast pen pals. Their relationship quickly escalates to the point where they make arrangements to run away together, which they do, prompting an island-wide manhunt. Needless to say, once they are discovered, the adults on the island do all in their power to discourage the relationship.[4]

---

3. In between, he adapted Roald Dahl's *Fantastic Mr. Fox* into a masterpiece of stop-motion animation.

4. The leading authority figure on the island is Captain Sharp (Bruce Willis), a police officer who takes a special interest in Sam. As is often the case with Anderson, it is their relationship—the father-son one—that constitutes the true backbone of the film. The

Wes constructs the perfect recipe for a parable of law and grace, which he delivers with both aplomb and heart. Writing for *The New Yorker*, Richard Brody spelled this out beautifully:

> The young lovers, with their innocent, daring, intensely sincere, and consecrated love (and the ultimate proof of that consecration...is their willingness to die for each other), have provoked a scandal. They are assumed by the authorities—parents, scoutmasters, scouts, and even the state...to be doing something indecent, immoral, intolerable. They're outlaws, and the law—the ostensible moral law—is after them. But in Anderson's view, they're on the side of the good, indeed, the highest good. And he conveys the notion...that when true passion is thwarted or frustrated, all hell—or, rather, heaven—breaks loose, with a deluge of divine vengeance against those who would keep the couple apart.[5]

Sam and Suzy, however, are not so much vindicated as delivered. Meaning, they are just as much in need of saving as the adults tracking them down. The storm intervenes on everyone, driving them all back to—no joke—church, which provides the backdrop for a number of the film's key scenes.[6] The colorfully named St. Jack's witnesses the hatching of Sam and Suzy's affection, provides refuge from the storm outside, and brings the community together in a crucial way. It is the place where judgment is handed down (via Tilda Swinton, in a scene-stealing performance as Social Services),

---

dialogue they share also happens to be some of the best Wes has penned. For example:

> SAM: I knew we'd get in trouble. We knew people would be worried, but we did it anyway. But something also happened, when we first met. Something that we didn't do on purpose. Something happened, to us.
>
> CAPTAIN SHARP: That's very eloquent. I can't argue against anything you are saying. Then again I don't have to because you're twelve.

5. Brody, Richard. "What To See This Weekend: *Moonrise Kingdom*, Twice" in *The New Yorker*. May 24, 2012.

6. Trinity Episcopal Church in Newport, RI.

and where the final word of grace is ultimately pronounced.[7]

The law—in the moving target form of parents, guardians, other scouts, even the government—hounds Suzy and Sam mercilessly, bringing them to the point of exhaustion, which also happens to be the top of the church steeple. Again, it turns out that the kids need to be unburdened of their stubbornness and fear just as much as their elders do. For their own part, despite how they are experienced by the youths, the generally well-meaning adults share a common woundedness and desire for mercy themselves. Everyone on the island is ultimately in the same stolen canoe, as it were.[8]

Grace in *Moonrise Kingdom* arrives at precisely the last moment possible, when Suzy and Sam have lost hope and are about to plummet willingly to their deaths. The form it takes is biblical, too: Captain Sharp offers to *adopt* undeserving Sam, who has put the sad deputy through quite an ordeal.[9] It is one-way love, pure and simple, occasioned by a storm so fierce that any insurance company would term it 'an act of God.'

The final scene of the movie finds Sam dressed in new clothes, a junior constable's uniform, aka those of his ersatz savior. The birds are chirping, the sun is shining, and everything points to rebirth. The irony that these new clothes would normally signify the law only makes a charming movie that much more so.

---

7. There is something undeniably cool about the vintage Sunday School *accoutrements* in *Moonrise*, e.g. the camp chapel, the church basement, the play itself. One can only hope that the current accessories of American church life will date as well. It's a long shot.

8. The Edward Norton scoutmaster subplot sticks out as particularly touching. He too is changed by the crisis—the rigmarole in the final scene at Camp Ivanhoe may not have changed outwardly, but inwardly it's a whole new beast. He is no longer alienated or exasperated by his young charges, but exudes a fresh confidence and warmth.

9. "For you did not receive the spirit of slavery to fall back into fear, but you have received the Spirit of adoption as sons, by whom we cry, 'Abba! Father!'" (Rom 8:15).

Moonrise Kingdom was the first film that Wes chose not to set in the present day. He decided to go further back in time for the follow-up, 2014's *The Grand Budapest Hotel*, the majority of which takes place in 1932, on the eve of the Second World War. The titular resort is located in the fictional country of the Republic of Zubrowka, an Austo-Hungarian wonderland of the most Andersonian vintage.

The pacing is also considerably faster than any other of his productions—a bonafide romp—so madcap, in fact, that recounting the plot feels like a fruitless task.[10] Suffice it to say, it involves a dead widow, some villainous heirs, a priceless painting, a girl with a birthmark that looks like Mexico, and a whole lot of cologne. More importantly, at the center of the story lies another mediated father-son relationship, between the flamboyant concierge M. Gustave (Ralph Fiennes, in a performance for the ages) and Moustafa (Tony Revolori), his resourceful lobby boy, from whose perspective the story is told.

At the time of its release, a number of critics remarked on the nostalgia inherent in *Moonrise Kingdom* and especially *The Grand Budapest Hotel*, a nostalgia for a world that "never existed."[11] Novelist Michael Chabon picked up on this sense of longing in a beautiful section of his introduction to *The Wes Anderson Collection*:

> The world is so big, so complicated, so replete with marvels and surprises that it takes years for most people to begin to no-

10. As has become a ritual with Wes Anderson films, the reviews inevitably feel an obligation to justify or even apologize for their love of the filmmaker, as if to proclaim one's unqualified admiration risks living into an undesirable archetype—or at least one that hampers the very individuality Wes personifies. Alas, there's no more reliable method of finding well-heeled young people wrestling with the law of Thou Shalt Not Be Predictable, or whatever hipness code fuels the contrarianism surrounding Wes, than by googling reviews his films.

11. See especially Dave Itzkoff's profile for *The New York Times*, "Casting Shadows on a Fanciful World: Wes Anderson Evokes Nostalgia in *The Grand Hotel Budapest*". Feb 28, 2014.

> tice that it is, also, irretrievably broken. We call this period of research 'childhood'...Along the way, he or she...struggles to reconcile this fact with the ache of cosmic nostalgia that arises, from time to time, in the researcher's heart: an intimation of vanished glory, of lost wholeness, a memory of the world unbroken. We call the moment at which this ache first arises 'adolescence.' The feeling haunts people all their lives.

The closest we can come to this half-remembered Eden are the composites we find in works of art. To paraphrase Walker Percy, a painting or a book or a song can tell us things we already knew but didn't know we knew, summoning emotions we are afraid to feel (but need to). This is very similar to what we mean when we talk about the abreactive potential of art.

The nostalgia vibe goes hand in hand with Wes' preoccupation with loss—of a marriage, of a parent, of a loved one, of a tail. Which is not to suggest that his films could be called morbid. Far from it. The sorrow makes the mending of Chabon's broken pieces that much more breathtaking. This holds true for *The Grand Budapest Hotel*. Here we are mourning—on the surface at least—the passing of an entire world, one filled with delicious pastries and bad romantic poetry, Caspar David Friedrich landscapes and Egon Schiele figure studies, secret societies and mountain top monasteries.

Yet as glorious as the window dressing may be, the occasion for the hijinks is the closest Wes has come to real menace or evil, namely, the rise of fascism. The candy-coated breathlessness runs so thick that he would have lost the tragic context had he not taken special care to frame the story within different eras: 1968, 1985, and the present day. The framing also makes it clear that Moustafa's film-length soliloquy is fundamentally one of grace, his response not just to being loved by a father figure, but being saved by one. To borrow Gustave's phrase, what does the "glimmer of civilization in this barbaric slaughterhouse we once called humanity" actually look like? It looks like a man giving his life for his adopted child, as Gustave ultimately does for Moustafa.

What feels like an epilogue is where the actual target of the nostalgia comes in. Come to find out, the grown-up 1968 Moustafa—the one narrating the entire story—is not pining for a particular time or place that may never have existed, but for specific people (Gustave and Agatha) who loved him at a cost to themselves. He is nostalgic for a mountaintop experience, pun intended, born once again out of catastrophe—not a meteorological but a political and personal one. Everything else pales in comparison to that sacrifice. The elder Moustafa comes alive to the extent that he feels connected with that one act of radical generosity.

But the film doesn't end there. Moustafa eventually purchases the hotel, by then a faded husk of its former majesty, refashioning it as a memorial, which then blossoms into an actual stone monument where followers pay homage. The story lives on as a beacon of something more potent than happiness, something very close to grace. Or you might say, something eternal.

Or not. That's just one man's opinion.

How to Put On a Killer Show According to

SCHOOL OF ROCK

by

BRYAN JARRELL

Jack Black's *School of Rock* has graciously given me one of my fondest memories from seminary. The student body was on a nine-hour bus trip together returning to school from a missionary conference, and a few of us brought DVDs along to play on the bus's AV system. After watching *Star Wars* and a few other film classics, we were frantically searching for the next movie we'd need to entertain our theologically savvy theater on wheels. Like a DJ at a rockin' dance party, the pressure was on to choose the perfect next feature or risk completely killing the vibe.

"*School of Rock* could work," one of us suggested. "But it has swear words in it," cautioned one critic. "I agree we could use a comedy; do we have anything better?" asked a third. "Will it offend some of our international students?" asked a fourth. No better comedies were found, so one of us bravely stumbled to the front of the bumpy charter bus to press play on this risky cinematic gamble.

Those international students I just mentioned...that year, a handful of students from Africa's more violent hotspots had joined the student body. Nigerian students whose churches had been attacked by the terrorist group Boko Haram, Sudanese students who had fled as refugees to Kenya because of civil war, Rwandan students who had lived through the 1994 genocide. All of them Christians with deep faiths forged in persecution and hardship. And all of them, within the *School of Rock*'s first ten minutes, were falling out of their chairs in uncontrollable laughter.

The scene on the bus was surreal. As Jack Black reached pinnacle Jack-Black-ness with his role as Dewey Finn, a rock-loving front man who snags a substitute teaching gig at the state's best prep school, the white Americans of the bus would politely chuckle. It was dark outside and our smart phones had died a few hours earlier, so *School of Rock* was the only boredom-killing tool we had left. But those same gags would send the international students at the front of the bus into howls of laughter! These strong, brilliant, solemn black men of the church, acquainted with those hardships Americans only see in the news, were reduced to schoolgirl giggles and guffaws of joy at Jack Black's silver screen shenanigans.

Their laughter and passion proved infectious. Before long, the whole busful of stodgy theology types was laughing along with these Africans, wiping away our own Jack Black-inspired tears.

In the world of intercultural communication, it is often said that humor is among the most difficult levels of communication to translate. I have absolutely no idea why the movie connected with these specific men—*School of Rock* has so much going for it! The movie features a ton of excellent music, with tracks from The Who, Led Zeppelin, The Ramones, Cream, The Doors, and more. The kid actors are adorable, especially once you learn they're also the musicians and singers on the soundtrack. Joan Cusack is delightful as the straight-laced principal trying to keep a legion of prep school parents satisfied.

Those are all wonderful aspects of the film. But if I had to guess why *School of Rock* has such wide appeal—and if there's one thing that has only grown more widespread and relevant since 2003, it's the outrageous performancism lampooned in the movie. Indeed, *School of Rock* encapsulates how a voice of grace can undermine (and outperform!) the rigors of a culture that places outsized importance on a person's utility.

It is no secret that the world, with its resumes and scorekeeping and ladder-climbing, makes little distinction between our performance and our value. Think of standardized tests, annual reviews, progress reports, etc. Unfortunately, the church often works that way, too. One's significance is measured by one's 'giftedness' or how much one volunteers or provides financially as a 'giving unit.' It's not hard for that view to be mistakenly translated vertically: One's standing before God becomes interpreted through the lens of how well we're doing here below.

The prep school where the movie takes place, Horace Green, comes with all the neuroses you would expect in a culture of performance: children striving to meet their parents' high demands, parents afraid for their children's success, teachers afraid of their principal's no-nonsense attitude, and a principal afraid of the parents' wrath and isolated by fear of her teachers.

When Jack Black's character commits a bit of harmless identity fraud to substitute teach at the school (suspend your disbelief!), we see someone whose love for rock drives out the fear of performance. Dewey Finn is annoyed by his brother's girlfriend (Sarah Silverman), but not afraid of her. He's worried about what getting caught will mean for his students and his chance at the battle of the bands, but not so much that he does the 'wise' thing and brings the class band project to closure. He is the only character in *School of Rock* who is not motivated by the fear of measuring up.

Observe how much Dewey has his pulse on the 'law of performance' when he gets going about gold stars and demerits and 'the man.' After Dewey declares all-day recess, star student Summer yelps incredulously, "How do we get gold stars if all we have is recess?" Can you hear the gasp of death in her voice? Dewey responds: "As long as I'm here, there will be no grades or gold stars or demerits. We're gonna have recess all the time...You're not hearing me, girl. I'm in charge now, OK? And I say recess. Go. Play and have fun, now." Can you see in your mind the wild, subversive passion in Dewey Finn's eyes?

It's fearless.

When Dewey later defends his antinomian-esque lawlessness to the students, he gives a heartbreaking but inspired lecture on "sticking it to the Man." Viewers realize that Dewey has been crushed by the same law that these students are trying so hard to uphold and live by. "So don't go wasting your time trying to make anything cool, or pure, or awesome, because The Man's just going to call you a fat, washed-up loser and crush your soul!" You can hear the prophetic voice of someone all-too-familiar with the weight of performing warning the class to run away and find acceptance elsewhere, because The Man has no love. The Man, like a reality TV panel of judges, has made that much painfully clear to Dewey. Indeed, The Man is a powerful metaphor for a law that by its very nature does not and cannot love. No exceptions. No mercy.

The escape from performancism here comes, of course, in the form of rock n' roll—an agent of grace and acceptance for schlub substitute teachers, overworked students, and stressed out school administrators. But the rock in *School of Rock* doesn't create a skip-school, disobey-parents, angst factory in the students—it spurs them on to freely and creatively follow their passions.

As Dewey and the students form their clandestine rock band in school, they are dancing, playing music, reading up on business management, designing fashion, programming computers, doing graphic design—they're actually learning! Not only that, but quiet students come out of their shells, insecure students find confidence, bullied students speak up for themselves, and bullies learn to tone it down. Not to mention, in an irony-of-all-ironies, rock n' roll makes Dewey into an incredible teacher. In the end (again, suspend your disbelief), even the parents come around, recognizing that joy, passion, and acceptance do more for their children than the pressure to perform and achieve ever could. Performing for grades and gold stars certainly didn't foster the growth these students experience.

In fact, remember how motivated Summer was for her gold stars? Here's how she responds to law-based approval later in the movie: "I didn't do it for the grade." Her motivation has changed. It's no longer about meeting some requirement or earning the right judgment—it's about play, fun, freedom, and joy.

School of Rock gives us a vision of a world in which joy and foolish passion trump law and performancism. Music in this movie is the voice of sympathy, the great identifier, the agent of grace which loves its listener apart from his or her track record and especially in failure. Not only that, but the music begets a closing performance more righteous than the laws of performance ever could. Here you don't have to suspend your disbelief—this is a real-life experience for many, including Mockingbird's own chief editor.[12]

So why then would we consider God as one to motivate us with

12. See: A Mess of Help: From the Crucified Soul of Rock N' Roll, by David Zahl.

a standard of performance when we can see through our own life experiences, and even our culture's (better) storytelling, that this doesn't work as well as 'the heart on fire'? Why should we think our value to God is based on our passion for him, our Bible study regimen, our giving, or our other work? The reality we see on screen in *School of Rock* is the same one we find in the New Testament: Coercion and leverage cannot hold a candle/lighter to the gold-star-trashing, demerit-thrashing, performance-ending work of the Crucified Savior.

Winners, Losers, and

LITTLE MISS SUNSHINE

by

NICK LANNON

With *Little Miss Sunshine*, one of the indie hits of 2006, Jonathan Dayton and Valerie Faris (directors) and Michael Arndt (writer) introduce us to the quirkily dysfunctional Hoover family. The youngest Hoover, Olive (Abigail Breslin), drives the plot. She is seven years old, and is invited to participate in the Little Miss Sunshine Pageant in Redondo Beach, CA. The trick is, the family lives in Albuquerque, is poor, and nobody trusts anybody enough to leave anybody behind. So they all pile into the family's VW bus and hit the road.

The driver is patriarch Richard (Greg Kinnear), author of a yet-to-be-published self-help, 'Nine Steps to Something-or-Other' book. His wife Sheryl (Toni Collette) is the manic glue that holds the family together. Sheryl's brother Frank (Steve Carrell) is fresh off a suicide attempt and may or may not be the world's preeminent Proust scholar, depending on who you ask. Richard's father (Alan

Arkin, who won an Oscar for the performance) is along for the ride too, having been kicked out of his retirement home for lewd behavior and rampant cocaine use. Completing the family constellation are Olive, the would-be pageant queen, and Dwayne (Paul Dano), a Nietzsche-reading would-be fighter pilot who, in his own words, "hates everyone." Quite the rogue's gallery.

A family such as this is certainly ripe for conflict, and much conflict arises on their two day trip across the American Southwest. The sharpest conflict, though, is one that has been raging since long before the Hoover's van pulled out of their driveway: Richard's 'Nine Steps' are driving everybody crazy. Fundamentally, the Nine Steps are like any self-help program: They purport to teach you to access that hidden capability inherent in everyone (or at least in 'winners') and then to help you use it to achieve your life goals. Richard is so drunk on his own Kool-Aid—and so blind to the pains of sufferers—that when Frank comes to their house direct from the hospital post-suicide attempt, he explains to Olive (over a family dinner at which Frank is present) that Frank "gave up on himself, which is something winners never do." As you might imagine, all the winners versus losers talk around the home has alienated his son, pushed away his father, and brought his marriage to the brink of divorce. But then, while on the road, Richard suffers the ultimate indignity, learning that he himself is a loser too: The book deal he's been counting on falls through, and his agent tells him that no one knows who he is and that no one cares about his nine steps.

The losing ways of the Hoovers are brought into sharp relief upon their eventual arrival at the Little Miss Sunshine Pageant. It is immediately obvious that Olive—sweet and precocious as she is—is no beauty queen. She's funny and confident, but she's also frumpy and awkward. There is a quiet push from the family, now closely bonded together due to the harrowing experiences they've shared on the road, to pull Olive out of the pageant.

Ultimately, Olive herself is asked what she'd like to do. She's clearly intimidated by the other girls, and has never been more sure that she's fat, but she decides to go on anyway. As the family expected, she is woefully out of place, and that's never more apparent than in the talent portion of the competition. But, amazingly, when Olive fails spectacularly (albeit joyously and hilariously) in her dance routine, the family runs up onto the stage and joins her in the dance, embracing their collective loser-hood.

And really, that's what *Little Miss Sunshine* is all about. It's about a man who is so afraid of being a loser that he creates a system that supposedly guarantees winning. Just follow the steps. But it turns out that it's not that easy. Success and peace aren't achieved by following some proscribed path up the proverbial mountain. In the end, 'winning' (in this case, symbolized by a happy family) only happens when the losing is acknowledged and embraced. The truth is that the path to follow isn't so much up the mountain as it is down through the valley of the shadow of death. As Christians, we might call this 'confession,' and draw the parallel to the law.

The law attempts to create a 'Nine Steps' style path to a good life, and to happiness, by giving us all kinds of things to do. Honor your father and your mother. Don't lie, cheat, or steal. Love your neighbor as yourself. Though these are all good things, the law *can't actually make us good*. It doesn't have the power. We see the path up the mountain, but we keep falling off. In other words, knowing the requirements (the nine—or however many—steps) doesn't give us the ability to accomplish them. When success isn't an option, confession becomes the only way out. It's only in realizing that we're losers that true winning is possible.

As long as Richard is convinced that he is a winner and that his family is full of losers, compassion and real love cannot exist. He will never connect with his suicidal brother-in-law across the winner/loser divide. It is impossible. It is only when Richard is forced by his failure to admit that he himself is a loser that he begins to see himself as *part* of this motley crew.

In Christianity, our peace is longer lasting than a Rick James song and a ridiculous family dance session. When the music stops, we know that our 'winning' is an eternal gift from another, a savior who lived up to all the requirements that showed us what losers we are, a savior who came down off the mountaintop and descended into the valley to be with us.

By our own power, we are all losers, and honorary members of the Hoover family. By the gift of Jesus Christ, we are adopted as sons and daughters of God. His victory becomes ours, forever.

A Mockingbird Guide to

MOVIES ABOUT JESUS

compiled by

PAUL F. M. ZAHL

It would be easy to overdo the preface to this little guide. There are many movies about Jesus.

There are also many singular and unusual movies about him—eccentric interpretations and odd approaches. And what Jesus are we talking about? The historical Jesus as portrayed so grittily and 'realistically' in Pasolini's *Gospel According to St. Matthew*? The modern Passion Play Jesus, yet one still with broadswords, red capes, and Roman centurions, as in *Jesus of Montreal*? Or *Godspell*, for heaven's sake, which is just as true as it can be (except for the resurrection) to St. Matthew.

We could have an argument about theology right here, right now. Paging Albert Schweitzer, and Martin Kaehler, and golly, John Dominic Crossan.

But I'd rather not do that.

I'd rather just talk about the movies, for some of them are wonderful. Therefore here goes: A short guide to movies about Jesus that work.

These are the ones, according to me—and I think I can say I've seen every one, except maybe the Godard and one or two to which I gave a deliberate miss because they felt, or rather the publicity about them felt, as if they were politically correct in an imposed sense—as I say, these are the ones I think communicate 'the power and the glory' of the man, who is for me the Savior of the World.

I've left out some of the silent ones, some of which still hold up. I've also left out Roberto Rossellini's *The Messiah*, from 1975, because it just doesn't work. It could have been so good, given the director, but it's a serious fail.

I have also left out *Godspell* (1973), which had a big impact on me when it first came out. It's just not quite the ticket as far as this particular list is concerned. Plus, it cops out—thuds out—at the end.

Fact is, this guide leaves out a number of serious movies that concern the life of Christ or have Jesus in them as a character. The 1935 version of *Last Days of Pompeii* comes to mind. The ending of that movie, in which Christ appears to the dying forgiven hero, is extremely stirring.

A Mockingbird Guide to Movies about Jesus, which this is, is going to naturally underline lives of Christ that don't gloss over or soften the distinction between the Gospel and the Law in His interactions with people. At least two cinematic lives of Christ that I can think of do gloss that over, so they will have to place on someone else's list. One of them, *The Last Temptation of Christ*, is a very good movie.

Here goes:

1) THE GOSPEL ACCORDING TO ST. MATTHEW (1964)

In my opinion this is still the best movie version of the life of Christ. From the soundtrack, which is inspired (J.S. Bach to the Missa Luba), to the literalness of Christ's miracles (the loaves and the fishes stand out, as does His walking on the Sea of Galilee), to the fiery power of the actor who plays Christ (especially in the Jerusalem section where He delivers the 'Woe's'), to the faces, every one of them, of His disciples: This is a wonder of a movie. I think Pasolini made it under the direct inspiration of a great man, Pope John XXIII. I don't think this movie will ever be superseded. Oh, and the angel who visits sleepy Joseph! I've seen the film thirty times, and the visitation scenes still don't fail me.

2) THE GREATEST STORY EVER TOLD (1965)

This version doesn't always get the credit it deserves. The script is extremely painstaking—Carl Sandburg was an active consultant, by the way—and the direction, by George Stevens, whose concept the film was, is perfect. Sometimes people complain about the Hollywood cameos, such as John Wayne's Centurion. With maybe that one exception, the cameos work, and are touching, such as Ed Wynn's as the Blind Man, and Carroll Baker's as Veronica. (There are many others.) Oh, and the king of cameos has got to be Sidney Poitier as Simon of Cyrene. It's just the most moving moment ever, when Max von Sydow, as Christ, thanks Sidney Poitier, as Simon, with one look.

The spiritual high point of the movie is the raising of Lazarus, just before the intermission. In that profoundly shot sequence, the actor Van Heflin bears powerful emotional witness to the miracle that Christ has done. That may be my second most favorite conversion-sequence in a Jesus movie. (The first is Charlton Heston's conversion as he observes Christ's humility during the travesty of Christ's trial before the Priests and Pontius Pilate. That, too, is unforgettable.)

3) BEN HUR (1959)

People rightly praise the silent version of *Ben Hur*, which came out in 1925. It is very good, and the scene 'down by the river,' in which women who are washing clothes talk about Christ's ministry—not to mention Christ's bloody footprints as He bears His Cross to Calvary—these are still powerful and raw even though they appear in a silent film. (Incidentally, the Crucifixion sequence in D.W. Griffith's *Intolerance* (1916) is something you shouldn't miss. It looks as if it is taking place in hell and Griffith and his cameraman were photographing it in hell. I don't know how they did it—in 1916.)

But for us the version of *Ben Hur* that will probably never date is the William Wyler version that was released in 1959. In particular, the Sermon on the Mount, Christ's *Via Dolorosa* on the way to His death, and the Crucifixion itself—one image of which is taken directly from a painting by James Tissot entitled "What Our Lord Saw from the Cross": These are magical moments, especially for Christians. I defy you to watch the third third of the 1959 *Ben Hur* and not be touched right down to the ground.

4) KING OF KINGS (1961)

Professional critics often try to pigeonhole or label a work of art. Thus *King of Kings* is sometimes called "I Was a Teenage Jesus," because Jeffrey Hunter was very young when he played the lead role. It is also labeled a 'Protestant' interpretation—or rather, a 'liberal Protestant' interpretation, because Philip Yordan's script downplays Christ's miracles and underlines very forcefully His teachings, especially the Sermon on the Mount.

King of Kings is really just a very good movie, perhaps a little more intimate in feeling or less like an epic than *Greatest Story*. The director, Nicholas Ray, likes close-ups more than George Stevens, so yes, he tends to humanize the drama.

But there are splendid jewels in *King of Kings*, especially that Sermon on the Mount, with Hunter striding through the crowd and captured by extremely fluid camera movement. And don't forget the 'God's-Eye-View' of The Last Supper, and, best of all, Christ's appearance, and sort of disappearance, at the very end, on the Sea of Galilee. This last scene and shot of *King of Kings* is one of the high points of all these movies.

While you're at it, don't miss the 1927 version of *King of Kings*. It's silent, and yet still excellent. A blind boy receiving his sight is one of the high notes of this 'battle axe' of a movie, which is actually not a battle axe at all. It was directed by Cecil B. DeMille.

5) THE ROBE (1953)

It is the sequences in Palestine that make this movie so religious and devout in the best way. Richard Burton and Victor Mature get caught up accidentally in Christ's Palm Sunday entry into Jerusalem, yet you see Christ Himself only in long shot. It's like Mizoguchi, and it's fabulous.

Then the Crucifixion itself, when Richard Burton as Marcellus navigates through the traditional lookers-on at the Cross, as if they are silent, watching chess pieces and he has been extruded into their timeless (theatrically static) roles: This sequence is one of the most effective and memorable of all Hollywood Crucifixions. Also, the sequence in which Dawn Addams, as Junia, sings the story of the Empty Tomb is not only moving, it is instructive, as that is the way many Gospel memories were preserved initially—and the moviemakers have demonstrated it.

People look down on *The Robe* as being 'Eisenhower-era'-religio-maudlin. But that's unfair. When people talk that way about *The Robe*, you can almost be sure they haven't actually seen it.

6) JESUS OF NAZARETH (1977)

This long, made-for television mini-series was directed by Franco Zeffirelli. It is very good, and have you ever seen it? Robert Powell plays Jesus.

What distinguishes this version of the life of Christ is that it is able to 'take its time' telling the story. *Jesus of Nazareth* is not compressed. Moreover, the Crucifixion sequence—that litmus test for the 'attitude' behind every one of these movies—is beautiful, extended, and moving. I believe Sir Laurence Olivier plays Nicodemus, and that it falls to Sir Laurence to read Isaiah 53 as the voiceover to Christ's sufferings. It is a perfect reading, and a perfect visual/verbal unity, and a perfect instantiation of the heart of the matter.

"Don't Forget the Motor City"—Don't Forget to See the 1977 version of *Jesus of Nazareth*.

7) THE PASSION OF THE CHRIST (2004)

Mel Gibson got a lot of grief for this movie. But it wasn't deserved. The main problem many people seemed to have with it, outside of their opinion of Mel Gibson himself, was the violence involved in the scourging of Christ. It was pretty intense. But I found that few of the film's 'liberal' detractors had actually been to the theater and seen the movie for themselves. (This travesty of criticism was parallel to the travesty of criticism that overtook *The Last Temptation of Christ* in 1988. But in the case of *The Last Temptation*, the criticism came from the religious right. And *they* never saw the movie, either.)

Anyway, *The Passion of the Christ* is cinematic while also being emotionally religious. Who can forget the teardrop coming down from the eye of God? And the Resurrection of Christ, in and from the Tomb. Gibson took major risks here, in the visual telling of the Greatest Story Ever Told. For my money, he succeeded.

I do find *The Passion of the Christ* to be a little on the 'heavy' side. What I mean is, I have to work myself up to seeing it, muster up my emotional strength to survive it. But when I do, which is about once every two years, then it makes a big impact and indites its message onto my chest as if I were Linda Blair in *The Exorcist*.

CONCLUSION

Well, I'm still tallying up in my mind all the *other* movies that tell the story of Jesus Christ, or engage with it directly. Then I start to think about the television shows over the years—right down to the *New Outer Limits* in the late 1990s, believe it or not—and MTV videos, such as that inspired video for "The Power of Love," by Frankie Goes to Hollywood.

But what I've given, I have given. The seven movies listed above are sure fire. They all reflect, tho' in different ways, a faithful and reverent 'take' on the life of Christ, yet not one that is boring or wooden. There *was* a quite wooden dramatization of His life made, which became a world-wide sensation because it was distributed free almost everywhere you could imagine. But it's pretty low octane, I have to tell you.

There have also been some good movies about characters in

the Gospel story other than Christ. For example, there is more than one good movie about Mary the Mother of Christ. There is also *The Big Fisherman* (1959), which is odd but a personal favorite of mine; and concerns mainly Peter, tho' in a somewhat fantastic Arabian background.

I leave these seven movies, seven rich and affecting treatments of the life of Christ, for you to see and feel and think about. Like Bach's *St. Matthew Passion*, they are probably the best that human beings can do to put into word and image an event that St. John said was so massive that "not even all the books in the world could contain the things he did" (21:25).

From Sadness to Gladness: Sin and Redemption in

ABOUT A BOY

by

R-J Heijmen

"When sin departs before His grace, then life and health come in its place." So goes the third verse of the Sussex Carol, an English Christmas tune of unknown origin, and it well sums up the transformation at the heart of *About a Boy* (2002). This unexpectedly affecting movie stars Hugh Grant, Toni Collette, Rachel Weisz, and Nicholas Hoult (of *Mad Max: Fury Road* notoriety), with Chris and Paul Weitz directing. It's based on a Nick Hornby novel and graced with a *Graduate*-level (pardon the pun) score from Badly Drawn Boy. If you haven't seen it (or don't remember it), do yourself a favor. And I promise, only very minor spoilers ahead.

The Sussex Carol is the background music for a Christmas dinner of misfits: an only child with a tragic bowl cut (Hoult), his clinically depressed mother (Collette) and deadbeat dad, dad's girlfriend, her clueless mother ("'Shake Ya Ass'? Is he Moroccan?") and a man who truly doesn't belong—Will (Grant). Will is a single, childless trust-funder. As one of his so-called friends points out a few minutes into the film, "You're thirty-eight, you've never had a job or a relationship that's lasted more than two months. You're a disaster. What is the point of your life?" Bloody hell indeed! Will's lifestyle is supported by the royalties from a song his father wrote decades earlier, allowing him to fill his days with meaningless activities and his apartment with objects that project an aura of 'cool' for an endless string of dalliances. Will loves his life, or says he does. John Donne (not Bon Jovi) may have opined that "no man is an island," but Will is more in agreement with the sentiment expressed in Simon & Garfunkel's "I am a Rock." He finds safety and peace in isolation.

Change begins to creep into Will's life, as it does for so many of us, in an act of baffling shamelessness and bewildering stupidity. Having found himself short on available female options, Will decides to give single moms a try. He joins a support group called SPAT (single parents alone together), in which he spins elaborate lies about a son, and from which he scores a date with Suzie, a promising blond. Unfortunately for him, she brings along not only her own child but also Marcus (Hoult), the hopelessly awkward pre-pubescent son of a fellow SPATer (Collette), who, by his very nature, squelches any romantic possibilities. He is the ultimate, shall we say, 'rooster inhibitor.' Even worse, when Will drops Marcus off at home after the date, they discover Marcus' mom passed out in a pool of her own suicidal pill-popping vomit, and Will is drawn into a very stormy archipelago indeed.

From this moment on, and unbeknownst to his mother, Marcus inserts himself into Will's life with ever-increasing regularity, tracking him home and showing up each day after school to have a snack and watch TV. At first Will resists, but Marcus is so persistent, and so undemanding, that it is eventually easier to have him around than not. In spite of himself, Will has made a friend.

At this point, it seems appropriate to take a step back and make a few theological associations. In this contemporary parable, Will is us. He is humanity. We may not all be trust-funders, but we wish we were, even though that would spell our doom. As C.S. Lewis astutely depicts in the *Great Divorce*, hell is sinful people getting whatever they want, whenever they want it. That kind of resourcing leads to ever-increasing alienation, both from others and from self. Furthermore, although Will is hurting, he thinks he's fine, or at least that he should be. He is so curved in on himself, *incurvatus in se*, that he cannot imagine any other option. He is a dead man, and dead men don't feel. Will's condition is a perfect example of what Luther called the bound will. He appears free, and yet he is trapped in his own isolating tendencies. He can make choices, but he cannot opt out of who he is. Will has everything, and yet he has nothing.

Marcus, shockingly, echoes Jesus, and this is made clear when his character is juxtaposed with writer Anne Lamott's profound conversion testimony from her book, *Traveling Mercies*. In the midst of the kinds of bad choices that always seem to lead us home, she writes:

> I had the feeling that a little cat was following me, wanting me to reach down and pick it up, wanting me to open the door and let it in. But I knew what would happen: you let a cat in one time, give it a little milk, and then it stays forever...When I went back to church, I was so hungover that I couldn't stand up for the songs...but the last song was so deep and raw and pure that I could not escape...I began to cry and left before the benediction, and I raced home and felt the little cat running at my heels...and I opened the door to my houseboat, and I stood there a minute, and then I hung my head and said "Fuck it: I quit." I took a long deep breath and said out loud, "All right. You can come in."

Marcus is the little cat. So small, so weak, so unrelenting that Will can't help but let him in. This is the miracle of Christianity—that the God of the universe comes to us as a baby, a penniless carpenter, a criminal on a cross. Rather than overwhelming us with the power of a full frontal assault, Jesus sneaks in under our defenses. He finds our cracks and works his way in, healing as he goes. So it is with Marcus and Will.

Marcus is also Christ-like in his unflinching assessment of Will's character. Marcus is the one who discovers that Will does not have a son, and he calls him out. Yet, like Christ, Marcus doesn't use this knowledge to condemn, but to connect. There is almost a sense of relief for Will at being known and not judged. Their initial interactions are reminiscent of Jesus and the woman at the well. Marcus names Will's sin, and yet offers him the living water of presence and relationship. Marcus demands almost nothing of Will (indeed, as Will says over and over again, he "doesn't do anything"—in and of itself a striking commentary on the divine/human relationship) save that he be allowed to stick around. But his faithfulness begins to chip away at Will's heart of stone.

It also bears saying that Marcus' mother, Fiona, represents the Law, both in her relationship with Marcus and with herself. There is no freedom in her self-righteous tree-huggerdom. Marcus is miserable. He wears absurd hand-made clothing to school (and receives the appropriate social penalty), lives completely out of touch with teenage culture, and remains crushed by the need to manage his mother's emotions. And in spite of all her crunchiest efforts, Fiona can never be enough—enough of a mom, enough of a person—to the point that death is preferable to life. Furthermore, when Fiona learns of Marcus and Will's relationship, her horror (somewhat rightly, I suppose) mirrors that of the Pharisees towards Jesus and 'sinners'—*you're hanging out with who?!* Thankfully, this toxic brew of judgment and despair isn't the end of the story for Fiona, but it is certainly where her journey out of depression begins.

All of which makes that Christmas dinner so powerful. Marcus has invited Will, his only friend (they are each other's only friend) to this crazy meal with his broken family. And just as it looks like it might all work out, the final guest shows up: Suzie, the blond from SPAT who, by now, has learned of Will's lies and deceit and, with Fiona, starts to lay into him. Will has nowhere to hide. He knows that he has behaved abominably and begins to visibly shrink, shame consuming his countenance. Will suggests that he leave; the ladies wholeheartedly agree. And then Marcus speaks up—shouts, actually. Will is *his* friend, he says, it is up to *him* whether Will stays or goes, and no one, least of all his mother, is perfect and has the right to judge. It is a John 8 moment. Those with righteous stones to throw drop them, back off, and Will's life is changed, redeemed. Sin, as the carol goes, is palpably chased away by grace, and life and health come in its place. The dead are raised, the dry bones made alive. I get goosebumps every time.

As promised, I will not divulge the movie's conclusion, but suffice it to say that Marcus' salvific work, his imputation of worth, begins to transform Will from the inside out, to such a degree that he commits brazen acts of love and self-sacrifice which previously would have been unthinkable. He makes more huge mistakes, to be sure, but his heart has begun to melt. As Will himself says, "Christmas at Marcus' gave me a warm fuzzy feeling, and I hold that feeling directly responsible for the strange events that followed." For a movie which stars a philanderer and shares a director with *American Pie*, *About a Boy* is a surprisingly insightful and helpful film. As the Sussex Carol says, "Men on earth" may be "sad," but the love of the "Redeemer makes us glad."

IT'S A WONDERFUL LIFE

The Most Terrifying (yet Wonderful) Movie Ever Made

by

RON FLOWERS

A much-beloved film shown ceaselessly around one holiday each year has been dubbed "the most terrifying Hollywood film ever made,"[13] "a terrifying, asphyxiating story....[a] nightmare account,"[14] and "one of the grimmest, most despairing portraits..."[15]

The holiday must be Halloween, right? The movie, *The Shining*? *The Exorcist*? Think again. Believe it or not, these quotes describe the Christmas classic, *It's a Wonderful Life*.

Seriously? The *It's a Wonderful Life* of "Buffalo Gals Won't You Come Out Tonight," and "every time a bell rings, an angel gets his wings"?

---

13. Rich Cohen, "It's a Wonderful Life: The Most Terrifying Movie Ever," *Salon*, Dec. 24, 2010.

14. Wendell Jameson, "Wonderful? Sorry, George, It's a Pitiful, Dreadful Life," *New York Times*, Dec. 18, 2008.

15. Mike D'Angelo, "It's a Wonderful Life," *A.V. Club*, Dec. 23, 2011.

Yes. While often portrayed on the surface as a saccharine classic overplayed during the Christmas season, the first one hundred minutes of *It's a Wonderful Life* recount the despairing tale of how the hopeful George Bailey becomes disillusioned by life and finds himself standing on a bridge considering suicide. At this moment his life does not seem quite so wonderful.

If you look at it from only an earthly perspective and remove the first five and the last ten minutes of the movie, the unfurling events of George Bailey's life demonstrate the "asphyxiating" feeling of life wrenching our illusion of control from our lifeless grasp. Without a few key scenes, *It's a Wonderful Life* would be a horrifyingly ironic title for a movie which offers George Bailey, and all of us, little wonder and ultimately no hope.

Fortunately, *It's a Wonderful Life* is the best (and perhaps only) movie to open with talking celestial objects. Granted, these heavenly orbs do not reflect the most convincing portrait of divine intervention. Still, along with the angel Clarence, they set the appropriate vertical context to accompany the horizontal story of George Bailey's (or any of our own) lives.

From a heavenly vantage point, Joseph recounts to Clarence the noteworthy events of George Bailey's life which lead him to his "crucial night" and the reason for Clarence's mission. The opening earthly scenes depict George as a child, in his happiest stage, playing with his friends and spending time with his friends at Mr. Gower's drugstore. George grew up a smart, talented young man who had planned his entire life:

> I know what I'm going to do tomorrow and the next day and the next year and the year after that. I'm shaking the dust of this crummy little town off my feet, and I'm going to see the world. Italy, Greece, the Parthenon, the Colosseum. Then I'm coming back to go to college and see what they know, and then I'm

> going to build things. I'm going to build air fields. I'm going to build skyscrapers a hundred stories high. I'm going to build bridges a mile long.

George has his life figured out. After working for four years to save for college, he reports his life's plans to his future wife Mary Hatch, just moments before learning his father has had a stroke. This is the first of a repeated string of unexpected turns which foil his immense plans one-by-one through circumstances beyond his control. Obligation repeatedly interferes.

George's dreams were fashioned in direct contrast to his father's day-to-day struggles at his small company, the Bailey Brothers' Building and Loan. Though low in profit margin, the Bailey Brothers' Building and Loan proves to be the only Bedford Falls institution not infiltrated by the insatiably greedy Scrooge-like businessman Henry F. Potter. On the night he dies, George's father, Peter Bailey, asks George to consider coming back to the Building and Loan, and George responds, "I couldn't. I couldn't face being cooped up for the rest of my life in a shabby little office." He laments to Potter about his Father, "Why he ever started this cheap, penny-ante Building and Loan, I'll never know."

George never leaves Bedford Falls. Opportunities arise, like when Sam Wainwright offers him a position on the ground floor of his plastics venture, but although George is tormented daily by the Building and Loan, he is bound by obligations beyond his conscious control. As he tells Mary (in the scene directly before their wedding), "I don't want any plastics. I don't want any ground floors, and I don't want to get married—ever—to anyone! You understand that? *I want to do what I want to do*!" He longs to get out, but he can't. He is paralyzed. He doesn't want the Building and Loan, but he can't get away from it.

George's acts are civically laudable—he provides home ownership to those who would otherwise be stuck in Potter's slums—but they are not born out of love. His self-sacrificing actions are generated out of obligation to his father's ideas. He valiantly tries to do all things for all people, and it buries him.

It's A Wonderful Life reveals that we are not free as we once expected. As time passes, the gap between what George wants to do and what he actually does widens. Ten to twelve years go by in less than five movie minutes as George teeters along, a respected businessman and father on the outside, but barely hanging on inside—until on Christmas Eve 1945 an unexpected crisis, again entirely beyond his control, sends him over the edge. George reaches the end of his rope.

In George's meltdown scene, we see that his dreams have been diminished to a worktable in the family room filled with models of buildings and bridges, the fragmentary remnants of his bold plans for the future. While outwardly managing the Building and Loan and scraping pennies, inwardly George has been longing to build skyscrapers and travel the world. Out of frustrations which have lingered and boiled up inside of him, he explodes to Mary and the kids about his measly job, the drafty house, and the brood of kids—"Why did we have to live here in the first place and stay around this measly, crummy old town?" The business's loss of $8,000 (roughly $105,000 in today's dollars) brings him to the ledge. The distance between where he wants to be and where he really is brings him to an imperturbable impasse.

Like George Bailey, none of us wants to fail. We do anything and everything we can to avoid failing. We fight and claw and hold on dearly to objects and identities which, in reality, are killing us. Like all of us, George can only turn away from himself as the instrument of his own salvation when this possibility has escaped him entirely.

Like George Bailey, we all are destined to fail, to reach an impasse where we see that all of our earthly efforts are not going to save us. It takes reaching that point to look away from ourselves for our salvation to the celestial object (Christ) who has already failed for all of us.

If *It's a Wonderful Life* existed only on a worldly plane, it *would* be a miserable life. For this reason, secular commentaries labeling the movie as "the most terrifying movie of all time" are spot on. If the movie, like our lives, did not begin (and end) with a heavenly perspective, when our blinders came off, the results would be horrifying. If George arrived at the end of his rope without Clarence's intervention, the graceless dystopia of Pottersville would be his (and our) reality. Our outlook would mirror the deathly stare of Ernie the cabdriver.

Thankfully, the "terrifying, asphyxiating" tale, though truthful, is not the entire story. After George's first prayer, "Help me," help does come, but not the monetary kind he has imagined. He asks for health, not death, but death is required for his rebirth—the death of all his grandiose plans and expectations in favor of an acquiescence ("I don't care what happens to me") to where God has brought him up to this point in his life. His prayer brings about the symbolic death of his pride, desires, and identity. Only through death can George see that his frustrations and disappointments were actually the well-meaning design of a creator bringing him to the place where he could look into reality and see the 'wonderful' side.

It's a Wonderful Life realistically depicts life's miserable side, the side which would triumph in the absence of Christ's intervening act. Our plans in life will fail, but paradoxically, the failure of our plans is what we desperately need and what Christ is calling us to. The "cheap, penny-ante Building and Loan" was the vocation God had brought him, not the one he wanted.

As with the sojourners on the road to Emmaeus, George's eyes are closed. It takes an outside source (Clarence, in his attempt to get his wings) to reveal to George the loving hand that has shaped his life, and the grace that has been bestowed upon him. Despite the talking clouds, the deepest truth of the movie is that his frustrations, his defeats, and even his ultimate collapse were orchestrated from another world.

In Pottersville, George sees a world without grace. It's a world in which we get what we desire and what we deserve. When the graceful institution of the Building and Loan collapses upon Peter Bailey's death, Potter's take-no-prisoners worldview prevails and sucks the grace right out of the town. Martini loses his business, Ernie his house, wife, and kids, and Uncle Billy goes to the insane asylum. Left to their own devices, the townspeople become depressed and isolated, and the community establishments evolve into avenues of escape.

It's a Wonderful Life reveals not only our need for grace but also how grace transforms its recipients. In contrast to Pottersville, the town of Bedford Falls thrives as a community of failures. The Building and Loan has issued them loans and built them houses, despite their inadequacies—"Take this loan to Ernie Bishop...I happen to know the bank turned down this loan, but he comes here, and we're building him a house worth five thousand dollars"—and therefore brought them to a place where they can spontaneously rescue George at his point of despair and bring him triumphantly into the Christmas celebration.

The community of Bedford Falls is made possible only by the

grace of the Bailey Building and Loan which credits the townspeople as righteous even when they are not creditworthy. Broken by the cruel law of Potter's Field, the imputation of the Building and Loan allows them to joyfully serve their vocations and care for their neighbors, like George when he reaches the end of his rope.

Frank Capra won five Academy Awards, none for this movie, but he counted *It's a Wonderful Life* as his favorite, although its box office failure bankrupted his production company and led the public to believe he had lost his touch after the war. Even more overtly Christian in its earlier drafts, Capra wrote it in response to a mounting trend towards atheism. The initial script ended with George on his knees reciting the Lord's Prayer.[16] Thankfully, Capra's edits were inspired and created one of the most moving death-resurrection sequences in all of film. It is powerful and possible only because God meets us in our point of greatest need, and where we have failed, he has overcome.

Though it's widely viewed as sentimental due to the ubiquitous holiday screenings, Capra's film looks at the stark reality of life and death and our human ambitions, and does not ignore the pain and frustration they cause. But it does not stop there. It reminds us that we have a heavenly father who looks down (figuratively) and says, "Poor George," and sends the whole town to rescue him on his "crucial night," lifting him up out of despair and calling him into an eternal Christmas party. *It's A Wonderful Life* is ultimately a story of a new birth, but a birth inescapably linked with death.[17] And for that we can all be grateful.

16. Cahill, Marie, *It's A Wonderful Life*, (1992), 105.

17. Eliot, T. S. "Journey of the Magi," (1927).

Law and Grace in

FROZEN

by

Michael Belote

As any parent with two ears is aware, Disney's movie *Frozen* became a major phenomenon (due in no small part to the impossibly catchy anthem "Let It Go"). What many miss is that *Frozen*—in addition to exuding the typical charm and humor we have come to expect from Disney—has a powerful theological message as well.

Frozen centers around the lives of two princesses, Elsa and Anna. Elsa, the elder sister, has a blessing/curse of magic—she is capable of creating anything cold, from snow to ice to storms. Anna, the younger sister, is a precocious, clumsy, and yet sincerely adorable girl.

When the two are young children, Elsa accidentally freezes Anna's mind. The local trolls are able to save her, but in the process they also extract the memories of seeing her sister perform magic. Fearful of a relapse of Anna's brain-freeze, Elsa and her parents agree to keep her magic hidden and secret from Anna as well as everyone else.

THE LAW CONDEMNS

As Elsa grows up, she becomes less and less able to control her magic. She spends her life focused on trying to keep her magic hidden and in control. Her fear of harming her sister or others leads her to live a life of isolation, as she attempts through sheer willpower to control the overwhelming magic bursting to come forth. She spends her life in her room, hidden from the outside world, gates to the castle closed: and, more significantly, the gates to her sister's heart closed.

However, her attempts to control her powers ultimately fail. Every time she becomes emotional, her magic comes back out again. This is a classic example of the theological principle of the Law, and it is just as clear as if Luther himself had described it. For Elsa, all of her attempts to will herself to "be the good girl you always have to be" fail—the Law has no power to save us from sin (Elsa's magic), but only to condemn. Just as theology tells us about the Law, Elsa finds that all her efforts only serve to increase her failures at controlling her magic.

Eventually this results in an embarrassing public fiasco, in which she is branded as a monstrous sorceress and has to flee into the wild mountains. Despite her best efforts at keeping the Law, her magic curse has manifested itself in a very public way, and she has been condemned for it.

Having found the Law a complete failure, in her exodus in the mountains Elsa actually feels a bit of freedom—indeed she goes completely to the opposite end of the spectrum. The anthem, "Let it Go," is her decision to go to the opposite extreme: Since her willpower cannot control her magic, then she should just let it out completely.

Her response (and the song's lyrics) are what theologians call antinomianism—an exaggeration of justification by faith: Instead of seeking out grace as the opposite of Law, the sinner rejects any moral constraint at all. Just as the antinomian believes that the failure of the Law means that sin may be allowed to run rampant, so too does Elsa believe that her failure to control her magic means she must now let it out in complete freedom.

Elsa's lyrics about magic could easily stand in for many a sinner's response to years of failed legalism:

> *Couldn't keep it in, heaven knows I tried.*
> *Don't let them in, don't let them see.*
> *Be the good girl you always have to be.*
> *Conceal, don't feel, don't let them know—well now they know!*
> *Let it go! Let it go! Can't hold it back anymore…*
> *Turn away and slam the door. I don't care what they're going to say,*
> *Let the storm rage on—the cold never bothered me anyway.*
> *Let it go! Let it go! That perfect girl is gone!*

She tried, and failed, to keep in her magic. Her will could not prevail over the power of magic (sin). And so, she decides to let it all go. Stop trying to be perfect and just let the storm rage, and to Hades with what anyone says.

However, this decision is not without an effect.

Legalism toward the individual has the strange effect of actually helping the community (by providing a highly moral individual) while simultaneously breaking the individual (by giving them the impossible task of saving themselves)—and so it was for Elsa. Antinomianism seems to provide freedom to the person fleeing legalism—but it is a false freedom. Though you may indeed be free from legalism, you quickly discover that the bondage of sin is even more destructive, both to your life and the lives of those around you.

We see precisely this happen in *Frozen:* Elsa is finally free, but in the process of her 'letting it go,' the entire kingdom becomes locked in an eternal winter.

GRACE SAVES

Now the film's focus shifts away from Elsa to her sister, Anna. Anna has never had much of a relationship with Elsa (due to Elsa's self-isolation). Nevertheless, Anna feels a love for her. She is not willing to allow her sister to be branded a monster, nor will she allow her kingdom to be locked in winter.

Anna chases after Elsa and tries to convince her to come back. Elsa refuses, saying that although she is alone, at least for once she is free. That is when Anna reveals the result of Elsa's antinomianism—the eternal winter affecting *everyone else* in the kingdom. It is true that 'letting it go' was a breath of fresh air to Elsa, but antinomianism was not the solution to the problem of the Law. As soon as Elsa realizes the impact she is having, she understands that she is helpless to solve it.

What can she do? She cannot isolate herself; she cannot fully engage her magic; she cannot control her magic through willpower. She is doomed to fail! Her case is hopeless. In pure emotion and frustration, Elsa radiates magic out from her, and even innocent Anna is affected—this time not with a frozen head, but a frozen heart.

The trolls' magic is again sought out, but the news is dire—a frozen heart is much worse than a frozen head. Only an act of True Love can save Anna now.

Now this is, of course, a Disney movie. And so the characters assume—as do we in the audience—that the act of True Love is a kiss. Anna (who throughout the movie is being pursued by two suitors) rushes around trying to find True Love's kiss to break the curse.

And if this were the purpose and solution of the film, it would be a typically enjoyable Disney film. But what makes *Frozen* so special is that a kiss is not True Love.

Anna rushes back, near freezing, to her fiancé for True Love's kiss. She is betrayed, however, and left to die. She then turns to her other suitor, seeking him out for the kiss which she believes will save her.

At the film's climax then, there is Anna, stumbling and near death, in a swirling ice storm, rushing toward a man for what she believes is the kiss needed to save her life. Then in the corner of her eye, she sees her sister. Elsa, believing that she has killed Anna, is mourning...and unbeknownst to her, the villain is sneaking up on her to deal a lethal blow.

Anna makes a split-second decision. She runs *away* from her beau, toward her sister. Just as the sword is coming down to kill her sister, Anna jumps in front of it, holding up her hand to block the blade.

Anna turns to ice. The sword is broken, the villain is defeated. Elsa (the sinner, the cause of all the problems) is saved. But Anna has died.

And then...something changes.

Anna begins to melt. Anna, once dead, lives again! Hallelujah!

The salvation for Elsa could never be the Law. Nor could it be antinomianism. It is in True Love—her willingness to sacrifice all that she is to save someone who does not deserve it.

It is at this moment that Anna becomes a type of Christ in *Frozen:* She (though innocent of Elsa's sorcery) willingly went to death to save someone (Elsa) who had never even made much of an attempt at a relationship. It was not because of anything Elsa did that Anna sacrificed herself; it was an undeserved love for Elsa that led to her willingly dying for her (cf: Rom 5:7-9).

The message of *Frozen* resonates with us because, like all great stories, it is a shadow of the One Great Story—that we were all cursed, all undeserving, and yet God died for us so that we might live. *Frozen* has it all: the condemnation of the Law, the false freedom promised by sin...and the true freedom that comes because someone loved us, died for us, and came back from the dead.

Jesus once said, "Greater love has no one than this: to lay down one's life for one's friends" (Jn 15:13). That is True Love. And True Love does, indeed, melt the frozen heart.

THE LOVERS, THE DREAMERS, THE MUPPETS, AND ME

by

David Zahl

The movie opens on a bright blue sky. There's a hot air balloon floating in the distance, and as the camera zooms in on the basket, a couple of instantly recognizable voices can be heard.

> FOZZIE: "What if we drift out to sea? What if we're never heard from again? What if there's a storm or we get struck by lightning?
>
> GONZO: "That would be neat!"
>
> KERMIT: "Listen, nothing's going to happen. This is just the opening credits."

Thus begins *The Great Muppet Caper*, our felted friends' second big screen adventure (1981). The fourth wall had scarcely been erected before it was broken. The exchange signaled that we were back in Jim Henson's hands, and all was well in the world.

Such winking at the adults in the theater has become commonplace in today's children's movies, but it was novel back then, one of the many reasons the public first fell in love with Kermit and crew. This was "family entertainment" aimed at children and adults in equal measure, proof that wholesome media could be smart, that absurdism didn't always entail cynicism.[18] In fact, the Muppets are an object lesson in the truism that inanity can flow from delight just as readily as pain.

There was something joyful about the entire, scruffy enterprise. You could tell that the creators were having a blast making these characters come to life. Indeed, nothing defines the Muppet magic more accurately than the spirit behind the work. This is why the various reboots have, by and large, been unsuccessful.

By all accounts Jim Henson was a bit of a saint. Read any biography of the man, and you will walk away almost suspicious of his overwhelming decency and personal integration, his unfailing optimism and boundless energy. What made the biggest impression on those around him was apparently *not* his astounding creativity but the passionate and compassionate way he lived.

In fact, some might say that Henson and his contemporary Fred Rogers comprise "the unfallen duo" of American public television. Both saw their work as a spiritual vocation; Rogers was an ordained Presbyterian, while Henson grew up in Christian Science—even teaching Sunday School in his 20s. Unlike Mr. Rogers, however, Henson reportedly distanced himself from his church as he grew older, downplaying sectarian concerns for the sake of reaching a wider audience with his amorphous message of hopes and dreams and rainbow connections.[19] Vestiges of Mary Baker Eddy do surface

18. One of the reasons why most Muppet reboots suffer. They overdo it on the adult stuff. It's a very delicate balance.

19. The urban legend that Henson died because of a Christian Science-based refusal to receive medial care is just that: an urban legend.

occasionally in his work, in the form of a can-do sunniness about the human condition that would be a lot more cloying if it were not dressed up in such zany colors.

Silliness is where Henson shone. The Muppets have never been able to resist a good pun—*The Muppet Show* in particular is a crash course in the power of corny wordplay. The abundant nonsense kept the feel-/do-good-ism from succumbing to the piety of political correctness. Frank Oz, Henson's great collaborator—literally the Bert to Henson's Ernie—once summed up their approach this way: "Whenever characters become self-important or sentimental in the Muppets, then there's always another character there to blow them up immediately."[20] That is, despite going on record about "people [being] basically good," the Muppet characters were wonderfully and truthfully drawn. Their bickering, broken collective was united by a shared ridiculousness: Fozzy was hopelessly insecure, Kermit was long-suffering, Piggy an egomaniac, Gonzo a self-described "weirdo." Animal was, well, Animal.

In the Muppets, the weaknesses tell the stories, not the strengths, and those weaknesses are frequently a source of humor.

Again, unlike so many other comedic talents, Henson did not derive his punch lines from a place of anger or despair. There was something sweet and, dare I say, loving at work in his poking of fun. You might even call it an affectionate absurdism. His faith in humanity began from an acknowledgement of limitation, not an illusion about perfectibility. He knew that joy flowed from honesty, rather than around it.

G. K. Chesterton once wrote, "It is the test of a good *religion* whether you can joke about it."[21] Sadly, humor is not generally

20. The quote from Oz, as well as the various quotes from Henson can all be found in *It's Not Easy Being Green (And Other Things To Consider)*, by Jim Henson, the Muppets and Friends, published by Hyperion in 2005.

21. From Chesterton's short essay, "Spiritualism."

something that characterizes today's Christian landscape—more the opposite. This is ironic, since a sinner saved by grace is someone whose identity is (theoretically, at least) found apart from their ever-changing and often hopeless abilities and attributes. Someone who is free not to take themselves so seriously.

What is self-deprecation, after all, if not an expression of freedom? In the realm of the Law, both secular and religious varieties, we must save face. Any weakness is seen as an affront to our righteousness before God and neighbor (and self). It is considered a threat, which is the opposite of funny. The Gospel of Jesus Christ announces that those stakes have been dismantled once and for all—that our ultimate righteousness is given rather than earned. Those things that once might have offended or wounded us have lost their sting. We can laugh at ourselves in the mirror.

Henson evinced something similar in his jokes. Where others found potential bitterness, he found the thread of human foibles, a lighthearted irreverence that was as universal as the appeal of his characters.

What about the stories he told? Henson may have preached self-belief, but the narratives he crafted almost always depicted individuals in desperate need of help from others. Despite the sometimes insufferable can't-we-all-just-get-along aspect of *Sesame Street* (and *Fraggle Rock*) much of Henson's work dealt with human suffering, both self-inflicted and otherwise.

1982's *The Dark Crystal*, for example, takes place in a broken, cursed world and tells the tale of a young "Gelfling"—a creature not unlike Tolkien's hobbits—who sets out on a quest to restore wholeness and harmony, all the while skirting the opposition of an evil race of Skesis who would make themselves gods. While the art direction is breathtaking, the film is far from perfect, lacking not only Henson's trademark wackiness but any narrative urgency. The title notwithstanding, few expected Jim and co. ever to deliver something that could legitimately be described as dreary or plodding in places. Yet where some see only pagan imagery, it's difficult not to detect a fable of Fall and Redemption, hubris and eucatastrophe. Jim may have embraced a "positive view of life," but his work reflects a larger truth.

Henson followed up *The Dark Crystal* with *Labyrinth* (1986), also known as the film where David Bowie dances around in an MC Escher painting wearing a Tina Turner wig. Meaning, he kept the ambitious set-pieces of *Crystal*, but served them up with an extra helping of whimsy, this time with the aid of Monty Python's Terry Jones. The film is a far more enjoyable experience, yet not without genuine menace. The premise finds a fifteen-year-old Jennifer Connelly impetuously bartering her baby brother away to a sinister goblin king (Bowie), before realizing her mistake. To rescue the child from certain doom, she is tasked with negotiating a series of mounting obstacles in a magical maze. You might say the film has a distinctly Pilgrim's Progress-like, um, progression.

Upon release *Labyrinth* flopped, and Henson was devastated. His vision was deemed too eccentric, too ugly for kids yet too goofy for adults. Some critics felt he was overly focused on technical achievements at the expense of heart. Not surprisingly, both *Crystal* and *Labyrinth* have gained substantial cult followings in the years since Henson's death in 1990.

As fascinating and worthwhile as those two films may be, they also illustrate what made the Muppets so special. In pursuing an older audience, something about Jim's core philosophy seems to have gotten obscured. All along he had evinced an understanding that, to truly reach another person, you must aim beyond the intellect, and even the constructed self, at the corner of the soul known as the inner child. Puppetry and humor were Jim's tools for penetrating adult defenses, not catering to them:

> At its best, [puppetry] is talking to a deeper part of you, and if you know that it's doing that, or you become aware of it, you lessen the ability to go straight in. Fairy tales certainly are in this category, as is a lot of fantasy–maybe everything is.
>
> The most sophisticated people I know–inside they're all children. We never really lose a certain sense we had when we were kids.

Children may not be innocent, but they *are* vulnerable. They are honest. They have yet to develop the elaborate defenses and rationalizations of adulthood. Perhaps that is why they so frequently experience awe and wonder. No wonder the kingdom of heaven belongs to such as these (Mk 10:13-16).

So the Muppets represent something unique: irreverent but not bitter, childlike without being childish, playful at all costs (except that of others), sincerely self-effacing, hopeful but seldom saccharine. Again, whenever the moralism threatens to suck the fun out of the proceedings, a character wryly undermines the seriousness, as if on cue.

For instance, in one of Henson's final projects, the excellent TV-special *The Muppets at Walt Disney World*, a downcast Kermit encounters cutie Raven-Symone, erstwhile star of *The Cosby Show*. She attempts to cheer him up by singing his signature tune, "The Rainbow Connection." After the first line, Kermit deadpans into the camera, "I don't believe this."[22] Of course, one would be hard-

---

22. Disney purchased the Muppets franchise in 2004, and, sadly, the two sensibilities have never meshed. The difference was made indelibly clear in *The Muppets at Walt Disney World*. In a word, the Muppets aren't afraid of irony.

pressed to find a system that affords the same life-affirming hilarity in the face of human striving and sin other than the Judeo-Christian one.

Naturally, the Muppets have largely steered clear of religion. That is, unless you count the priceless scene in *The Muppet Movie* when Kermit and Fozzie encounter Dr. Teeth and his Electric Mayhem band practicing in a church, and Fozzie quips, "They don't look like Presbyterians to me." The closest they've come to the subject actually happened after Jim died, in *The Muppet Christmas Carol*, oddly enough one of the most faithful and moving adaptations of Dickens' classic ever put on screen. Paul Williams delivered his first Muppet songs since *The Muppet Movie*, Michael Caine made a devastating Scrooge, and the religious element wasn't muted in the slightest. In fact, the final five minutes are about as powerful an illustration of rebirth on the other side of repentance as Hollywood is likely to produce any time soon.

While the post-Henson outings have all had something to recommend them, Jim's absence has been acutely felt, not the least in the character of Kermit, who Henson voiced. One almost wishes the Muppet-verse had had the good sense to retire the little green guy when Jim shuffled off the planet. Kermit's scenes are too often marred by the nagging (and distracting) feeling that we're dealing with an imposter—a toad in frog's clothing, if you will. Fortunately, nothing is stopping us from re-watching the originals.

Like any institution (or ministry, for that matter), the sustainability of the Muppets says very little about their ultimate impact or significance. What Henson gave us is gift enough—enough to reacquaint even the most Sam the Eagle-ish of us with our inner Muppet and laugh ourselves silly. In other words, it's okay if they are never heard from again; this is just the closing line of the essay.

TOY STORY

A Journey of Heroic Repentance

by

Jeremiah Lawson

In Pixar's best movies, the conflict often plays out inside the main character's head. This might be why people who are into more conventional man vs man or man vs nature stories find Pixar villains disappointing. In *Toy Story*, Woody is not the hero simply because he beats the bad guys but because he is on a steady path of repenting of his own biases and fears.

When we first meet Woody, he is the chosen, favorite toy of a boy named Andy, and while he has urged other toys to trust in Andy's benevolence, Woody's own trust in Andy (who, for Woody, can be construed as God) is shaken by the arrival of a new toy, Buzz Lightyear

After he attempts to knock Buzz off the windowsill, in classic storytelling irony, he loses the trust of all his friends, even Slinky-Dog. Thanks to bad luck and his own envy, Woody finds himself trapped with Buzz in the home of toy-destroying Sid Phillips.

Woody and Buzz must be literally imprisoned in order to confront their respective fears and delusions. When Woody admits that he should be strapped to the rocket, he is able to see the wickedness in his heart and repent. He is also able to encourage Buzz, making him realize what a great toy he is, and that not being a real space ranger does not mean he has no value. This frees Woody to face his great fear that compared to the space ranger he could not possibly be loved or wanted by Andy. Together they are not only able to escape but to save Sid's toys from continual torture, and are finally reunited with Andy and his other toys.

We see the beginning of a compelling character study in the *Toy Story* journey. Those toys that seek to save and control their lives lose everything while those who sacrifice for Andy and other toys find they are allowed to keep their status as Andy's beloved.

In the second film, Woody fears that Andy will no longer want him if he is broken, and that the boy will one day grow up and no longer play with him. Buzz was deluded into believing he was a real space ranger in the first installment. Woody's great temptation in *Toy Story 2* is to trade in his identity as Andy's toy and friend of Buzz and the other toys, to become a rare collector's item. In an ironic reversal, Buzz is given the opportunity to remind Woody of what his real identity is and who really loves him. Having seen his fears and envy cause so much harm in the first film, Woody does not take very long to have a change of heart. He is tempted to stay with the Roundup Gang, but Buzz convinces him that his home is with Andy. Woody quickly sees that he was looking for fulfillment and love in the wrong place. He turns back to the love of his friends. Graciously, he offers Jessie and Bullseye the opportunity to join him and return to Andy's house.

Of course, the Prospector won't have this! He hated spending decade after decade watching every *other* toy get played with while he collected dust on a shelf. The envy and wrath that nearly destroyed Woody in the first Toy Story have completely consumed the Prospector. He serves as a grim reminder of what Woody could have become.

By *Toy Story 3*, our protagonist is completely reconciled to Andy's faithfulness and goodness. Woody has been in the family for at least two generations, so he is not going to be shelved or given away, and his friends know it. They fear Andy will not be so generous to them, and they will be sold off or, worse, thrown away. Woody's new conflict is with his own friends, as he must convince them to put their faith in Andy's goodness and generosity.

Woody's friends hedge their bets and get themselves donated to the Sunnyside daycare. There they are greeted by new toys, led by Lots-O'-Huggin. But appearances could not be more deceptive and, as one toy tells Woody, "Sunnyside is a place of ruin and despair ruled by an evil bear who smells of strawberries."

Lotso, like the Prospector before him, is the culmination of all the things Woody could have chosen to be. Not content merely to control the terms of his own life, he must exercise control over others as well. It's not enough to be the top toy in the heart of a child; he must be the self-contained master of his own destiny even when the lives and livelihood of other toys are at stake. As a toy that was lost, and who made the arduous trek back to his home only to see that he had been literally replaced, Lotso now rejects the very nature of what it means to be a toy: not merely knowing the joys of being played with but also the risk of being lost, abandoned, and replaced. As a former friend of Lotso says, "Something inside him changed." Lotso broke and could no longer be what he once was.

Where Woody sees his identity as emerging from the shared

experience of playtime with Andy, Lotso defines the lot of a toy in darker terms: "You are a piece of plastic. You were *made* to be thrown away...We're all just trash waiting to be thrown away. That's all a toy is."

Lotso would rather throw fellow toys into a landfill to be burned than concede that any child who owned a toy could really love it. Woody has met a toy so hardened against grief that he repays mercy with murder. When Woody and his friends reach out to save the twisted teddy bear, he betrays them for their help and leaves them to burn up. (Fittingly they are saved by still more cast-off toys!)

In the end, Lotso, who reveled in his power to be free of any need for a child's love, and scoffed at the mercy offered to him even by those he sought to destroy, is left pinned to the grill of a truck hurtling down the freeway. He never realized that the day-care children he hated after his owner replaced him were the only people preserving the fragile dominion he had fashioned for himself.

Much has been written on the touching final scene with Andy. He gives his toys to a little girl and introduces them: "Now Woody, he's been my pal for as long as I can remember. He's brave, like a cowboy should be. And kind, and smart...He'll be there for you, no matter what." Think of it as "Well done, good and faithful servant," for a toy. While Lotso says Woody is just a piece of trash, Andy describes Woody as a hero among heroes. We see in three films that Woody lives up to all that Andy says of him. Yet Woody's path is not one of triumph but a journey of heroic repentance.

Ten Great

WOODY ALLEN MOVIES

compiled by

JOHN AND DAVID ZAHL

The American independent film scene has bloomed so exquisitely in recent years that it is easy to forget the *original* homegrown alternative to Hollywood: Woody Allen. As troubling as aspects of the writer-director's personal life may be, his work speaks for itself, from the gorgeous cinematography and reliably brilliant ensemble work to the hilarious insights into male-female dynamics and admirably bleak takes on existential questions. It is possible to go wrong with his filmography though, simply given how extensive it is. Here is where the newcomer might start:

1) ANNIE HALL (1977)

The ultimate intro, bridging his early comedy with the more mature filmmaking that would define his most brilliant period. *Annie Hall* is the gateway into the world of Woody Allen. Notice the existential themes, the insight into what lies behind the curtain in romance, and the enduring ending, which holds up. Plus, there's the groundbreaking editing, and Diane Keaton in her quintessential role.

2) BROADWAY DANNY ROSE (1984)

More subtle than *Annie Hall*, and also more closely tied to Christian themes (humility, betrayal/forgiveness, the failure of religion as a means to control), the film is entirely driven by questions of legitimate vs. illegitimate love and the need for comfort in a superficial world. The closing Thanksgiving scene beautifully captures the vibe of early house churches from the Book of Acts, and the black and white photography is timelessly beautiful. *BDR* also happens to be Christopher Guest's favorite film.

3) MANHATTAN (1979)

The darker (and more profound), fully realized extension of what began in *Annie Hall*. Arguably Woody's very best movie from a critical standpoint, but with less hope...

4) STARDUST MEMORIES (1980)

...which is where *Stardust Memories* picks up. A smaller, riskier movie, full of classic Woody Allen moments and atheistic musings, albeit the sad, face-in-the-window variety (jazz heaven!). Those who've seen it will not be surprised that *Stardust Memories* was hated by critics at the time of its release. Yet the satire remains trenchant all these years later, and the relationship material still packs a punch. Charlotte Rampling's portrayal of mental illness is as haunting as any ever put to film.

5) HANNAH AND HER SISTERS (1986)

Well-rounded Woody, the apex of his peak period in the mid-to-late 1980s. Woody's ability to write for women (which he gives Diane Keaton credit for) is unparalleled. Sophisticated and full of heart without sacrificing humor, the chemistry of the three principal actresses is something to marvel at. As with all of his best films, the theme of subtext (i.e., motivation), the true story just beneath the surface, is the key to this movie. To real life too, one might add.

6) RADIO DAYS (1987)

Woody's romantic biopic about his upbringing in Brooklyn, *Radio Days* is a seamless mix of nostalgia, pathos and gags. A return to his more humorous material while retaining the winsome sentimentality. Take the gas-pipe!

7) HUSBANDS AND WIVES (1992)

The film that came out right before his life exploded. A devastatingly transparent portrait of marriage, divorce, and mid-life crises among the educated classes. The scene with the aerobics instructor at the party talking about astrology is one of the all-time great Woody Allen movie moments. Not the place to start, but if you've seen some of the ones mentioned above, watch this next. It was the last of the films made during his 'great' period.

8) BANANAS (1971)

No Woody Allen list would be complete without a taste of the slapstick and screwball comedy that propelled him to fame. While most of the early comedies are unbalanced, *Bananas* is the most consistent, rife with some of the twentieth century's greatest antics and one-liners. See if you can spot a short cameo from a young Sylvester Stallone, in his first film.

9) CRIMES AND MISDEMEANORS (1989)

Arguably Allen's very best movie. Something of an homage to Dostoyevsky, this one brims with Christian material (and is dead serious about it too), primarily related to the conscience beset with the baggage of sin. To those who find the dour notes off-putting, well, any honest depiction of life without God *should* be as depressing as Woody paints it here. Its low placement on this list is due only to the fact that *Crimes and Misdemeanors* is best appreciated as a Woody Allen film rather than, say, another great American dramedy.

10) ALICE (1990)

Quirky, fun, zany, a nice intro to the magical realism that has come to define the later period Woody Allen movies. *Alice* centers on the titular Upper East Side housewife, played by Mia Farrow, and the mid-life questions she finds herself asking about what it means to live purposefully. It takes the supernatural help of a Chinese herbal doctor to get her on track, but you'll love the ending.

HONORABLE MENTIONS/NEXT STEPS

Midnight in Paris (2011), *Bullets Over Broadway* (1994), *Manhattan Murder Mystery* (1993), *Sleeper* (1973), and the "Oedipus Wrecks" portion of *New York Stories* (1989).

The Pomade Won't Save You Now: Salvation and Sorrow in

O BROTHER WHERE ART THOU?

by

Lizzie Stallings

Redemption, it seems, is a product of self-reliance. And a palm-sized jar of pomade. At least this logic applies as far as Ulysses Everett T. McGill is concerned.

In the Coen Brothers' Depression-era adaptation of *The Odyssey*, Everett (George Clooney) and his two accomplices, Pete (John Turturro) and Delmar (Tim Blake Nelson), escape their labor sentence on a penal farm in Mississippi with the intent of recapturing Everett's hidden treasure, a sum worth 1.2 million dollars. The three covertly travel through cornfields, farmhouses, and town squares, traversing the all-too-familiar path of the impoverished American South while adopting a series of deceptive identities to throw off the law that pursues them.

The men find themselves in unlikely circumstances of all kinds: First they escape arrest with help from Pete's car-stealing nephew, then they pick up a young musician named Tommy who claims to have sold his soul to the devil; they are drugged by alluring 'sirens,' attacked by a manipulative 'cyclops,' implicated by an adrenaline-addicted bank robber, chased by corrupt politicians, and nearly killed by a blood-thirsty gang of Ku Klux Klan members. Perhaps the least anticipated thread, however, is the subtly ballooning fame of the trio's alter-ego, The Soggy Bottom Boys. They create this impromptu band in attempts to make some fast cash at a roadside recording studio shortly after their initial escape, and the single they record, "I Am a Man of Constant Sorrow" (based on Bob Dylan's of the same name[23]), quickly catapults the group to fame. It goes like this:

> *I am a man of constant sorrow…*
> *For six long years I've been in trouble*
> *No pleasure here on earth I found*
> *For in this world I'm bound to ramble*
> *I have no friends to help me now*

The melancholy song tells of a long, aimless journey ahead. The final lines, however, offer some hope: "But there is one promise that is given / I'll meet you on God's golden shore."

The Soggy Bottom Boys' subplot occurs alongside the rest of the action, so while the men themselves (Everett, Pete, and Delmar) attempt to remain incognito, their doppelgänger band becomes a sensation—despite the public believing that they're a crew of "negro one-hit-wonders." Their records fly off the shelves while they evade the law. The lyrics perform rather like a confessional, with Everett admitting his consistent state of rambling, uncertain despair. He has broken the law and avoided the consequences, and thus his life has been one of Sorrow.

---

23. Originally published by one Dick Burnett and first popularized by The Stanley Brothers.

However, it is the very notion of 'law' existing in the escapees' absurdist world that makes this real-life adaptation of Homer's mythological epic nearly as folkloric itself; each new character surpasses the last in his hypocrisy, with scenes dripping in ridiculous irony throughout the film. And yet, every one of these characters insists that his or her conventions are rational. These conventions are Machiavellian to the core—tactics to 'meet the goal' or 'get the gold' or just survive in the *O Brother* universe. In a realm entirely devoid of financial and moral certainty, acquiring the upper hand is really the only objective worth chasing, and thus all rules bend to meet this Grail. Everett's song, then, is a sarcastic justification of his felonious conduct; The Soggy Bottom Boys and their lyrics are about as ironic as it gets.

To understand this individualized state of morality, though, first one must understand a few of the protagonists and their opponents. These whimsical individuals, forced (or so they'd claim) to extreme behavior during the severe economic drought, loosely (but not explicitly) embody the canon of deadly sins.

To begin, we have Ulysses Everett T. McGill, i.e. 'Pride' the slick, handsome, and arrogant ringleader of the fleeing threesome. From the first scene, it is obvious that Everett fancies himself a man of reason; his logic, he presumes, will save them from any and all situations. His confidence is overwhelming, but he is also neurotic, and his obsession with having perpetually gelled hair reveals his compulsion for self-perfection throughout the film. Without his Dapper Dan, Everett McGill is a witless man.

Perhaps his most poignant quality, though, is his satirical relationship with religion. As the calamitous events influencing these three begin to resemble mystic intervention with increasing transparency, Everett reacts with quipped statements like: "Well, ain't it a small world, spiritually speaking. Pete and Delmar just been baptized and saved. I guess I'm the only one that remains unaffiliated." Of course, in the final scene of the movie, as a noose is being placed around his neck and the end looms near, the man drops to his knees in an uncharacteristic fit of distress, crying out to God to save him, despite his being guilty of "pride and short dealing." When a flood then washes through to save them, he responds:

> Well, any human being will cast about in a moment of stress. No, the fact is, they're flooding this valley so they can hydroelectric up the whole durn state...Out with the old spiritual mumbo jumbo, the superstitions, and the backward ways. We're gonna see a brave new world where they run everybody a wire and hook us all up to a grid. Yes, sir, a veritable age of reason. Like the one they had in France. Not a moment too soon.

While Everett is speaking, however, "I Am a Man of Constant Sorrow," an admission of weakness and woe, spreads like wildfire, contradicting his "reasoning ways."

The rest of his companions are no less ironic.[24] Wingman 2, or Pete Hogwallop, i.e. 'Lust,' is a countryman of the most stereotypical proportions. He is hot-blooded and quickly aroused, which serves to nearly kill him when he, Everett, and Delmar stumble upon three women singing and bathing on rocks in a stream. He succumbs to their advances and when his comrades awake, they find his clothes sans Pete, and believe he has been turned into a toad "on account o' the fornicatin'!" (Ultimately, they find him in a movie

24. While not necessarily embodying a deadly sin, Wingman 1, also known as Delmar O'Donnell, betrays a charming hint of irony as well: a simple and impressionable man, he is incarcerated for robbing a Piggly Wiggly. After escaping, he "gets himself baptized" in a cult-like service that he, Pete, and Everett encounter by a river. From that point forward, his reliance on God only strengthens, and he carries his baptism like an indulgence, an abstract shield protecting him from ultimate harm. Every exploit on their way to the stolen-treasure is in the name of the Lord, because Delmar "has been saved!"

theater and free him from his recapture so they can pursue 'the treasure' once more.)

Big Dan Teague, i.e. 'Gluttony' and 'Greed' combined (his enormous girth representative of his vices, it seems), serves as one of the heroes' greatest foes, as a one-eyed Bible salesman and member of the Ku Klux Klan who robs the men of their money after luring them into an isolated picnic on the country side. He dies at the hands of a lynch mob, which Everett, Pete, and Delmar interrupt to save Tommy, who also faces death-by-racists. Big Dan is ultimately crushed (we presume) beneath the weight of a burning cross as it crashes over his head.

Pappy O'Daniel, i.e. 'Greed' as well, is an unscrupulous politician feening for re-election. He will stop at nothing to achieve his goal, and thus at the end of the movie he endorses the Soggy Bottom Boys (who have snuck onstage to stop Everett's wife from marrying another man) and absolves them of their crimes, promising to protect them from the law, having seen how popular they are with the townspeople.

Next, we have Homer Stokes, who, as potentially the most villainous of them all, embodies multiple vices. He promises to be a "servant of the little man," fighting against "nepotism, rascalism, cronyism" and, most importantly, Pappy O'Daniel in the upcoming election. Then, in the scene with the KKK, he is revealed as the head of the mob, tearing off his mask to curse Everett, Pete, and Delmar for thwarting the terrorists' attempt to "preserve [the town's] hallowed culture and heritage!"

Finally, there is Sheriff Cooley, i.e. 'Wrath,' a relentless policeman who chases Everett, Pete, and Delmar to the very end, attempting to hang them all for foiling him time after time. Given that execution is too extreme for their crimes, they insist that Pappy

O'Daniel has pardoned them (as the Soggy Bottom Boys), crying "It ain't the law!" Cooley states: "The law? The law is a human institution."

O Brother presents us with a set of predictable eccentrics living according to their own rules, pitted together and against one another in scenarios created as the effects of adherence to (or dismissal of) constitutional law. Legally speaking, every one of these men has broken this law somehow or another, and yet they believe their actions are justifiable, implicitly moral and redemptive in their own unique right. Everett has to save his marriage, Delmar has to buy back his farm. Pete insists on family loyalty, and Homer wants to reestablish purity in a "misceginatin' world." Their corruptions are well-founded; in a world of impoverished debauchery, the ends seems to justify the means. The characters' objectives range from reasonable to grotesquely dogmatic, but regardless these men believe they are upholding a standard. The constitutional law only holds weight when they need it to, which skews the morals of the *O Brother* universe even further.

Everett, Delmar, Pete, and their enemies represent their values with fervor, but this symbolic fervor does not bring them to the treasure, nor to power, nor to security. Their respective ideals, or those results that will bring them fulfillment, none of them save these men from their transgressions. One by one, these characters meet a near-fatal—or completely fatal—end. Their rules, or the created morals to which they adhere, fail them. Big Dan dies and Homer falls out of public favor. Pete is re-arrested then almost hanged along with Everett and Delmar, and though Everett gets his wife back, their final conversation ends in strife.

And yet there is one factor woven throughout the storyline, one factor to which every character—big and small—relates: the song.

The Soggy Bottom Boys are champions to the people because, despite their failures as individuals, they sing the truth.

They are Men of Constant Sorrow, all of them, attempting to make some sense out of a world robbed of morality and security. The economy is depressed, but the people of *O Brother* are *op*pressed, and thus they try to create mini-redemptions for themselves, objectives to aim for amidst the swirling dust and moneyless desperation of their realities. Everett, for one, has a plan: If his hair is perfectly gelled, his words sound, and his marriage saved, his sorrows will be erased. He will be well, and the world will be on his side once more. However, as *O Brother* proves time and time again, plans fall through, hopes are dashed, and expectations become jokes for the audience's pleasure.

The ironies and hypocrisies breed absurdity, but against the grain of satire The Soggy Bottom Boys spin a yarn more honest and more reliable than any bout of reasoning that Everett, Delmar, or Pete could convey. Their self-constructed rules for survival emerge as twisted logic, and yet they cling tight to these structured hopes for deliverance.

The title of the film asks: "O Brother, where art thou?" Everett, Pete, and Delmar seem to be asking this same question throughout. They turn to themselves and each other. They turn to the world. "O Brother, where art thou? Where do we meet? What do we have in common?" The Soggy Bottom Boys answer: We have the Sorrow. There is trouble and there will be trouble, but at the end of that trouble, we will see one another "on God's golden shore."

Just Another Word for Nothing Left to Lose:
The American Lie of an

EASY RIDER

by

Ethan Richardson

Flow, river, flow
Let your waters wash down
Take me from this road
To some other town

It is a disservice to lump *Easy Rider* into the slews of American 'counterculture' or 'indie' films of the late 1960s and early 70s. It's not that these descriptors aren't accurate–both are quite true–or that it wasn't a hippie film, standing against those "scissor-happy, beautify America" typesetters that George Hanson (Jack Nicholson) classifies in the film. What makes it different, though, is that its critique is too inclusive, too comprehensive, to merely stand against the mainstream. As Peter Fonda said in *Shaking the Cage*, a documentary about the making of the film, *Easy Rider*'s indictment was aimed at nothing less than the whole of America: "We don't let anyone out of the theater…you can't put it under the seat in the theater–you have to truck it home with you."

From the beginning, Fonda and Hopper (producer and director, respectively) sought to create a true-to-life American Road Odyssey, a spur-studded tribute to freedom–the engined outlaw–the "Machine Western" as Fonda described it at Cannes. You see it in the names of Fonda's and Hopper's characters, Wyatt and Billy. You see it in the fringed leather, the fireside chats, the repeated references to independence. It is a modern rendering of two paper-cut cowboys, and yet, its rendering here, on a couple of motorcycles, pushes the tradition of American freedom to its outer reaches. Hopper described the term 'easy rider' as a man who lives off of a whore, not as her pimp, but as her financially dependent lover. For a movie spent predominantly on two badass bikes, with Peter Fonda riding across America like a cowboy, the title drastically discolors the picture of freedom we're given. Its pursuit suddenly feels rigged.

Take the flag. The American flag is almost like a supporting actor in the film. It is decaled on Wyatt's teardrop gas tank, on his helmet, on the back of his black leather jumpsuit. It feels as though it is multiplied in the hopes it compounds the freedom. And yet the very symbol of freedom is immediately a showy caricature, a heroic impracticality. The California chopper itself was all about style and swagger. It had painful consequences for a cross-country journey, as Fonda would later admit after his days of shooting on the bike. And don't forget about the tube of drug money, shoved secretively in the American gas tank, an ominous image of greed behind the stars and bars.

Take the commune. The confounding hippie retreat, where lovers commingle and babies run naked and disregarded; comers and goers are spiritual messengers. Amid the abundant drug use, it feels like a valiant effort at free living, but a dire one; an image sticks of serious-faced young men and women sowing seed on hard, dry dirt. You get the picture that the communal living idea doesn't seem all that ridiculous, but it is only that: an idea. When it comes to letting loose from the old institutions, let alone feeding themselves, they're on fallow ground.

Take the jail scene, or any of the scenes following for that matter, and you see an ill-conceived fellowship of 'free men,' whose interactions with the world around them stir only defensive reactions. Hopper and Fonda are imprisoned for joining a parade, a celebration. They sleep outside because hotel rooms are suddenly booked up when they arrive. Nicholson as the ACLU lawyer (lawyers of liberty!) George Hanson, someone who would be lumped in with the respectable elite, joins the chopper voyage and, despite his comely appearance, becomes lumped in as one of the "freaks" at the Louisiana diner. No one likes to see the freaks of freedom, but what's worse is one of 'us' becoming one of 'them.' George, before his murder, delivers the pivotal monologue (the monologue that started Jack Nicholson's career) on humanity's complicated relationship with freedom.

> Talking about it and *being* it is two different things. It's real hard to be free when you are bought and sold in the marketplace. 'Course don't tell anybody they're not free, because they're gonna get real busy killing and maiming to prove to you that they are. They're going to talk to you and talk to you about individual freedom. But when they see a free individual it is going to scare them...it makes them dangerous.

Kierkegaard describes anxiety as "quivering at the edge of freedom," that freedom understood by fearful human beings is actually a dangerous proposition. Christ's freedom certainly did not lead him into safety. His life's trajectory makes sense of George's speech. And yet, Paul's letter to the Galatians tells us that Christ's gift for us is nothing short of the same: "It is for freedom that Christ has set us free."[25]

We are left at the end of the campfire scene thinking that George Hanson is giving something like the last rites of the hippie age, a glorifying salute to the kind of life being lived in the commune. *You will be free, and they will kill you for it.* Hanson seems to be pointing them back to the yurt, as if to say the age of peace and love really was the arrival of perfect freedom.

But that picture gets complicated in the buildup to the final scene. The chopper duo finally lands on the other side of New Orleans—after a weekend of prostitutes, acid, and graveyards—and the completion of their journey feels more like a hangover than a culmination. Camping out once again, Billy is glad to have arrived at freedom's gate, money still secure in the teardrop-tank. He tells Wyatt the moral of the story: "You go for the big money and you're free, you dig?" For Billy, freedom is still bound to the American Dream of acquisition—freedom is getting things and keeping them. Freedom is take-the-money-and-run; it is retirement in Florida. Wyatt doesn't agree: "We blew it." He rolls over to go to sleep, and the American flag on his leather jacket rolls over with him, like it's dead. After hitting it big, even this idea of freedom is wrong. It isn't freedom at all.

In the final scene, after the bikes blow up, after the ride is over, the camera pans out over the wreckage. As it pulls up and away from the crash, we see laid out the road that led them there, and the heavy, rolling river to its side. Fonda here insinuates an answer for the problem of freedom. In an interview about that final scene, he remembers telling Bob Dylan what a ballad for the Easy Rider

25. Gal 5:1

might be: "You see, there's the road that man builds, and we can see that, and there's the river, and that's the road that God builds, and so you can see what happens on the road that man builds." Hence the "Ballad."

> *The river flows*
> *It flows to the sea*
> *Wherever that river goes*
> *That's where I want to be*

The movie makes known that no man is truly free, but bound up in himself, in his own conception of freedom. Freedom then, for the likes of Dylan and the Byrds, the final sounds of the film, has to do with being led. Not leading, not taking, not running. It is a surrender unto the road of God, a baptism into the river, a falling in and letting go.

Put Down the Gun, Honey Bunny:
The "Realer than Real" World of

QUENTIN TARANTINO

by

BRYAN JARRELL

It is a Hollywood legend that Tarantino's love of film started in his childhood. He dropped out of high school to pursue acting school at age fifteen, though he soon dropped out of acting school too. His next move would be finding work at a video rental store, a now mostly extinct vocation. Even before this rental job, Tarantino had a love for films, including the lower budget B-movie cult classics most moviegoers wouldn't recognize. QT testifies that this video rental job would be the catalyst for his moviemaking career, giving him full access to the best films ever created—even the ones no one else had ever seen. The word 'autodidact' is often used to describe Tarantino, who once told the BBC, "When people ask me if I went to film school I tell them 'no, I went to films.'" The man's life always revolved around movies, and the movie world that defined the first twenty years of Tarantino's life would become the foundation for his directing career.

While working as a rental store clerk, Tarantino met a Hollywood producer at a party, who convinced him to try writing a screenplay, which was eventually sold and made into a movie. Seeing potential in Tarantino's writing, the pair were then able to bring actor Harvey Keitel into their first independent film, 1992's *Reservoir Dogs*, a violent heist film and psychological thriller that played with chronology and, remarkably, didn't actually show the heist. The film impressed audiences at the famous Cannes Film Festival and brought Tarantino into the attention of Hollywood's business elite. In 1994, Tarantino released *Pulp Fiction* to near universal acclaim. A mashup of multiple storylines about a seedy Los Angeles underworld, *Fiction* showcased creative dialogue, exposed viewers to nauseating levels of violence, and drew out uniquely stellar acting from an all-star cast. *Fiction* won top honors at Cannes and gained the Hollywood accolades necessary to solidify Tarantino's future in directing.

To date, Quentin Tarantino has released a total of eight films. Alongside the already mentioned *Reservoir Dogs* and *Pulp Fiction*, QT directed *Jackie Brown*, the two-part *Kill Bill* series, *Death Proof*, *Inglorious Basterds*, *Django Unchained*, and *The Hateful Eight*. When Tarantino wasn't directing, he would occasionally step in to help produce a film, or advocate for a smaller film's wider release. Both *Fiction* and *Django* garnered Academy Award wins for Tarantino's screenplays, and his actors have often been nominated for (and won) their own awards.

All this to say, Tarantino loves movies, and he's good at making them. So when viewers sit down to enjoy one of his films, what can they expect?

DIALOGUE

Some of the most entertaining parts of Tarantino movies are listening to his characters interact. When *Pulp Fiction* introduces viewers to mafiosos Vince and Jules, the two are riding in a car discussing how different the "little things" are between Europe and the U.S., like the fact that McDonalds' famous 'Quarter Pounder with Cheese' is called a 'Royale with Cheese' in France because of the metric system. Tarantino gives the hitmen quirky, seemingly natural, lines instead of relying on dialogue to move the plot forward.

ACTORS

Tarantino is known for his creative casting, finding the perfect actor for the perfect part. Samuel L. Jackson makes appearances in most of Tarantino's movies. Christoph Waltz and Uma Thurman gained international fame for respectively portraying Col. Hans Landa in *Inglorious Basterds* and Mia Wallace in *Pulp Fiction*. John Travolta's work in *Fiction* resurrected his acting career, distancing him from his roles in *Saturday Night Fever* and *Grease*. Look for famous actors throughout Tarantino's work, especially in places you'd least expect them.

MUSIC/SOUNDTRACK

Japanese katana battles are overdubbed with mariachi music, torture scenes are juxtaposed by 70's pop. David Bowie sings over Nazi-occupied France, and antebellum Django rides off into the sunset to the funky bass grooves of disco and soul. Creative music choices are a key part of Tarantino's storytelling. Keep an ear out—these quirky musical choices are also clues to how a scene should be understood.

EASTER EGGS

Throughout his relatively short filmography of seven movies, there's a growing list of sight gags, repeated shots, and inside jokes that add another layer of visual storytelling. For example, most of

Tarantino's films include a Mexican Standoff, where enemies have loaded guns pointed at one another, creating the tension of a mutually assured destruction scenario. Most of Tarantino's films involve characters wearing black and white suits. As new Tarantino movies are released, devoted fans will be looking for these visual bread crumbs that link his filmography across multiple decades.

CINEMATIC HOMAGE

For movie watchers with a critical eye, Tarantino is easily caught borrowing (or, pejoratively, plagiarizing) scenes, ideas, tropes, and shots from other movies. This is perhaps the most important tool to have handy when watching a QT film because it adds a level of context to the film's story. Sometimes these allusions are absurdly obscure. At the beginning of *Jackie Brown*, titular airline stewardess Jackie is shot standing still on an airport moving walkway, with the camera moving the same speed and tracking her in the frame. The effect is that Jackie looks to be standing still while the airport background behind her is moving. This shot is identical to the opening of 1967's *The Graduate*, where recent college graduate Benjamin Braddock (Dustin Hoffman) is similarly tracked on an airport moving walkway. QT is telling the viewers that the same malaise that led one character to an unwise affair with Mrs. Robinson leads the other character to unwisely transport money for a weapons dealer. But he only uses the lens of the camera to say it.[26]

26. As an aside, good readers of the Bible will already have had practice at this skill. When John writes of seven trumpet judgments in Revelation, readers are right to think back to Jericho's walls in the book of Judges, which fell to the ground after seven blasts of the war trumpet. When Jesus groans, "My God, my God, why have you forsaken me?" readers are wise to return to Psalm 22. If it helps, think of Tarantino movies as cinematic Bibles where the viewer is invited to create the cross-referencing footnotes, although viewers wanting more entertainment and fewer mental hoops will still enjoy the experience.

VIOLENCE

The most well known trademark of Tarantino's films is violence. And to be clear, Tarantino's violence is not limited to the bloody shootouts or limb-removing sword fights that make headlines. Our director has no qualms about using verbal violence, whether it's expletives or racial slurs, nor does he shy away from sexual violence. Psychopaths, revenging crusaders, gangsters, and assassins populate Tarantino's cinematic world, creating much of the conflict that drives these film's storylines.

The question for more nuanced viewers is not 'what' but 'why.' Does Tarantino's violence have a purpose in his films? The answer is unequivocally Y-E-S. There is meaning behind Tarantino's violence, and it has everything to do with the "realer than real world" in which Tarantino's movies take place.

THE "REALER THAN REAL" WORLD

Reservoir Dogs, *Pulp Fiction*, *Jackie Brown*, *Inglorious Basterds*, and *Django Unchained* all take place in the same movie universe. QT has said so himself, calling the stories and characters in them "realer than the real world." These five movies create a cinematic universe defined by power, drugs, violence, lust, and survival of the fittest. The law at its most ideal—whether it exists in the form of police, government, religion, social pressure—does not exist, except to be lampooned or dismissed. Tarantino World is *Lord of the Flies* meets the Wild West American Frontier, where 'good' and 'bad' are less accurate descriptions of people than 'strong' and 'weak.'

Everybody has weapons in this Tarantino World. It's no coincidence that a scared old lady shoots Mr. Orange in *Reservoir Dogs*, or that a secret shooter hides in the bathroom in the first act of *Pulp Fiction*. Weapons represent power, the assertion of control over other people. Cars become weapons, razor blades and gasoline become weapons, snakes become weapons. When watching Tarantino films, keep an eye out for who has weapons and how those weapons are used. It will say something about the character. The ubiquity of weapons shows us that Tarantino's "realer than real" world is built on a giant hidden Mexican standoff, where assertions of power are met with equal assertions of violence.

In Tarantino World's history, there are no oppressors, or at least there are no oppressors for very long. Those they oppress quickly overthrow them. Hitler and crew are killed in *Inglorious Basterds* by a combination of players: a Nazi defector who sees the war's coming end, a French Jewish girl and her black lover, and a team of American Jewish commandos led by Aldo the Apache. In *Django Unchained*, a black slave and a sophisticated European bounty hunter outwit white Southern men of wealth and power.

Tarantino's "realer than real" world is, by virtue of his "realer than real" title, a world of judgment against our own 'fake' world. Tarantino gives us selfish characters, tragic characters, or, to borrow language from the Bible, sinful characters. It is not Tarantino who anesthetizes violence, as the critics might say—it is our world that refuses to acknowledge the real violence Tarantino portrays. Critics who see Tarantino's films as desensitizing, amoral, or nihilist haven't looked close enough. These films betray a voice of righteous judgment, a cinematic version of Southern 'Gothic' writer Flannery O'Connor minus the Roman Catholicism. The prophetic word of judgment buried in Tarantino's films is that no one is righteous—no, not one.

Take for example, the message of *Inglorious Basterds*. Its fictional World War II plot revolves around the premier of the newest Nazi propaganda film. Hitler and the rest of the Nazi high command are all planning to attend the premiere, and a plot to kill the

Nazi high command is set in motion by the secretly Jewish theater owner and the team of American commandos. Tarantino frequently shows his audience scenes from the Nazi premiere: As the brave Nazi sniper in the belltower kills dozens, hundreds, of Allied soldiers, the Nazi leaders in attendance cheer and clap with joy. We moviegoers, of course, are unimpressed, maybe even offended, at the Nazi propaganda; but we moviegoers know that the American commandos and the Jewish theater owner have their plans, and so we wait patiently through these propaganda scenes for our good guys to strike.

When the revenge hammer does fall, it falls hard. The violence in the scene is appalling. Nazi officials are burned alive, struck down by gunfire, blown up by bombs. Blood squirts onto theater walls. Bullets pour into Hitler's face, disfiguring it into a bloody mess. The whole movie has led to this climactic moment: The plots are successful, the theater explodes with the Nazi leadership inside, and the war is over. We are even given a patriotic cherry on top: The slippery Col. Landa is given a swastika scar on his forehead in a final act of judgment.

Our joy at the Nazis' cinematic defeat is not at all different from their joy at the Allies' destruction in the propaganda film. When it comes to propaganda, says Tarantino, we are just as guilty as the Nazis. "You, the viewers, are more like the Nazis than you care to admit," says *Basterds* through the violence, explosions, and irony. "You both enjoy films which flatter your ideals and your ways of life."

The same word of judgment can be found in *Django Unchained*. Here, QT attacks films that present sanitized images of the American South, where happy, wealthy white plantation families and their equally happy black servants boldly overcome whatever challenges they face (usually these challenges are caused by Northerners). These slave-free depictions of the American South are not real, and Tarantino sees it as his duty to inject some reality back into that genre. While *Django*'s plot revolves around the rescue of Django's beloved wife Broomhilda, the message of the film stands clear: Here is the 'real' antebellum South, with ignorant Bible-thumping slave drivers, cruel and paranoid plantation owners, idiotic, bumbling proto-Klansmen, and a society of violent racists with no notion of real justice. These are caricatures, for sure, but since normal images of antebellum slavery rarely elicit strong emotions in our time, Tarantino increases the violence to provide the shock the audience should have appropriate to the subject. As the climactic shootouts progress, Django is no longer killing to rescue his bride, but he is killing the Rhett Butler and Scarlett O'Hara versions of the American South, along with our notions of a glorified American History.

The film world of Tarantino is so complex, but its purpose is clear: No one is righteous in Tarantino World. If Tarantino created a full-blown Western movie, the cowboys would all have black hats, and there would be no sheriff. Rarely with Tarantino do we get the luxury of classifying characters as good or bad—most of them are a grey mix of both. Like visual representations of what the Apostle Paul calls "the flesh," Tarantino's characters are driven to self-preservation at the expense of all the other characters, curved in on themselves to reflect that same reality back at the movie's viewers.

PUT DOWN THE GUN, HONEY BUNNY: REDEMPTION AND PULP FICTION

If all of Tarantino's other films are words of judgment against films that portray a rose-tinted view of the world, void of injustice, violence, and greed, *Pulp Fiction* is the exception. It gives us a glimpse at real characters that, surprisingly, uniquely, unexpectedly, become agents of grace. In the rest of Tarantino world, we cannot find characters interested in anything outside of self-preservation, revenge, reunion with a spouse, money, or survival. Despite the overwhelming violence of *Pulp Fiction*, two characters experience moments of divine grace, which translate into a desire to love others—including their enemies.

The first redemption happens when boxer Butch Coolidge (Bruce Willis), who was supposed to throw his big fight, wins big and double-crosses mob boss Marcellus Wallace. Having bet on himself, Butch is now rich for life, and flees the city with lover Fabienne, trying to avoid Wallace's hitmen. In a jarring string of events, Butch and Wallace end up bound at gunpoint and locked in the basement of a pawn shop owned by deviant sexual predators. While these two predators sexually assault Wallace, Butch escapes, knowing that he can now run free from Wallace's influence. On the way out of the pawn shop, he has a change of heart. Taking a Japanese samurai sword from the front counter, Butch returns to the basement and rescues Wallace, who in return promises Butch's safety if he leaves LA and keeps the day's events a secret.

Tellingly, as Butch leaves, he takes the keys to a motorcycle from one of the dead rapists. Riding as a free man to meet Fabienne, the audience can see the word 'grace' clearly emblazoned on the side of the chopper. Tarantino wants us to see an unselfish act of grace, where the empathy of one man leads to the (admittedly temporary) salvation of a second. Debts are cancelled, enemies are loved, and (some) sinners are forgiven. Is there a better name than 'grace' for a motorcycle ridden by the man who rescued his enemy?

A second redemption happens when hitman Jules Winnfield

(Samuel L. Jackson) encounters a divine miracle. After Jules famously quotes a fictional Bible verse and executes some teens who tried to take his mob boss's briefcase, a hidden gunman jumps out from the bathroom and fires six close range shots at Jules and hitman friend Vince (John Travolta). All six bullets in the revolver miss, much to the shock of the hitmen who stop to check their bodies for wounds before retaliating. They quickly dispatch the once-hidden gunman, and a bewildered Jules turns and stares at the bullet holes in the wall behind him.

"This was divine intervention," declares Jules. "You know what divine intervention is?"

A sarcastic Vince replies: "I think so. It means God came down from heaven and stopped the bullets?"

"That's right. That's exactly what it means," says Jules, emphatically. "God came down from heaven and stopped these motherfucking bullets."

The two argue over their good fortune throughout the film—were they lucky or were they blessed? Was the shooting a miracle or a freak accident? Jules officially interprets the shooting as a divine sign, and plans to retire as a hitman that very morning. Vince remains skeptical.

Arriving at a diner for breakfast, they continue their conversation about miracles and freak accidents. As Jules reaffirms his intentions to retire, musing that he doesn't know why God chose to intervene, Pumpkin and Honey Bunny begin robbing the diner. As the thieves attempt to steal the mob boss's briefcase, Jules pulls a gun on Pumpkin, and the scene quickly turns into a Mexican Standoff. With all four characters a hair trigger from death, Jules takes charge, delivering a monologue that many consider Samuel L. Jackson's finest acting moment:

> There's a passage I got memorized. Ezekiel 25:17: "The path of the righteous man is beset on all sides by the inequities of the selfish and the tyranny of evil men. Blessed is he who, in the name of charity and goodwill, shepherds the weak through the valley of darkness...I will strike down upon thee with great vengeance and furious anger those who attempt to poison and destroy my brothers. And you will know I am the Lord when I lay my vengeance upon you." I been sayin' that shit for years. And if you ever heard it, it meant your ass. I never really questioned what it meant. I thought it was just a cold blooded thing to say to a motherfucker 'fore you popped a cap in his ass. But I saw some shit this mornin' made me think twice.
>
> Now I'm thinkin' it could mean *you're* the evil man. And I'm the righteous man. And Mr. .45 here, he's the shepherd protecting my righteous ass in the valley of darkness. Or it could mean you're the righteous man and I'm the shepherd and it's the world that's evil and selfish. I'd like that.
>
> But that shit ain't the truth. The truth is you're the weak, and I'm the tyranny of evil men. But I'm trying. I'm tryin' real hard to be a shepherd.

Jules lowers his gun, laying it on the table. The power of the scene is staggering. A redeemed Jules spares the restaurant robbers, keeping the briefcase, but giving them $1,500 of his own personal money. Jules buys their freedom from his own wallet. If he gives them his money, they are no longer thieves deserving of his wrath, but simply recipients of his generosity. Jules confesses that he is the tyranny of evil men, struggling to turn over a new leaf, and slowly puts down his gun. Remember, in Tarantino World, it is unspoken but true that everyone is out for their own self-preservation. Lowering a weapon is unheard of, and yet Jules makes himself vulnerable so he can end the Mexican standoff. That level of self-sacrifice—that willingness to die to save others—is as redemptive as it comes, whether it takes the form of a New Testament crucifixion or a gangster uncocking his gun. When Tarantino needs to portray redemption, he can't help but draw on the image of Jesus, who showed the world just how radical real redemption can be. Jules's isn't a Christ figure by any stretch—but he is someone saved by grace, "paying it forward" to equally undeserving criminals.

ARIVOIR, SHOSHANA!

Again, the rabbit hole here with Tarantino's filmography is very, very deep. It's a filmography full of original sin, with characters that play the foil to expose the viewer's own sinfulness. There is no self-justification, no righteousness, no pretense in these films. Aside from Butch the boxer and Jules the hitman, there is no love of God, love of neighbor, or love of enemy. Of vengeance, anger, and craziness, there is plenty. But there is very little grace, almost no forgiveness, and only whispers of divine love, which reflect the world as it 'really' is.

And yet, there is one last relationship worth mentioning—the love that our director has for cinema. Rarely do we meet a cinephile of his caliber, someone who eats and breathes and sleeps 35mm technicolor film. It's not hard to imagine that the younger Tarantino found respite in the Grindhouse theaters of his childhood, watching with starry eyes the Gunslingers and Shaolin Monks and Foxy Browns of the 60's and 70's while other kids played sports or joined the yearbook club. As welcoming voices of non-judgment and friendship, movies were an agent of grace to Tarantino the kid, so it's no surprise that Tarantino the director has devoted his life to the gospel of motion pictures.

In a way, despite the genre mishmashes, violence, and rabbit holes, all of Tarantino's films are love stories between the director and his medium. Tarantino is a disciple of cinema, not out of some slavish need for validation, but because in the world of motion pictures, he finds his heart "strangely warmed." He makes no room for cinema sins like sexism and racism, pollyanna characters in pollyanna cultures, or fake stories about a reality that doesn't exist. Instead, like a hitman who retires because of a religious experience, or the pearl merchant who sells his whole stock to acquire a single, perfect, unblemished pearl, Tarantino, full of gratitude, gives his life for the sake of his craft.

The lesson here is clear: Tarantino loves movies because movies loved him first. That love creates passion, discipleship, fidelity, and creativity in the director, which results in some of the best characters and films to hit the silver screen. By soaking his screenplays in the reality of original sin, rejecting characters that refuse to acknowledge their conflicted souls, and leaving just enough room for the possibility of divine redemption, Tarantino invites viewers to follow him down the rabbit hole of cinematic history to find the same love he has found.

The Comforts of Irony and the Terror of Earnestness

METROPOLITAN

by

William McDavid

Mockingbird favorite Whit Stillman's wonderful debut film, *Metropolitan*, is a social commentary which continually crosses over, wryly and adroitly, into the domain of religious experience, Law and Gospel, anxiety and trust. It follows a young group of debutantes and their escorts in New York City, those sons and daughters of established wealth whose socio-economic trajectory has, in their twenties, stalled out. They are the natural members of a generation of new, white aristocracy ('Urban *Haute Bourgeoisie*,' or UHB), waiting in the wings but, as the prodigious intellectual-cum-self-parody Charlie puts it, "Downward social mobility…I think that's the direction we're all heading in."

But for now they're mostly just stalling, poised between upward momentum and inertial stillness. In addition to the quite absurd out-loud thinker Charlie, there is Nick (Stillman/Baumbach favorite, Chris Eigeman), an obnoxious cynic with deep insight and dry humor; Tom, a well-mannered and well-read intellectual but of "limited resources," who is magnetized to the deb circuit though he morally opposes it in principle; and Fred, a drunk who's the closest Stillman comes here to slapstick. On the female side, there's Audrey, a reserved, good-girl type with a crush on Tom; Jane, a dry-witted realist enamored of Nick's penchant for critical honesty; Cynthia, a free spirit; and Sally Fowler, a blonde who hosts get-togethers at her apartment during the deb season with the above group, known as the Sally Fowler Rat Pack, or SFRP.

Two disclaimers: First, if I've described the female characters mostly in terms of the male ones, then that's only because Stillman builds a satiric element of male initiative into *Metropolitan*'s world; second, the prevalence of acronyms in the movie playfully reflects the easy familiarity and determined non-showiness common to all the denizens of the SFRP.

Tom is introduced to the pre-existing world of Sally Fowler apartment gatherings almost by chance, and the charms of this world are so lulling that he almost gives up his Fourierian socialism. Audrey soon develops a crush on him, but Tom's continuing attachment to his ex-girlfriend, Serena, brings the group into closer contact with an intolerable member of the titled aristocracy: Rick von Sloneker.

Von Sloneker is certainly Stillman's most memorable villain; although he's reputedly done terrible things to girls, his real sin, by UHB standards, is *trying*.

To see von Sloneker's variance with WASP-y, or UHB-y, values, we first turn to Charlie's prediction of how the doom of the aristocracy, or "downward social mobility," will take place:

> Take those of our fathers who grew up very well off. Maybe their careers started out well enough. But just when their contemporaries really began accomplishing things, they started

> quitting, not openly, but in other ways—"rising above" office politics, refusing to compete and risk open failure...where even if they were total failures no one would know it.

One core value of Stillman's young aristocracy is 'social grace,' meaning a basic giftedness and natural aptitude for navigating people and society. To people who really value social grace, something like the term 'networking,' for example, may be an almost intolerable word—to think that forming profitable friendships is something dependent on practice, intention, or effort! Anything one does not do naturally, as a result of proper upbringing and good sense, reeks of artificiality. And so trying too hard must be avoided, because that would be a violation of the basic trust that given one's social context, one cannot fail to succeed—barring, perhaps, serious addiction or a DUI in the wrong state.

This basic trust in social grace is the world Stillman's characters inhabit and, for all its faults, it has real charm, to the point that some analogy can be made between this trust and religious trust. Meaning: If one has the basic confidence that all things will be well, regardless of where they are now, there is a simple freedom to say and do almost anything, and that freedom tends to produce wit, humor, and something akin to joy. The person who deliberately tries to earn his future well-being—financial or religious—does violence to grace's assurance in the first place. Trying implies control, which violates destiny—and destiny alone confers freedom, by taking the weight off the present.

And so we see how it's so funny and apt that von Sloneker is the villain: He is the 'douchebag' who violates coolness by trying to earn it, violates social destiny by being so aggressive, whether that be calling Audrey a prude or punching Nick in the face. And worse, von Sloneker lacks irony: His straightforwardness is unreflectedly self-justifying, an unselfconscious effort to exert his will and communicate something. Nick, who hates him, represents the apogee of the UHB with regard to his self-awareness and cynicism and irony. Regardless of how well or poorly he treats women, Nick must always hate him and discredit him.

And yet, there's a problem with the 'ub': Times are changing, or at least they seem to be, and the guarantees of the past don't seem to apply with the same force to *this* generation. The inability to try and fail—which is the very characteristic of their culture—is somehow the thing that seems to be paralyzing them. Though the film was written in the late eighties, it's hard to place the exact cultural timeline of why their fathers had an inability to try and fail. To take a simplified guess—they likely weren't war veterans.

But what matters now is this paralysis and that, amidst the advantages of trust funds and Ivy League degrees, things seem less sure than they were. They may be fine financially, but what about purpose, identity, prestige?

Charlie recognizes the threat of failure better than anyone, and his defense is a strangely passionate fatalism. He just assumes that they'll fail and there's nothing anyone can do about it. A man at a bar near the end talks with Charlie, and exposes the absurdity of Charlie's fatalism: "'Doomed?' That would make it easier. We just fail without being doomed."

For Nick, on the other hand, the solution is an irony which he deploys against the threat of inertia or 'downward social mobility.' He never tries and fails because he never tries, never attempts to say anything sincere, except when that loathsome von Sloneker guy is brought up. Nick's running social commentary is the film's most constant voice of cynical truth; but his deconstruction of the other characters' efforts and motivations, while usually true, is motivated by a need to prove that their effort and earnestness will get them no further than his own cynicism will get him.

And yet Nick, with his perceptiveness, conspires with Audrey (she's the real architect, according to Stillman), to bring Tom, a young red-headed ideologue, into the group. Tom, as a trust-fund kid with a Princeton education, fits well into the group socially, though he's been financially strapped since his parents' divorce three years earlier. While Tom isn't really a 'triehard,' his earnestness does make the viewer (and more than one of the characters) question why Nick likes him so much. Nick replies that he's basically a good guy, but apart from that and perhaps a loyalty to Audrey, it's possible Nick's attracted to him because Nick's parents were divorced too.

Divorce shakes their providential sense of well-being, putting Nick and Tom emotionally in touch with the reality which Charlie vocalized. Thus Nick's defensive irony and Tom's defensive ideology: They have both fallen, at different times, through the cracks in their providential world—they know 'downward mobility' of some sort firsthand. And Nick's inclusion of Tom in the group is a good deed, whether for him or for Audrey or both—and it's in earnestness that Stillman finds hope for the quickly-disintegrating SFRP.

Nick reveals Tom's ideology for the travesty it is, midwifing Tom into a world beyond Fourier. (And yes, I'm trying not to lose sight of the movie's utter absurdity). Once Tom starts reading Selena's letters (while Audrey cries—on Christmas Day! Hope dawns before 'orgy week'!), Nick's role in the movie is drawing to a close, first as the groomer of Tom—since he, the movie's hero, is starting on the path to 'redemption,' and second as the film's sardonic Tiresias—since the prophet of failure can neither predict nor assimilate true romance.

(Okay, so 'true romance' is a strong term for a mostly Quixotic quest to save Audrey from that evil von Sloneker's house in the Hamptons. Wherever Stillman makes a serious point, there's a stroke of satire lying just behind it. The style matches the content; the movie itself could never be accused of saying anything *too* serious, and that's a major part of its charm.)

The great irony of Nick's and the others' preoccupation with social grace is that von Sloneker, who seems to be breaking good form by being so damn sincere and effortful, is that he actually exudes effortlessness. His overt machismo and arrogance don't come from a place of trying to earn his social stature, but rather the opposite. The irony is that von Sloneker actually *does* possess socio-economic providence, in the sense of a title, which gives him the freedom to not take it all that seriously. Indeed, it is out of the freedom of social grace that he's willing to try and fail; the SFRP crew hate effort as an offense to grace precisely because their grace is fragile.

And so von Sloneker is the ultimate threat at the movie's end, when Audrey—the 'goodie-goodie'—is out at the Hamptons with him; Charlie and Tom imagine the worst debauchery. The film's ending is appropriately mild for a comedy of manners: It turns out von Sloneker was more lazy than manipulative, and he's happy to get rid of the straight-laced Audrey. The other surprise for Tom and Charlie is that women actually *do* have agency—even (gasp!) the mild-seeming ones like Audrey—and aren't pawns for the von Slonekers of the world.

But she appreciates the gesture, and the sincerity of Tom's concern for her wins her over, and provides the movie's happy ending. Luckily for Tom, true feeling doesn't mean sap or grand gestures of love; the grand gesture itself is humorously misguided, and they speak with playful obliquity about their feelings for one another and intent to make things work.

The ironic form, once it assumes an earnest content by being pulled outside of itself by love, is redeemed in a sense. And I don't want to get too Christian-y here, but the Christmas setting and opening/closing snippets of "A Mighty Fortress Is Our God" would make it almost untrue to Stillman *not* to go there, briefly. Nick's affection for Tom and not-so-gentle unmasking of his Fourierism allows Tom to break through his defensive shell, which leads to a pursuit of Audrey, which is really only an assent to the affection she's expressed for him. The movements of grace here are real and powerful. And the movie ends up not being elitist at all, simply because the anxiety of Stillman's 'UHB,' the fear of trying and failing, and the corresponding effort to *not* make an effort are universally human tendencies, and ones which demand love both to break through fatalism and to redeem the failures we make "without being doomed" to.

By its end, the film itself reaches the same point which Tom and Audrey do: the ability to use irony not as defense or refusal to speak seriously, but as a nuanced form for expressing earnest thoughts and real emotions.

In the first four or so minutes, in the course of one of his intellectual rambles, Charlie makes an argument for the existence of God:

> When you think to yourself—and most of our waking life is taken up thinking to ourselves—you must have that feeling that your thoughts aren't entirely wasted, that in some sense they are being heard. Rationally, they aren't; you're entirely alone. Even the people to whom we are closest can have no idea of what is going on in our minds. But we aren't devastated by loneliness because, at a hardly conscious level, we don't accept

> that we're entirely alone. I think this sensation of being silently listened to with total comprehension—something you never find in real life—represents our innate belief in a supreme being, some all-comprehending intelligence.

Of course, Charlie's God *would* be someone with the patience to listen to him with and the weirdness to understand him. Half the time, no one else knows what he's saying; as a kid, he tried to communicate with seagulls. But that doesn't at all detract from the hope he expresses here. The immensely clever and yet constantly self-parodying dialogues of these characters need something to invest them with meaning, need some touchstone in reality. But even these characters' fears of von Sloneker, self-describing acronyms, arguments over defunct socialists and, yes, cha-cha dancing are perhaps "no more ridiculous than life itself." All the absurdity is invested with a deep lovability, and Stillman's process of aestheticizing absurdity, writing the script from a perspective where it all *does* have meaning, even meaning in its aimlessness—*that's* a true risk, and one that doesn't fail.

Nine Documentaries

FOR THE GRACE ADDICT

compiled by

JOHN ZAHL

UNDEFEATED (2011)

The real-life *Friday Night Lights*, *Undefeated* is a crash course not only in grace-centered coaching, but in fatherhood and ministry. The filmmakers were somehow able to capture the infectious, transforming power of grace (in practice) on film, not just once or twice, but with about nine major wallops to the old ticker! No wonder it won the Academy Award for Best Documentary 2011. Love for the loveless shown.

RISING SON: THE LEGEND OF SKATEBOARDER CHRISTIAN HOSOI (2006)

Ever wondered what the conversion of a hopeless case by God's grace alone looks like? Look no further than this short documentary on the coolest professional skateboarder of the 1980s. The stamp of God's call upon Christian's life from long before he could recognize it is something to behold. Hosoi's signature move was called "the Christ air" for crying out loud! He now serves as a pastor for a massive Vineyard church.

UNGUARDED (2011)

Extreme cases create circumstances where grace abounds. This is one of them. How does God redeem—and make something beautiful—out of failure? *Unguarded* provides a moving example of the answer our faith affirms.

BUCK (2011)

Can love really achieve that which the law fails to do? *Buck* says yes and backs it up with examples galore, including an amazing portrait of adoption and a father-son story about a pair of gloves that will leave your heart on the floor and your eyes streaming.

THE CRUISE (1998)

This one is top-drawer, but not for the faint of heart. It tracks the brilliant and mercurial Timothy "Speed" Levitch, Manhattan's greatest tour guide, through his ups and downs. The 9/11 material is uncanny in its strange, prophetic apprehension, and the confession on the Brooklyn Bridge is not to be believed. This one is primarily a portrait of idol worship, and wasted genius, but to an extent that is mind-blowing.

RIZE (2005)

God sees hope in the most forgotten places...and His ways are not our ways. No film better makes this point than *Rize*. Imagine a spiritual movement taking form in a gang-ridden ghetto, where instead of joining gangs, kids join troops of birthday party clowns. As a result they rise (rize!) above the troubles that plague their daily lives. Be sure to notice how, in the end, the local church plays an immensely positive and pivotal role.

THE KING OF KONG (2007)

The ascendancy of the underdog, and the greatest documentary villain yet discovered. Can there be a new high-score contender in the world of arcade Donkey Kong gaming? The world says "No," but God says "Yes." If you watch the deleted scenes on the DVD, you may not be surprised to find out that St. Wiebe also writes praise songs in his spare time.

BILL CUNNINGHAM NEW YORK (2010)

Another beautiful portrait of good-ole-fashioned faith in a modern world and God's ability to shine even in a place where everything sparkles. Cunningham is the Pope Francis of fashion (with Grace Codington being runner up). See also: *The September Issue* for Law/Gospel themes writ large in fashion.

MAKE BELIEVE (2010)

"And a child shall lead them..." Who is the best teen magician in the world? He has been plucked, like King David, from the rural pastures—in this case, of Japan. Before him every (teen magician) knee shall bow.

Holly Golightly and the Knight in Shining Armor Complex

BREAKFAST AT TIFFANY'S

by

EMILY HORNSBY

A 2013 *Onion* headline reads: "College-Aged Female Finds Unlikely Kindred Spirit in Audrey Hepburn." The article (which is about a girl named Emily and set in Charlottesville…) writes that "While no one would ever suspect it, [Emily] has a *Breakfast at Tiffany's* poster hanging in her dorm room." While I swear that I am not the basis for the fictional Emily of Charlottesville quoted in this article, at least two different posters of Audrey have adorned my walls in past years, and I have watched *Breakfast at Tiffany's* more times than I can count. But what is the big deal with Audrey Hepburn anyways? What is it about the doe-eyed, pencil-thin starlet that continues to inspire dorm decoration nationwide and fashion collections every season?

Most females would probably say similar things: She's beautiful in a classy, sophisticated way, she's quirky and elegant in equal measure, she has impeccable style, etc. I'd say the majority of her timeless appeal comes from the characters she's played, especially the iconic Holly Golightly. Holly is fun and spontaneous, she's gorgeous and impossibly thin (and skinniness is next to godliness, after all), and she can play "Moon River" on the guitar and pull off a towel headscarf at the same time. But she's also a total mess. She drinks too much and can't keep track of any of her belongings, including her cat, Cat. Her quirky flaws make her relatable, if only by anchoring her down just before she sails over the horizon of unattainable loveliness. A little while ago I talked to a friend right after she'd watched *Breakfast at Tiffany's* for the first time. She said that she didn't understand why every girl is so enamored with Holly Golightly when she's completely out of touch with reality and pretty unintelligent. She does, after all, implicate herself in a mobster drug ring as a result of her own naïveté. If you take physicality out of the equation (ha!), Holly Golightly does not have many desirable traits. My wiser-than-most friend concluded: "I found the movie tragic. To me, it was about how screwed up her life is."

But it's her helpless messiness that makes her romantic—that makes her eyes just as lost as they are starry, betraying every look as a silent plea for help. It's endearing when she leaves a shoe in the refrigerator or wakes Mr. Yunioshi up yet again because she's lost her key. She's a beautiful mess, and that's precisely the allure.

Holly Golightly is incomplete until the handsome and sympathetic Paul Varjak comes along, finds her shoes, and saves her from herself. In a word, he fixes her. And yet, the Holly Golightly model of dependence is much more appealing than what we often see today. Modern women, and especially female characters, seem to be pushed in two directions at once: to be both cute—read submissive—and sexy—read, well, sexy. Nearly every female archetypal character is centered on dependence—on the need for a man. To be cute is to be childlike and helpless, in need of both guidance and protection. To be sexy is to be the object of another's desire—a desire that, sadly, has come to mean the validation of a woman's worth. The magic equation for finding romance is then vulnerability plus physical perfection. So, compared to a baby-talking Paris Hilton, who wouldn't pick a broken but elegant New York socialite as a sort of role model?

There's a sweet surrender in identifying with a beautiful mess like Holly Golightly because most of us are hyper-aware of our inability to keep it together. The female need for a savior is often mistaken as the need for a male hero to ride in on horseback, sweep the woman off her feet, and make her right by loving her. Holly, a beautiful klutz, is the perfect recipient of human love, because her beauty and klutziness merit her romantic salvation. And so, when being a hopeless screw-up qualifies you for a salvific romance, it's hard to resist admiring—even emulating—a damsel in distress. You can embrace your sloppiness, put a sexy spin on it, and wait until a Prince Charming moves into your building, or so the cultural imperative goes.

The damsel in distress is alive and well in movies and TV today, especially with the surge in superhero flicks—think Mary Jane and Lois Lane, for example. The season two finale of *Girls* played off of this knight-in-shining-armor complex note for note. Hannah is at her absolute messiest: Her OCD has flared up, and she's just given herself a horrendous haircut. In a moment of sloppy weakness, she calls Adam and (while they undo the whole man-to-the-rescue thing in season three) it is impossible not to smile as Adam runs, heroic and shirtless, through the streets of Brooklyn as the romantic string music builds. That episode, however, made me feel a very modern, third-wave-feminist guilt for my flushed excitement as

Adam came to the rescue, because it's weak to admit to the desire for a man, especially one in any kind of saving role. Which I know may be a little ironic for someone who (theoretically) believes that all of us are in need of saving, men and women alike, and that if we were to insist on rescue on our terms it wouldn't really be much of a rescue. But I digress.

It might seem, at first glance, that this is an area where these (often restrictive) societal norms actually make it easier for women to recognize the need for a savior. Men, on the other hand, are pressured to be the stoic aggressor/winners. But drawing comparisons between the culturally conditioned female need for a human male savior and the innate need for a divine savior is dangerous (and a little awkward). According to the synopsis on its back cover, *Captivating* by John and Stasi Eldredge (the female counterpart to John Eldredge's *Wild at Heart*), relies heavily on appealing to a woman's desire to be "the Beauty" who gets "swept up into a romance." I have not actually read *Captivating*, and I have friends who speak highly of it, but it is nevertheless an example of a common phenomenon: using the language of romance to describe a woman's relationship with God.

Of course, the Bible uses this language too (Isaiah 62:5, for example[27]). What I am wary of is focusing too much on romance in trying to understand how a woman relates to God. Many contemporary Christian messages for women seem to split their time between a Song-of-Solomon-esque reading of the Bible and advice on finding a good man. One of the problems with the Jesus-as-boyfriend model is that it drags all of the female romantic complexes behind it—especially when you add language about beauty. Even worse, it

27. "For as a young man marries a young woman, so shall your builder marry you, and as the bridegroom rejoices over the bride, so shall your God rejoice over you."

seems to reinforce with spiritual backing the cultural lie that beauty and romance are the primary measuring sticks of a woman's value. It would be great to see more media from Christian women speaking of God as a best friend, not just a bridegroom.

In the final scene of *Breakfast at Tiffany's*, Paul tells Holly he loves her. She brushes him off, saying she won't let anyone put her in a cage. Paul argues that loving her is the opposite of encaging her; his love will free her from the cage she has built for herself. *If* we pretend Paul is Jesus, this is a pretty apt summation of the gospel—except that, once again, the man is the Christ-figure.

Fortunately we're starting to see more stories in which both men and women are portrayed as messy and incapable of saving each other, and, while they may not be romantic, they're refreshing. Take *Celeste and Jesse Forever*, starring Rashida Jones and Andy Samberg, for example. Celeste and Jesse are a separated couple who remain best friends until they start seeing other people. Misleadingly labeled a romantic comedy, it's a heartbreaking movie about the difficulty of ending a relationship with someone you still love. Despite the small mound of used tissues at my side, I felt lighter after watching it. Rom-coms are fun until the credits start rolling and you're back in your own unromantic life, wondering why Richard Gere hasn't pulled up in a white limo yet (*Pretty Woman*, anyone?).

We all fail every day at loving each other, and watching this play out onscreen reminds us that no one is alone in the hurt and struggle. It's a welcome reminder that we don't have to rely on Paul Varjak or any man (or woman) to redeem broken lives and broken hearts.

Pathological Optimism and Crucified Lives in

SILVER LININGS PLAYBOOK

by

Ethan Richardson

> Instead, you can walk backwards into life—
> Undo your steps and gain ground as you yield...
> —Mark Jarman

If David O. Russell's 2012 film *Silver Linings Playbook* is a playbook at all, it's for one hell of a losing team. One needs only to look at the coach for proof: Pat (Bradley Cooper), a husband on a restraining order, hopes to get on the healing train so he can get his old life back. He has just been released from a psych ward in Baltimore for his bipolar disorder, which surfaced violently when he caught his wife Nikki in the shower with a coworker. Needless to say, Pat has some work to do, but he needs Nikki back. So he has structured his new life around good stuff, all the things he thinks he should have done for her before: physical exercise, therapy, and reading all the books she teaches in her high school class. Despite the circumstances, Pat's new mantra is optimism—"Excelsior!" (Ever upward!)—and he is determined to find the silver lining in everything.

Pat's story soon becomes entwined with that of Tiffany (Jennifer Lawrence), a friend of a friend, who has an equally checkered past. She's a young widow, and her grief has slowly spiraled her into a lot of bad relationships and an ugly reputation. She tells Pat she sees Nikki from time to time, and so agrees to help Pat with his effort to win her back. The offer comes under one condition, though: Pat must agree to be her dance partner in an upcoming competition. Eager to show Nikki he's a transformed man, Pat agrees.

As willing as he is to work to get Nikki back, Pat still seems incapable of changing his tune. He still has moments of rage; he still can't hear his wedding song, "La Cherie Amour," without completely flipping out.

In short, it seems that, as much as he wills to fix the situation he's in, he's equally *un*willing to face the issue within himself.

There is a breakthrough scene in a diner—it's Halloween and everyone around Pat and Tiffany has costumes on—where Tiffany listens to him and discovers, "You think that I'm crazier than you." Pat can't deny it. He, in fact, does believe that Tiffany is crazier than he is, that he is in a "superior mental illness category." Tiffany is aghast—the audience, too, knows she's further down the road to recovery than Pat is. At least she's not hiding from who she is. She walks out of the diner and, for the first time, Pat sees that there might be a gap between who he is and who he *thinks* he is.

He later relays the conversation in his therapist's office. He tells his therapist that Tiffany said she "likes (the crazy) parts of herself along with all the other parts of herself, and can I say the same?" The therapist asks him if he *can* say the same. Pat responds: "Is that...? You're asking me, you're really asking me that question? With all my crazy, sad—? Are you nuts?"

It is not nuts, and it is not until Pat can see that he is, in fact, *worse off* than Tiffany that he can begin to work on things. Until he can come to grips with the depth of his self-delusions, he is spinning his wheels. And this isn't just true of Pat. Anyone has the ability to disassociate themselves from the *truth* about themselves. It is a terrible power. It can kill intimacy in relationships and it can prevent healing help.

Of course, in a world of 'normal people,' it is also a necessary defense mechanism. In our day and age, susceptible to what John Jeremiah Sullivan calls "the pathology of pathologization," no one wants to be a pathology. So we live our lives in a state of perpetual self-justification. We remember and forget things selectively; we tell ourselves stories that allow us to see the world (and ourselves!) in a way that fits our script. This is especially true when we believe we are supposed to have changed. In their book *Mistakes Were Made (But Not By Me)*, social psychologists Carol Tavris and Elliot Aronson describe it like this:

> At the simplest level, memory soothes out the wrinkles of dissonance by enabling the confirmation bias to hum along, selectively causing us to forget discrepant, disconfirming information about beliefs we hold dear...
>
> For most people, the self-concept is based on a belief in change, improvement, and growth. For some of us, it's based on a belief that we have changed completely; indeed, the past self seems like an entirely different person. When people have had a religious conversion, survived a disaster, suffered through cancer, or recovered from an addiction, they often feel transformed; the former self, they say, is 'not me.'

If this is pathological, it is not just Pat's pathology but everyone's. Including the rest of the cast. His father (Robert De Niro) is a bookie, but he'd rather see himself as a man of faith. His mother, a patsy. His brother, a narcissist. There isn't a character with a speaking part that doesn't have one foot in the looney bin. This is one of the remarkable unspokens of *Silver Linings*: Not one character is permitted the abnormality of 'normal.' Everybody is working something out.

Which is why another target of the film is the inherent optimism of contemporary American (and, we could add, Christian) values. The writer and director David O. Russell is explicitly attacking the merits of an 'it's all good' philosophy. In fact, according to Pat's story, the more we invest in our personal incarnations of 'Excelsior' philosophy, the harder our fall will be when our hidden wounds come to the surface.

In his interview in the first issue of *The Mockingbird*, author Francis Spufford says about the same. He describes the "cruel optimism" of contemporary culture, the inherent perfectionism of clothing advertisements and celebrity coverage—and, at the other end of the spectrum, the people who wind up at the sharp end of those indirect accusations. People who are addicted, overweight, lonely, self-destructive. And so this optimism, which glorifies all the extraordinary things 'ordinary' people are capable of achieving, demands that we simultaneously deny the contrary evidence we gather in our lives every day.

> You expect the best, you expect the best, you expect the best, you're gonna be surprised with the worst when it comes. You stick your fingers in your ears and you default back to expecting the best again and that takes care of the cruelty *and* the optimism. It seems to me to be an amazingly effortful way to live... it becomes a deep relief just to be a sinner.

Effortful, indeed. As with all of us, Pat's denial of the truth in himself stems from a deep-seated belief that acknowledging (entertaining?) our inner-crazy can't possibly be the way to healing. In a world that loves the semantics of ascent, talking about what's in the basement feels like a bad move for your life prospects.

And yet, complete disclosure is what love—*real* love—does. Real love doesn't hold up aspirational mantras or push for the you you *should* be; love shows you who you already are, right now. It "gets down to the bottom of it." And so, Pat begins to see himself at the same time he begins to see he is *really* loved, not by Nikki, but by Tiffany. As the weeks go on, Pat and Tiffany practicing for their big competition, Tiffany continuing to stalk Pat on his daily runs, Tiffany continuing to listen as Pat spews his name-it-and-claim-it 'Excelsior' nonsense, Pat begins to realize that there might be a life better suited for who he *actually is*. In other words, Tiffany's persistence has shown him the difference between love and deserving.

Relationships are where we most often see the 'theology of the cross' at work in our lives. This is because, on the whole, relationships follow the cruciform nature of our life experiences—the Christian understanding of Christ's cross tells us that strange power resides in moments of weakness, and that new life can resurge from dead places. Why else do we find solace with such needy love songs ("God Only Knows What I'd Be Without You") and delight in such forgotten ordinaries (*Beauty and the Beast*, *The Hunchback of Notre Dame*)? The theology of the cross promises hope for those who are burned out, beat up, rejected or reviled. It puts the climax of God's incarnation in the center of their predicament.

Pat's transformation is no different. Despite the will to change, despite the new tools he has (Excelsior!) to get back to the life he had, he cannot do it. He cannot make the self he wishes to be. That self is *dead.* Only in being loved—unconditionally, in a time of shame-inducing, ugly need—is he transformed. In other words, it happens *to* him. Love drags him into newness of life through a dance routine he never would have chosen himself.

The *denouement*, as in all rom-coms, hinges upon the decision between the old and the new. After their less-than-professional, all-too-lovable performance in the dance competition, it turns out, Nikki has been sitting in the crowd admiring. At the climax of his recovery, now that he has found new life, and is acceptable again in Nikki's eyes, will Pat choose the love he was fighting so hard to earn? Or the love that chased him down his neighborhood roads? Because it is a romantic comedy, you might guess where he's headed when the lights go up in the ballroom, but you won't guess how much it will make you cry. It's not meant to be a surprise, anyways. How can he go back to what is dead? For Pat, the old is gone, and the new has come (2 Cor 5:17).

The Common Mess of

PUNCH-DRUNK LOVE

by

Joe Nooft

The 90's were a golden age for children's movies. With the birth of Pixar in '95 and the far too premature peak of Nickelodeon Movies in the latter part of the decade, there surely was never a better time for school to be in session. There was, however, one common denominator, shared by nearly all children's films, that seriously irked me: the implausibly catastrophic wreckage scene. Toys exploded out of bins, liberated animals ran rampant, food fights left walls and ceilings caked with condiments, articles of clothing fell victim to irreversible stains. And the worst part about it was that the clean-up scene was virtually nonexistent. Audiences were left to believe that the mess just...lingered.

Take for instance a scene from Nickelodeon's first film, *Harriet the Spy*. The classmates whom Harriet has spied on conspire to avenge their compromised reputations by dumping buckets of blue paint all over her. To make matters worse, the little devils pretend to help clean Harriet up, but really they just spread the paint all over her. The passive art teacher, of course, offers no aid to a humiliated Harriet. The audience never sees Harriet properly cleaned up. She is left stained.

This mess scene is a G-rated version of Harriet hitting rock bottom. It's effectively disorienting, but beneficial in allowing the viewer to experience the character's cringe-worthy tension of being left messy. This terrifying feeling, this tailspin out of control, is the aura that Paul Thomas Anderson's *Punch-Drunk Love* incubates. The movie's messy, and the audience is implicated in the mess.

In *Punch-Drunk Love*, Adam Sandler delivers a more emotionally nuanced performance than we're used to, taking on the role of Barry Egan. Barry is a single, friendless, insecure man content to skulk through life sheepishly avoiding all of its pressure points. His only community exists within the encasement of his seven nagging sisters. While the sisters receive limited screen time, it is clear that their primary function in Barry's life is to make him thoroughly miserable. They fire infiltrating questions at Barry with menacing repetition, covering their overwhelming disapproval of his life with a veneer of sisterly care. This is established early in the film when a few of the sisters call Barry to pressure him into attending a family party:

> SISTER ONE: Are you going to this party?
>
> SISTER TWO: I'm just calling to make sure that you show up at this party tonight.
>
> SISTER THREE: You going to the party tonight?...What time are you going to be there? You can't be late. I'm serious. Seriously. You can't be late. You can't just not show up like you do. Seriously.

The bludgeoning is nonstop, and Barry responds, "Yes I am," with a forced calmness, to each sister. But to Barry's surprise, Sister Four doesn't call; she shows up at his workplace. She, of course, asks him if he plans on being at the party, and he, in turn, delivers the same soft-spoken confirmation. But a wrench is tossed into Barry's well oiled, conflict-avoiding machine. She informs him that she would like to bring a female co-worker for Barry to "meet." Sister Four's intentions seem innocent enough, but with the awkwardness of the blind date and the nagging of his sisters awaiting him at the party, Barry is pushed into flight mode. He backs himself into a corner, Sister Four hovering over him. He responds to the threat of this dreadful night with a sliver of appropriate vulnerability: "Yeah, I don't want to do that. I don't do stuff like that…There's an outside chance I don't even come tonight…Please don't [bring her]." Sister Four doesn't make any promises; she just bullies him into confirming his attendance. Barry attends the party, relieved to find that the proposed date is not there.

Despite Barry's best efforts to orchestrate an ordinary night, things go south pretty quickly. Barry ends up kicking out a couple panels from a sliding glass door—according to his sisters, something that he's done in the past. His action is the inevitable response to the constant antagonizing from his sisters. But Barry's outburst helps him loosen his grip on life.

In the shadow of Barry's temper tantrum he opens up a bit, admitting to his brother-in-law that he doesn't "like himself sometimes." He asks for help, before breaking down and crying hysterically. His brother-in-law doesn't quite know how to handle the situation, and Barry's play for empathy falls flat. So, he turns to more controllable comforts. First, he stockpiles Healthy Choice pudding packets in an effort to win a cheap air travel promo, but he runs into some small print technicalities. Next, he calls a phone sex hotline, but receives more of a headache than any sort of tangible enjoyment. What Barry wants more than pleasure is connection: a reciprocated love or even 'like.' His half-hearted searches come up empty again and again until, ironically, what he is searching for finds him. *She* finds him. *She* is Sister Four's co-worker, Lena Leonard, played by Emily Watson, whom Barry has already met, somewhat serendipitously, in the beginning of the film. When Lena enters Barry's life, she slowly loosens his white knuckle grip from life's proverbial steering wheel of control.

Paul Thomas Anderson meticulously creates a surreal and emotionally exhaustive experience in *PDL*. Vivid blues and reds and pinks highlight the emotion of a scene. Gloomy Barry wears a striking, royal blue suit for nearly the entire film. Silhouetted, shifty lighting turns bright and white-washed in the blink of an eye, giving the audience a window into Barry's capricious state of mind. Jon Brion's brilliantly frantic and bipolar score moves rapidly from heartwarming to horrific, and is often used to raise tension in expectedly mundane moments. This sensually rich backdrop accents Barry's anxieties.

As a result, Barry's life often appears unrealistic and a bit over-dramatic. Therefore, it's hard to engage with his inner conflict even though it's familiar to all of us. In fact, it wasn't until my third viewing of *PDL* that I began to wonder whether Anderson was choosing to show his audience Barry's perceived life rather than his real life. Let me explain. Perhaps you can relate to the act of formulating imaginative outcomes, composing conversations in your head before they actually happen. I know I can. For example, before I walk into a situation where I anticipate negative consequences, I will fabricate a make-believe conversation, beginning to end. It's a defense mechanism, a blueprint to maintain control. Usually in my perceived reality I am very much like Barry: subtle, kind-hearted, a pitied person. The perceived opposition, on the contrary, is cruel, bloodthirsty, and confrontational, similar to the portrayal of Barry's sisters in *PDL*. Thus I prepare myself to take a defensive stance. How should I hide my feelings of guilt and embarrassment? Here I plot out a frail admittance of mistake followed by a twisted rebuttal to eliminate the consequences of my wrongdoing. The real fangs come out in the opposition's final blow. This is the part of my make-believe conversation where I hear that I was absolutely wrong in every way—that I'm a giant screw-up whose attempt to camouflage his flaws has failed miserably.

This is how I think of *Punch-Drunk Love*: as a long warm up round for Barry before he enters into the boxing ring of reality. When the audience witnesses Barry's sisters fire encroaching questions at him, what we are really seeing and hearing is how Barry projects and expects his sisters to respond disapprovingly to his life. When Sister Four attempts to play matchmaker and Barry backs himself into a corner, we see a more figurative depiction of Barry's insecurities. Not often do people literally corner themselves mid-conversation. Perhaps the reason Barry's defensive responses appear so blemished on-screen is because we are being shown Barry's bullshit-formulation process. What the audience sees is a different kind of reality, one that most if not all of us are personally familiar with. It's a projected or anticipated reality. Until I saw Barry's life through this unique lens, I was unable to truly connect with him as a character.

Who isn't familiar with the fatigue that comes with trying to control our perception and identity? It is a universal struggle, and one that has all but paralyzed Barry. Everywhere he looks for help, he encounters a wall: His family is hostile, the sex hotline brings in unwelcome drama, and his pudding plot to fly away never takes off. This is where Lena Leonard, *PDL*'s only other character who sticks around from start to finish, comes in. Lena shuts down Barry's BS factory. Instead of turning a blind eye towards Barry's dark places, his crippling attempts at control and his projections that keep him from intimacy, Lena inspires him to accept their existence. She acknowledges his shortcomings and allows him to walk free from his failings. In doing so, Lena gifts Barry the space to pursue her.

As *PDL* enters its third act, Lena has undoubtedly compiled enough insight from Sister Four to steer her far away from Barry, but instead, she draws closer to him. In response to her love, he no longer wishes to hide. Instead, he longs to tell Lena about himself, even the ugly parts, because he knows that she accepts the real Barry. Her attention transforms him into a new man. In fact the only scene in the film where Barry is not wearing his tacky blue suit, is in bed with Lena, wearing a bathrobe. Stripped of his fabrications, all that's left is pure, intimate Barry. When the heartwarming sections of Jon Brion's score play in scenes like these, the tense musical moments can finally be recognized as not only valuable but also essential in showing Barry's maturation.

In acquiring this love, Barry's mess surfaces for all to see. But Barry finds that he is still loved despite this mess. Don't we all need that kind of love? Couldn't we all use a love that covers our faults with its transforming power? Couldn't we all use *A Punch-Drunk Love?* (Eph 2:1-10).

It's Gonna Last You for the Rest of Your Life: Sanctification According to

GROUNDHOG DAY

by

Matt Schneider

I have a tradition of watching the film *Groundhog Day* every year around February 2. Repeated viewings are a fitting homage given the movie's plot, which has weatherman Phil Connors (Bill Murray) reliving Groundhog Day over and over and over again for what seems like eternity. In the story only Phil knows what's happened the previous Groundhog Days, but everyone else wakes up as if they are living it for the first time. This existential tale says a lot about human nature, particularly the realities of sanctification (that is, the process of becoming holy).

Many of us influenced by Protestant Reformation theology often explain that we are weak on sanctification. We regard Christians as being not terribly different from non-Christians, in that our flawed human nature persists, despite our saving faith, baptism, and best efforts. Such an understanding flies in the face of prevailing notions that Christians are or should be inherently nicer and holier people.

In this respect, *Groundhog Day* serves as a good analogy for how sanctification works (or any kind of real personal growth for that matter). It is not necessarily something we can achieve by our own will and strength. When Phil tries to live up to the standards of perfection held by his love interest Rita (Andie MacDowell), he falls endlessly short.

Consider when Rita describes her vision of the "perfect guy":

> RITA: Well first of all, he's too humble to know he's perfect.
> PHIL: That's me.
> RITA: He's intelligent, supportive, funny.
> PHIL: Intelligent, supportive, funny. Me, me, me.
> RITA: He's got a good body, but he doesn't have to look in the mirror every two minutes.
> PHIL: I have a great body, and sometimes I go months without looking...
> RITA: He likes animals and children, and he'll change poopy diapers.
> PHIL: Does he have to use the word "poopy"? I am really close on this one. Really, really close.

Although Phil says he's close, we're in on the secret that he is egocentric and embittered, essentially the opposite of what Rita desires. Yet he is too smitten to give up his attempt to attain Rita's vision of perfection.

Phil later feigns compatibility after learning Rita's favorite drink is a sweet vermouth on the rocks with a twist.[28] Despite this being a cocktail Phil obviously detests, over the course of the next repeated days he orders this drink in her presence at a bar much to Rita's surprise. But his ploy doesn't stop here, as he also attempts to match her sentimentalism. "What shall we drink to?" Rita asks.

28. This drink is now commonly known as 'The Groundhog Day.'

He jokes, "To the groundhog!" A disappointed Rita says, "I always drink to world peace." The next day he explains, "I like to say a prayer and drink to world peace," before offering her white chocolate, which makes her sick. The process repeats itself, world without end, with Phil constantly upping the ante only to fall short on some new and unforeseen point.

Phil is motivated by all the wrong factors, and somehow Rita tacitly picks up on his manipulative inauthenticity. She smells the rat! Even Phil himself doesn't like who he is becoming by pretending to be perfect—it's all lies. He burns himself out trying to live up to Rita's unachievable and oppressive standards, becoming somewhat maniacal in the process. The film depicts Phil's desperation and decline as Rita literally slaps him in the face for a variety of untold reasons during a montage of new Groundhog Days: Slap, slap, slap, slap, slap.

Thank goodness Phil eventually accepts his plight and the futility of trying to become Rita's perfect guy. One Groundhog Day he stops his charade and opens up to Rita, telling her the whole truth about his situation and sharing his emotions. Despite Phil's crazy story, Rita surprisingly shows him some compassion, saying, "Maybe I should spend the day with you as an objective witness, just to see what happens."

On this day Phil repents of his old ways and admits his genuine love for Rita as she innocently falls asleep in his room. While in previous scenes Phil attempts to commit suicide to stop the endless cycle of Groundhog Days, in this scene we witness a more powerful death—a death of the old self-centered, sleazy, and bitter Phil with his ulterior motives: "The first time I saw you something happened to me. I never told you, but I knew that I wanted to hold you as hard as I could. I don't deserve someone like you. But if I ever could, I swear I would love you for the rest of my life."

Phil has a sort of conversion here after bottoming out. This is the film's fulcrum, the point where transformation finally begins, and it happens not because he tries so hard to become the vision of Rita's perfect guy. Rather, he gives up, resigning himself to the endless cycle of Groundhog Day in Punxsutawney. He takes up piano and ice sculpting because he is actually interested in learning these skills for their own sake. He tries to save an old beggar's life over and over again because he begins to genuinely care. He becomes altruistic, daily saving the same boy falling from a tree and fixing flat tires for little old ladies. He has died to his old self and his desire to win Rita over. Interestingly, it is only at this point, when his disattachment becomes complete, that Rita actually falls for Phil, and the unseen forces at work end his twilight zone of repeated Groundhog Days.

There has been fan discussion of how much time elapses for Phil in his time loop. Harold Ramis, the director of the film, states in the DVD commentary that he believes ten years pass, but he has been quoted elsewhere explaining that it could be thirty or forty, or maybe even ten thousand. As Phil says during a particularly suicidal phase while reporting on Punxsutawney Phil, the famous groundhog who predicts how long winter will last: "You want a prediction about the weather, you're asking the wrong Phil. I'll give you a winter prediction. It's gonna be cold, it's gonna be gray, and it's gonna last you for the rest of your life."

Sanctification is similar, is it not? A long, frustrating, humbling process—and it's gonna last you for the rest of your life! It seems to finally come about only when we accept our imperfection and inability to live up to anybody's (including God's) standards of the perfect guy or gal, dying to our selfish desires for victory and acknowledging that we remain sinners in and of ourselves. In God's sight we are accepted as if we were not flawed, because of Jesus Christ. It is at these points of surrender in our lives that God's grace begins to bear fruit, just as it does with Phil when he finally submits himself to the realities of Groundhog Day.

Growing up with

GREASE AND FERRIS BUELLER

by

David Peterson

Across the board, the movies that I continue to go back to contributed possible answers to the persisting adolescent question, "Who do I really want to be?" Or, more accurately, "Whom do I most want to be like?" Between Sean Astin, River Phoenix, Wil Wheaton, Tom Hanks, Ralph Macchio, C. Thomas Howell, Matt Dillon, Matthew Broderick and John Travolta I compiled a fairly diverse assortment of filmic role models. These were some pretty cool cats. Looking back, I see I wasn't nearly as successful at emulating their quirks as I thought. Still, watching these movies over and over shaped some of my lasting thoughts around relationships, camaraderie, and what it means to be an American male. From Ferris Bueller and Danny Zuko, specifically, I came to see that being known is cooler than being cool.

I used to watch *Ferris Bueller's Day Off* before the first day of school every year. When going back to class was the last thing I wanted to do, watching Ferris and Cameron blow it off was pretty encouraging. Ferris's antics with the principal and his reputation as a "righteous dude" amongst the "sportos, the motorheads, the geeks, sluts, bloods, wastoids, dweebies, dickheads" are the stuff of aspirational teenage lore. Ferris's easy demeanor, cool clothes, and taste for adventure make him the ultimate model for right behavior. In his desire to make his big day out in the city memorable, he also captures the adolescent desire to stand out.

However, as I projected my stresses and worries onto Ferris, seeing how they would translate in his world, I naturally began to relate more to his anxious friend, Cameron. A popular interpretation of the movie is that Ferris is merely a construct of Cameron's imagination, existing to push him out of his comfort zone and force him to face up to his numerous insecurities.

While Ferris successfully propels Cameron towards independence and self-confidence, their relationship runs deeper than that. Near the beginning of the movie, Ferris calls up his friend to announce he's taking the day off and wants some company. Cameron moans and groans and claims he's too sick to join him. "I'm so disappointed in Cameron," Ferris tells the camera. "Twenty bucks says he's sitting in his car debating whether he should go out." Of course, he's right. The scene shifts to Cameron's driveway where the perfectly healthy teen delivers a tortured monologue about the pros and cons of joining up with Ferris. The joke is on Cameron's melodramatic self-loathing and hypochondria, but there's humor and comfort in the fact that Ferris isn't afraid to step back and rag on his pal, making fun of his imagined poor health and girl problems, among other things. But he also encourages Cameron to open up, bringing out his sense of humor and having his back when disaster strikes later. Like Ferris and Cameron, my friends and I tease each other, but we also understand that there is serious comfort in being known. So, when stepping out and making a splash proves futile, the example of friendship remains. Clearly, a day off like Ferris Bueller's can't be replicated, but sharing memories and knowing one another outlive the desire to be unique.

Another character that captured my imagination was *Grease*'s Danny Zuko, played memorably by John Travolta. When I was thirteen, I went through a serious Zuko phase, watching *Grease* twice a week for almost an entire school year, memorizing all the lines, and even doing my rendition of his signature shoulder roll in our school's Shakespeare production. Needless to say, *Grease* secured a special place in my heart that year.

Danny and the T-Birds handled their mundane concerns with the brash cockiness typical of adolescence. Their strange mix of detached cynicism and surprising enthusiasm helped the movie define a moment of growing up for me, even though their self-assured jaunts generally turned ridiculous as they tried to fashion an identity from a world of possibilities.

Despite the affected coolness of the Pink Ladies and the T-Birds, the girls and boys have flashes of emotion that are refreshing. From attending the football pep rally to fixing up Kenickie's pile of junk, from the making mayhem at the school dance to celebrating at the graduation carnival, the characters exude that adolescent feeling that what they are doing at a given moment is the most important thing they will do their whole lives. In one such episode, Danny struts around the track and tries to dramatically clear a series of hurdles to catch the attention of Sandy (Olivia Newton-John), but he trips and falls on his face. Lo and behold, she comes to his aid. His friends would be mortified, and if he was able to step back and examine himself with the cool, detached glance that the cynical greasers prize, he would be too. But in the moment he's unaware of anyone's opinion but hers. He's the perfectly coiffed greaser with the heart of gold, a veritable King David! His exaggerated machismo, although off-putting in its libidinal supercharge, is nicely countered by the enthusiasm he pours into winning over Sandy.

From their frolic on a beautiful secluded beach in the opening scene to their flight into heaven aboard Greased Lightning in the final number, Sandy and Danny's romance holds the hopeful promise of transcending the dumpy confines of Rydell High. The cold open on the beach is short and sweet, like their summer fling (after all, they sing, it "don't mean a thing"). "Danny, is this the end?" Sandy asks as the waves crash and the romantic music plays. "Of course not. It's only the beginning," he responds, clearly willing to say anything at this point. When they head back to Rydell and literally face the music from their friends in "Summer Nights," it is clear that, in order to sustain the flame, Danny and Sandy will face their respective conflicts of identity.

Danny and Sandy's romance, in this way, features earnest attempts at mutual submission. Ephesians 5:21 reads, "Submit to one another out of reverence for Christ." In their respective transformations over the school year, Danny and Sandy work to surrender their own identities and submit to each other's. After seeing Sandy on a date with the quarterback, Danny decides that the way to her heart is to become a straight-shooting jock, so he goes out for a few sports. The bumbling Coach Calhoun (Sid Caesar), tells him at tryouts, "The first thing you have to do is to change."

"Well, I know, that's why I'm here, ya know, to change," Danny says.

Calhoun means change out of his jeans and leather jacket,

but the message is clear and touching: Danny wants to change for Sandy. The gossipy Pink Ladies, on the other hand, want Sandy to forget about Danny and realize that "Men are rats." However, when she watches Danny win heroically on Thunder Road, she decides to ask for a makeover from beauty school dropout Frenchy (Didi Conn), to adopt the look of her clique. The specifics of her transformation and the reasoning behind it appear smutty, but the idea of both parties taking on new identities for the other is wholesome. Driving into the sky as the credits roll, they both know "You're the one that I want."

In contrast to Ferris, who remains invincible for the extent of his day off, Danny is knocked from his superior perch in the middle of the movie when things with Sandy aren't working out. Courting her, he dips and dodges away from his friends, and his identity as top dog is uncertain. He wants to please all the people in his life, but as he struggles to get the girl, the things that used to matter to him don't seem quite as important. In Danny's moments of weakness—exposed at the pep rally, stranded at the drive in, Cha-Cha'ed at the dance—he fails to keep up his carefully crafted, grandiose self-image. The too-cool façade fades to reveal an earnest guy who's emotionally invested in his friends and painfully aware of their opinions of him. When the movie closes, Danny has come a long way. His hair is still perfectly combed and he hasn't toned down the pelvic thrusts, but he has humbled himself to change for Sandy and he has settled into a new rapport with the T-Birds.

My favorite teenage characters met me at the obnoxious adolescent stage when I was certain that if the world didn't revolve around me, I was crucial in some way to its orbit. I looked at their subtleties of dress and manner and thought, here are some likeminded individuals I can learn a thing or two from. But Ferris and Danny and the rest of my favorite teenage characters weren't the selfish egotists that I at first thought. Ferris squeezed the marrow out of every day with his pals, and built strong relationships; Danny learned the hard way that trying to be cool could only get him so far. Together, they spoke to the power of the gospel in a good story and in sharing life with others.

TRAINWRECK

Afraid of a Love That There's No Cure For

by

Charlotte Getz

Some readers will want to stalk me down and slash my tires when I say this: I hated most of Judd Apatow's *Trainwreck*. Like *really* hated it. I watched it at my parents' house, and, as any self-assured thirty-one-year old girl would do, I held my finger over the 'stop' button all two hours and five minutes of the movie, lest my parents walk in during one of the many salacious scenes; there are parts of this movie that would make a seasoned hooker blush. My disdain dramatically shriveled though, in the manner of having a wart frozen off the bottom of your foot, in the last five minutes of the movie. But I'm getting ahead of myself. Let's back up to the ninety-eight percent that made me want to hide under a blanket.

The protagonist, Amy (played by Amy Schumer, who also wrote the screenplay), is a mess from the get-go. I'll be blunt: She's a slut, an alcoholic, she's mean, and she has ridiculous friends at a meaningless job (at least from the easy vantage point of *my* polished pedestal). In the opening scene, in a flashback from her childhood, Amy's dad explains to her and her younger sister that he's divorcing their mother because "monogamy isn't realistic." Because Amy is a girl who worships her father, this memory sets the stage for her own sad view of relationships. Really, it sets the stage for her entire worldview: that her job, relationships, and sexual exploits, should all be geared towards *her* pleasure and convenience. If someone in her life doesn't fit into those narrow parameters, she can't deal with it. The minute someone asks anything at all of her, she pushes them away.

The worst part is, Amy doesn't see any of this. In a voiceover at the beginning of the movie, as she's wearing a skimpy dress while leaving a strange apartment after a late-night hookup, she says, "Don't judge me fuckers. I'm just a sexual girl, okay? I am fine. I am in control." The way Amy sees it, she is living the life; but she is totally blind to how pathetic she looks hung-over, limping down the sidewalk with mussed hair and smeared mascara at seven in the morning.

Donald Miller, an author who has a lot to say about the construct of an effective story, posted on Twitter about the characteristics of a great *villain*:[29]

- A backstory of brokenness
- Unredeemed and unforgiven pain
- A twisted vision for a better world
- Minions rather than friends or a team
- An unwillingness to admit to any fault or weakness

Look familiar? Amy fits more into the category of *villain* than hero. This is not what I wanted when I paid ten jillion dollars to rent this

29. Miller, Donald [@DonaldMiller]. (2015, November 4). [tweet]

movie! It's terribly uncomfortable to watch someone contentedly spiraling into a nosedive and refusing to press the 'eject' button.

What I really hated about *Trainwreck* was how much of myself I saw in the movie's protagonist—or antagonist—or whatever tragic, off-color breed of contemporary heroine Amy Schumer has written herself into. Maybe we don't share all of the crass, nuanced similarities, but we both wholeheartedly convince ourselves that we are the rulers of our own, self-made kingdoms—and it's all good. You'll note that this is really the beginning of the Christian narrative.

Enter Aaron (played by Bill Hader). Aaron is an athletic surgeon for the Knicks whose star is on the rise. If that weren't enough, he's also involved in Doctors Without Borders. By all accounts, Aaron is a real American hero and Amy, a writer for a men's magazine, is assigned to interview him. He is immediately endearing (sort of handsome, a little nerdy, very smart, and friends with the likes of Lebron James). He's perfect. The absurd thing is that Aaron seems to be enamored of *Amy* as well.

When he calls her the morning after their first date, Amy is convinced it's a butt-dial. "No, I dialed you with my fingers," he says, confused. That is what undeserved love feels like. A butt-dial. An accident. We look over both shoulders astonished: Certainly you don't mean, *me*.

In spite of her picky, judgmental aloofness, Aaron chooses her. He doesn't wait for her to stop drinking, or to be nicer and less selfish. Against all rationale, he seems to like her just as she is. But here's the really obnoxious thing: After Amy reluctantly agrees to date him, while there's sort of a love montage, nothing about her really *changes* (other than that she's finally in a monogamous relationship). It's obnoxious because she doesn't deserve him. Amy is still a silly, hypercritical alcoholic.

Then Amy's dad—her favorite person in the world—passes away. This is the point when in any other movie the protagonist would break. They would have a come-to-Jesus moment and face all of their flops and flaws. Will Amy finally realize the chink in her own armor and then rise from the proverbial ashes?

No. Directly after the funeral she says something nasty to her nephew and accuses her sister of never really even liking their dad.

Right then Aaron says to her, "I just want you to know I really care about you, and I love you." He loves her. Right there in the middle of her messy, stone cold death.

Maybe now we will see the thaw that we've been waiting for?

Nope. She's pissed about his timing.

A few weeks later, on a night when Aaron is to receive an award from Doctors Without Borders, at the height of his perfection, Amy hits what the viewer now assumes will be rock bottom. She walks out on his acceptance speech to answer a critical work call from her editor about running an article ("Are You Gay, or is She Just Boring?"), and then she smokes a joint in the hallway.

Aaron, with his trophy in tow, finds her. The sight of him there carrying this hard-earned award is just too much for her.

> AMY: What are we doing? What do you want? Why are you with me?
>
> AARON: I love you.
>
> AMY: Why do you keep saying that?
>
> AARON: Because I mean it! I love you, I'm crazy about you! What do you want me to say?
>
> AMY: What's wrong with you that you want to be with me? I'm a drinker!
>
> AARON: I don't care.
>
> AMY: I've been with a lot of guys.
>
> AARON: I don't care. How many?

Next to Aaron, the picture of righteousness, Amy is so overwhelmed by herself that she pushes him away for good. Following their breakup, she finally hits the bottom of the frigid, empty barrel. She gets wasted, tries to sleep with her sixteen-year-old intern, and subsequently gets fired from her job. At long last, this movie takes a turn for the bearable.

Tail between her legs, she visits her sister for the first time since their dad's funeral. When her sister tries to brush off her apology, Amy says, "No, I'm really sorry. I want you to know that I act like everything you do in your life is so wrong and stupid, but it's just because I don't think I can have that. I'm not okay. I'm not okay. I know what I am. I know who I am. And I'm broken."

Here are Donald Miller's elements of a great *hero*:

- A backstory of brokenness
- A crippling self-doubt
- A reluctant willingness to take action
- A calling that is larger than him- or herself and somehow represents a deep longing in the audience

Both hero and villain are broken, but the real distinguishing mark of a hero is an admission that something is not right with them, and then a hesitant step forward.

I hated most of *Trainwreck* because I don't usually sit down to watch a movie to partake in *painful reality*; I have enough of that in my own life. Amy's spiral lasts at least twenty minutes longer than your typical movie protagonist's. This is frustratingly, unnervingly authentic. I wanted to grab her by the ponytail and yell, "Pull the ripcord, you asshole!" I (like her) am a tragic, off-color, contemporary heroine. I am an asshole. You are an asshole! Do we need to be reminded of it in our down time?

Maybe we do. Because the final moments of this movie are

absolute soul candy.

Amy, who previously mocked cheerleaders, surprises Aaron by performing a dance routine with the Knicks City Dancers. She's *almost* good, *almost* bad—which is as much as any normal girl can hope for next to a Knicks cheerleader. Aaron is mystified. She's sort of awkward, missing some of the steps, and her high kick doesn't even come close to cutting it. But she's having a hell of a time up there. Aaron yells, "You're really good!" And she really is. Then the music switches to this David Cassidy classic:

> *I think I love you,*
> *So what am I so afraid of?*
> *I'm afraid that I'm not sure of*
> *A love there is no cure for.*

These lyrics sum up so much of the problem and solution of this movie, and the problem and solution for any ruined human. We are revolting, we are loved beyond reason or measure. This love may initially feel like a curse (in that up next to it, we find ourselves so critically in need), but it is ultimately *the cure*.

Each day that I wake, *this* heroine must accept the butt-dial of Jesus (which is actually a finger dial). With palms weakly open, I confess my dire brokenness, and then awkwardly dance onward. *What am I so afraid of?*

The Sun Never Sets on the Romantic Comedy (Until It Does)

BEFORE MIDNIGHT

by

CHARLOTTE HORNSBY

"I'm tired of movies about romance," my mom said one day, scanning Netflix. "They're all about falling in love and never about staying in it."

I was twenty-one when she said this, had never fallen in love, and was convinced that I had already passed my prime. Romantic comedies tortured me. I loved the intoxicating feeling of seeing lovers meet on screen, but when the movie was over I would wallow in the indulgent, lovesick question, "When will it be my turn?" It never really occurred to me that rom-coms were selling me an incomplete picture, that movies about love always ended before married life began.

Then I saw Richard Linklater's *Before Midnight* (2013). It was the follow-up to two films about falling in love, *Before Sunrise* (1995) and *Before Sunset* (2004), and it started ten years into a couple's life together. It was ugly and angry and difficult, unlike any romance

I'd ever seen. As soon as I left the theater, I called my mom.

Before I get into what makes *Before Midnight* different, I want to examine what makes every other rom-com the same. Namely, they almost always begin with a 'meet-cute.' A meet-cute is the script-writer's shorthand for the cute scene in which the guy and girl first meet; it's the catalyst for the romance that follows. (Billy Wilder once landed a screenwriting gig on the strength of the meet-cute he proposed: The guy wants to buy a pajama top, but only the top, because he sleeps without pants. The salesman refuses to sell top and bottom separately. A girl comes up to the counter to buy pajamas for her father, who, as fate would have it, only sleeps in pants.)

The bar for meet-cutes has dropped since Billy Wilder's time, and the majority of rom-coms I've seen seem to believe that if you follow two attractive people independently for ten minutes and then put them in the same room (the man clever and candid, the woman disarmingly pure) then just about any interaction will do. Throw in a few problems (she's an independent bookstore owner, he's the head of a corporate chain), heighten the stakes (she could lose her job if he finds out she's not who she says she is), and it's just a matter of jumping a few hurdles until they end up in each other's arms. The pleasure of the fated timing of the meet-cute—when the two people who were always supposed to meet finally meet!—and the relief when all the hurdles between them are overcome ultimately distracts from the true question that brought us to the movie to begin with: "Is this love?"

A good scenario is clearly not enough. In my own love life, reading coincidence as destiny has had disastrous results. Shortly after my mom's remark, I decided to turn a rom-com into reality. (Does our parents' advice stand a chance against the seductive language of cinema?) I met a boy, who was about to leave for Cuba, at a rooftop party in Manhattan. This was my chance to will the meet-cute of my dreams into existence. Borrowing a scene between Hugh Grant and Julia Roberts from *Notting Hill*, I convinced this boy to hop the fence in Tompkins Square Park so we could kiss on the grass only to get arrested a minute later by the NYPD. This was only one of my many misguided attempts at romance in which the story of our meeting was stronger than our connection.

If films have the power and perspective to show us that we are not alone in our failures, that we are bound together by the gulf between what we want to happen to us and what does happen to us, then the rom-com formula is clearly failing us.

Enter the *Before* films. At first blush the opening scene in *Before Sunrise* seems to present the most unrealistic, coinkydink-turned-act-of-God meet-cute in the history of the genre. Here are all the clichés of a movie-land meet-cute as if plucked from the impulse-purchase aisle of the rom-com gift shop: A train skirting the Austrian countryside. A dog-eared philosophy book. A boy with a Leo DiCaprio cow-lick and a plump-lipped blue-eyed French girl on her way to Paris. But while the premise is disappointing in its unlikeliness and bourgeois exclusivity ('love finds you when you most expect it—in Europe when you're young'), the exchange between boy and girl goes beyond shared physical attraction and a clever repartee.

The scene opens on a married couple in their forties arguing on the train, a clever counterweight to a scene about young love.[30] The couple bickers in German, but their volume is enough to disturb Celine, who is trying to read across the aisle. She moves back a few seats to sit across from Jesse, who takes note. Celine pretends

30. It is also a pretty spot-on bit of foreshadowing for the last scene in *Before Midnight*, which didn't yet exist (but we'll get to that).

to read while quietly checking out Jesse who feigns interest in his own book. A few seats ahead, the couple's argument climaxes and the wife storms away down the aisle, past Jesse, who is delighted for an excuse to talk to Celine. He asks if she has any idea what they were arguing about.

> CELINE: Yeah, no. I'm sorry my German is not very good... Have you ever heard that as couples get older they lose their ability to hear each other?
>
> JESSE: No.
>
> CELINE: Well supposedly men lose the ability to hear higher pitched sounds and women eventually lose their ability to hear on the lower end. I guess they sort of nullify each other or something.
>
> JESSE: I guess. Nature's way of allowing couples to grow old together without killing each other.

They share a smile. One reason this dialogue has more personality than your average meet-cute is that it wasn't written by one man alone at his desk dreaming up a conversation between himself and an imaginary dream girl (whose defining personality trait is her beauty). Richard Linklater co-wrote the first script with a female writing partner, Kim Krizan, and then workshopped and revised the script through conversations and improvisations with actors Julie Delpy and Ethan Hawke so that every exchange would feel candid and sincere. The result is two hours of dialogue where the substance of the conversation is equally weighted between the male and female leads.[31]

In an interview with *The Guardian*, Ethan Hawke says of the

---

31. Delpy and Hawke identified with their characters' dialogue so much that years after *Before Sunrise* was released the actors started an email chain in the voices of Celine and Jesse, continuing the story where the first film left off. This email chain would lay the groundwork for the second film, *Before Sunset*.

film, "The way you make a movie like this interesting is to blur the line between performer and character. You don't have any plot to hide behind." One of the most notable differences between *Before Sunrise* and any film in its genre is the defiant absence of plot. A typical rom-com gets its momentum from its obstacle-course plot (guy meets girl, guy loses girl, guy runs into a press conference, down the tarmac or up the stairs to the New Year's Eve party, confesses his love, and gets the girl back). Yet Linklater has made a reputation for himself by crafting films that rely solely on dialogue to hold the audience's attention (*Slacker*, *Waking Life*). Celine and Jesse's exchange on the train keeps going. And going. And going. When his stop comes, Jesse convinces Celine to get off with him so they can keep talking and the pair talk their way through the streets of Vienna, a record store, a carnival, a park, a cathedral, a cemetery and back to the train station. This movie, it turns out, is one two-hour long meet-cute.

So how does it hold our attention? The question "Is this love?" is what really drives the piece, and the Linklater-Delpy-Hawke team makes their best case for it. Celine and Jesse take turns sharing about spiritual experiences, fear of death, doubt in the opposite sex, their hopes, fascinations, and obsessions, all with a zealous drive that seems to scream, "This is me! These are all the things I care about!" While their views differ in almost every category, they respect each other's point of view and take great pleasure in each other's company. When the two cling to each other as the sun rises, waiting for Celine's train, we do feel that they've found love, or at least a rare connection worth pursuing. We want it to keep going because we thirst for that connection in our own lives.

Yet how much can we really know about someone in our first twenty-four hours of meeting them? Even if the conversation plumbs the depths an average rom-com won't even acknowledge (death! supernatural experience!), it is still just a conversation (with, spoiler alert, sex that turns out to be largely a debate about whether to have sex). We don't know how either behave when faced with a conflict. Can Jesse share responsibility? Is Celine able to forgive? We also don't know what their conversation looks like after a year together, after ten years. It's one thing to connect with someone over shared tastes and values. It's another thing entirely to share a life with him.

Enter *Before Midnight*, the third film in a trilogy that just kept writing itself. After two films about their ache to be together, Celine and Jesse are finally together, twenty years after their first meeting, and they're having a rough time. In a rambling conversation that constitutes the first act, writers Linklater, Hawke, and Delpy try to catch the audience up to speed on what's happened in the past nine years in as organic a manner as possible (Jesse left his wife and his son in Chicago; he and Celine had twins). But if all seems calm as the pair joke about being bad parents and driving past the Greek ruins while their kids are asleep, the groundwork is also being laid for the explosive third act, a thirty minute-long fight where every stored up hurt and sacrifice from the past nine years becomes ammunition:

> JESSE: So this is now how you want to be spending this evening? I mean, this is what you wanted to be doing?
>
> CELINE: Well you started it.
>
> JESSE: You are the one who will not shut up about it. But if you want to talk about it—I mean really talk about it—I would prefer to have an unemotional, rational conversation. I mean, do you think we could do that? Would that be possible?
>
> CELINE: Here we go.

In this fight, Celine and Jesse are dealing with the consequences of the decisions they made to be together, of a reality forged by compromise. This last act is so far from the conventions of dream factory rom-coms that it doesn't have a name. It's the anti-meet-cute and it doesn't look or sound like any romantic comedy I've ever seen. It looks and sounds like love as we live it. And if *Before Sunrise* and *Before Sunset* gave us an incomplete picture of life in love, it's because they were both movies about attraction, compatibility, and intimacy before commitment, before anything had been given up. Now in *Before Midnight* we see what it looks like to try to stay together: the unglamorous exhaustion of two people with separate sets of desires, the kids who depend on them, and a finite amount of time. It looks tough.

And yet, as I watch Celine and Jesse argue, I can't help but feel kind of honored that a couple is letting me see them act like this. The desires they each entered the relationship with, Celine's desire for a fulfilling job and Jesse's desire to have visiting rights with his son, are not mutually possible and the sacrifices have been painful. "Do you remember that time," Jesse asks, "when you were like thirty-five minutes late to pick the girls up from school, and you were so stressed out 'cause you knew they were somewhere out on the playground wondering what the hell happened to you? Okay, that is the way that I feel all the time." These decisions have shaped their present, and it's not a balanced ledger or the life they'd planned, and it's littered with regrets.

I met my own Jesse the month that *Before Midnight* came out. I was tired of the grind of the city, hungry for adventure and convinced that dating in New York was impossible. I was about to leave for good, but I stayed an extra month to act in an adaptation of "The Seagull," which my roommate had written. We were rehearsing in the park one day, and I struck up a conversation with an actor who had just joined our cast. He was handsome and easy to talk to and seemed to understand everything I loved about film. And he was married. I couldn't believe my bad luck. After overhearing him say something about his wife, I immediately stopped talking to him for the rest of the rehearsals (never stopping to think that he could be referring to his wife in the play.) The play went up for a one-night run in the Lower East Side, and I got to flirt and kiss and seduce on stage in a way I never really had in real life. It was a triumphant exit from a city that had been one string of disappointments. As soon as the play was over I was about to head out, when Jesse stopped me.

"You were great tonight," he said.

"Thanks," I answered. "Are you married?"

He wasn't. He came to my going away party, and a year later I came back.

Stories that end with a kiss are only harmful when they reinforce the daydream that finding our other is the struggle and everything after is easy. I'm two years past my own meet-cute, and I know more about myself and Jesse than when we met. Our love is playful and explosive and complex, and it's still very, very young. There isn't a lot I can learn from stories about other people my age at this stage in the game. I look to the older Celine and Jesse of *Before Midnight* to remind myself that the journey towards fulfillment doesn't end when we find our mate. Your partner is not your destination. But as Celine thought as she looked out the train window, thank God he asked to sit with me for the ride.

The Progress of the Human Soul in

THE MAGNIFICENT AMBERSONS

A Footnote to Orson Welles

by

Paul F. M. Zahl

This is a footnote to Orson Welles, not a study.

Welles' very famous movie *The Magnificent Ambersons* (1942) has been so written up by so many people and in so many forms and forums that I don't even want to begin by thinking of this as anything more than a footnote.

Seriously, if you start visiting the enormous literature on this movie, on its supposed several versions and afterlife, and the complex whys and wherefores of artistic authorship and legacy in relation to a seemingly fathomless work of art, you end up getting caught in tar. The movie is that big a deal!

One thing I have noticed, though, is that no one, or at least no one I have yet read in the world of film studies, has looked at the truly bizarre ending of the source material, which is Booth Tarkington's novel *The Magnificent Ambersons*, published in 1918.

People are interested, and justifiably interested, in the originally intended and even physically lost ending to Orson Welles' movie. But the really strange thing is the ending of Booth Tarkington's book on which it was based.

I say that because this is a note that relates to Mockingbird and the religious interest of Mockingbird.

Something happens at the end of *The Magnificent Ambersons*, the novel, which is so surprising and so moving—and also so incredible because it is supernatural—that its omission in Welles' movie, and in every version of his movie, is of interest. Because this element is completely missing in the Welles version, the motivation for his ending seems rushed and unsatisfactory to the viewer. Even with the next-to-last scene in Welles' original version, which is 'Eugene Morgan's' visit to 'Aunt Fanny' in a run-down boarding house—a scene which has apparently been cut, and now lost, almost from the time it was shot—the last scene in the movie, which has not been lost, would still be missing the presence of a physical angel. For it is an angel who appears to Eugene Morgan in the last chapter of *The Magnificent Ambersons*. Three times!

Something occurs in Chapter XXXV, the last chapter of the novel, which converts a subtle and somewhat gloomy novel into a transcendent ghost story. This is the part Welles never shot, and must never have intended to shoot; but which actually makes sense of everything, and transforms the novel into a transcendent epiphany of heaven on earth.

DISTINCT AND CONSTANT: WHY EUGENE MORGAN VISITED MRS. HORNER IN NEW YORK

Georgie Minifer (played by Tim Holt in the movie) has been hit by a car while he was crossing the street. His total adversary in life, Eugene Morgan (played by Joseph Cotten), reads a short paragraph about it in the newspaper while he is on a train to New York. Eugene writes a letter to his daughter Lucy (played by Anne Baxter) when he gets to New York, in which he speaks of the effect the news of Georgie's accident has had on him. He says that the accident made him think of Georgie's mother, Isobel (played by Dolores Costello), and that her "distinct" and "constant" image was before him.

When Eugene arrives at his New York hotel, a letter is waiting for him from Lucy, reporting Georgie's accident. Their letters have crossed. In her own letter, Lucy uses the words "distinct" and "constant" to refer to the way she found herself thinking about Isobel when she heard of Georgie's accident. Lucy's use of the exact words that *Eugene* had used, in a letter replying to his that she could not possibly have seen yet, strikes him as very odd. He thinks there must be some kind of message in this, so he resolves to do something that is even more odd.

He decides to visit a medium.

That is the background to Eugene Morgan's out-of-character conversation with Mrs. Horner, the medium (played by no one in the movie because her character does not appear in the movie).

There follows a scene that is unique in Booth Tarkington, and possibly unique in American realistic literature of that era. None of it appears in Orson Welles' movie version of *The Magnificent Ambersons*.

EUGENE MORGAN'S CONVERSATION WITH LOPA: HOW ISOBEL PIERCED THE VEIL

Mrs. Horner's mediumistic 'other' is named Lopa. When Mrs. Horner goes into a trance, she becomes Lopa. It is therefore Lopa who addresses Eugene Morgan.

Lopa begins to speak with people who are living in the afterworld. One of them is, she guesses—or rather, Eugene guesses—Isobel Amberson. Remember, Isobel was Eugene's true love, from whom Isobel's son, Georgie Minifer, had separated him. Isobel is extremely eager, urgently eager, to give, through Lopa (Mrs. Horner), a message to Eugene. Isobel's message, repeated twice, is "Be kind." There is no question in the book that this is Isobel's word to Eugene, her lost but also true love. And Eugene receives it that way.

Later in the chapter, Tarkington represents Eugene's doubts concerning Mrs. Horner and Lopa, after he leaves Mrs. Horner. Eugene is an engineer, as the reader knows well, and a rational man in every circumstance. But not in this circumstance. In the matter of romantic love, specifically his love for Isobel Amberson, Eugene Morgan is open to anything. He loves her that much.

It shouldn't surprise the reader that on the way back to Midland (i.e., Indianapolis), Eugene sees Isobel outside his train window. She is an angel accompanying the train, an "ethereal figure" with "an infinite wistfulness."

When Eugene arrives in Midland, he proceeds straight to the hospital where Georgie Minifer is, and where Eugene's daughter Lucy is. There, in the hospital room, Georgie asks Eugene for his forgiveness. Eugene gives it to him. It is also clear that Lucy Morgan and George Minifer will get married.

Here is the last sentence of Booth Tarkington's *The Magnificent Ambersons*:

> But for Eugene another radiance filled the room. He knew that he had been true at last to his true love, and that through him she had brought her boy under shelter again. Her eyes would look wistful no more.

TARKINGTON'S ENDING AND WELLES' ENDING

Orson Welles ended his movie with a scene that is controversial today, and has been so almost ever since the film was released. It is controversial because it is not absolutely certain who really directed the scene; plus, the scene that supposedly preceded it in the original cut version of the film is not available.

That latter scene apparently portrayed the visit of Eugene Morgan to the boarding house where Aunt Fanny (portrayed by Agnes Moorehead) lived, to give her the news of Georgie's accident. The last scene in the movie, which we *do* have and was intended to follow the boarding house scene, shows Eugene and Aunt Fanny leaving Georgie's hospital room together. Eugene says something similar to the last lines of Tarkington's novel. There is also an implication that Aunt Fanny and Eugene will end up together.

What my footnote to Orson Welles is showing is that the movie version of *The Magnificent Ambersons*, magical as it truly is, leaves out the higher magic of Booth Tarkington's book. Booth Tarkington's book hinges on the supernatural appearance of Isobel Amberson's "shade." Eugene Morgan's sudden change of heart in relation to his Oedipal antagonist Georgie Minifer can only be explained by his dead beloved's intervention from beyond the veil. Eugene believes that in forgiving Georgie, he is following direct instructions from beyond.

In the Welles version, on the other hand, the peace of mind achieved by Eugene at the end lacks that force of motivation. Is he forgiving Georgie for the sake of the still-living Fanny? Or is he doing so for the sake of his daughter Lucy? And yet in the movie he does invoke Isobel at the end. Only Isobel, or her memory, could fuel the fire of transcendent absolution that suffuses that final shot—tho' without explanation.

The message of both the book and the movie version of *The Magnificent Ambersons* is the message of 1 Corinthians 13:8: "Love never ends." The difference between the book and the movie, however, is that the book objectifies the sentiment, because Isobel herself is *still alive*; the movie, on the other hand, subjectifies it, because Isobel lives within the memory of Eugene Morgan.

I prefer the ending of the book.

WHY DID ORSON WELLES IGNORE THE ENDING OF THE BOOK?

Here is a footnote to a footnote.

Whatever the pros and cons are of the movie's ending, or of its proposed ending, or of the finally cut ending—in other words, the ending Welles intended as well as the ending as cut by the studio—whatever the pros and cons are of whatever version we see or wish to see—Orson Welles chose not to film the ending of *The Magnificent Ambersons* as Booth Tarkington wrote it. There is not a millimeter of film that concerns the appearance to Eugene Morgan of his departed Isobel Amberson through the medium of Lopa. It's not there.

Why did Welles do nothing with Tarkington's surprising supernatural conclusion to his great book?

The only solid thing I know of that we might be able to go on is something Welles himself said. I think it was in an interview with the French magazine *Cahiers du Cinema.* Welles said, "In my opinion, there are two things that can absolutely not be carried to the screen: the realistic presentation of the sexual act and praying to God."

Ironically enough, there is a touching scene in *The Magnificent Ambersons* that shows Georgie Minifer asking forgiveness on his knees at the side of his mother's bed after she has died. It looks a lot like "praying to God," to quote Welles against himself.

Nevertheless, if this is what Orson Welles believed about what could not be shown on the screen, then the appearance of Isobel Amberson to Eugene Morgan, both outside his speeding train and through the spiritualist medium, Mrs. Horner, would probably qualify. How do you show a *real* ghost? It's very hard to do. Even in Robert Wise's movie *The Haunting* (1963), which is about as good a movie ghost story as there is, you never really see the ghost(s). They are just strongly implied.

I think Orson Welles' reticence about depicting 'acts' of religion in a movie probably applies to his artistic response to Booth Tarkington's ending of *The Magnificent Ambersons*. Thus the movie, while being hypnotic and moving in so many ways, and visually at the summit of film art, is not as profound as the novel on which it was based. That is because in the novel on which it was based, love never ends because people never end. There is no final death in the glowing world of Eugene Morgan, Isobel Amberson, Lucy Morgan, and Georgie Minifer.

I Want You to Hit Me as Hard as You Can

FIGHT CLUB

by

NICK LANNON

The Christian musician Brian Doerksen wrote a song, "Refiner's Fire," that will be familiar to many. I haven't heard it in a while, but it was a staple of my youth group and college fellowship days, and it's simple enough that I'll never forget it:

Purify my heart
Let me be as gold and precious silver
Purify my heart
Let me be as gold, pure gold

Refiner's fire
My heart's one desire
Is to be holy
Set apart for You, Lord
I choose to be holy
Set apart for You, my Master
Ready to do Your will

During all the hundreds of singings of those lyrics, it didn't really dawn on me what I was saying. To the extent that I thought about the lyrics at all, I was simply expressing a desire for God to come in and make me holy. But, as the saying goes, be careful what you wish for. Because seriously. A refiner's fire? That sounds awful.

The verse of Scripture that Doerksen is certainly alluding to is Malachi 3:2b-3, which reads, "For he is like a refiner's fire and like fullers' soap; he will sit as a refiner and purifier of silver, and he will purify the descendants of Levi and refine them like gold and silver, until they present offerings to the Lord in righteousness." It wasn't until years later, when I saw *Fight Club*, that I began to understand what God's refining fire might actually be like.

There's a scene in that film, directed by David Fincher and written by Jim Uhls (based on Chuck Palahniuk's cult novel), that features Brad Pitt's character teaching Edward Norton's character to make soap. Already the parallels between Malachi and *Fight Club* begin coming to light.

Pitt's character, Tyler Durden, embodies everything Norton's unnamed narrator aspires to be. While Norton numbs himself with designer catalogs and cute theories about life ("Everything on an airplane is single-serving, even the relationships"), Durden makes accurate, incisive speeches about the ugly truths of American consumer culture. "The things [we] own end up owning [us]," he says. And, more colorfully, "[Expletive] Martha Stewart. She's polishing the brass on the *Titanic*...it's all going down."

Through a series of circumstances too intricate to go into here, Norton comes to live with Pitt and begins to lose his beloved trappings of Americana—his job, his yin-and-yang coffee table, and his refrigerator full of artisanal mustard. Pitt, though, still thinks Norton is being a poser, acting like he's ready to let it all go but, in actuality, too afraid to really take the plunge. So Pitt decides to teach Norton about the fuller's soap…and the refiner's fire.

One of the key ingredients to making soap, it turns out, is lye, a strongly alkaline solution capable of producing a brutal chemical burn on the skin. After asking Norton for his hand, Pitt shakes lye onto the back of it. "It'll hurt more than you've ever been burned," Pitt says, "and you will have a scar." When Norton tries to escape the pain by retreating into what he calls "guided meditation," imagining a peaceful forest of beatific trees, Pitt snaps him back to reality: "Stay with the pain. Don't shut this out… *This* is your pain, *this* is your burning hand, it's *right here*."

This is what the refiner's fire is actually like. This is what goes into the fuller's soap. It's not wonderful; it's terrible. This is the bad news of Christianity: To make you holy, God must burn away your sin. To redeem you, he must first destroy you. This is your pain, it's right here.

Norton, like any one of us, tries to get the pain to stop. "I get it!" he shouts. We say much the same: "I understand what you want from me! I'll do better!" But God knows that all we really want is an escape. "What you're feeling is premature enlightenment," Pitt retorts. "This is the greatest moment of your life, man, and you're off somewhere missing it!" Before he allows Norton to soak his hand in vinegar, neutralizing the burn, Pitt demands that he embrace the pain: "First you have to give up. You have to know…not fear… *know*…that someday, you're gonna die." Frustrated, Norton says, "You don't know how this feels!" only to have Pitt hold up the back of his own hand, revealing a chemical burn scar of his own. After the music quiets and Norton gains some composure, Pitt makes his final statement: "It's only after we've lost everything that we're free to do anything."

This is a conversion experience of the first order, an example of what we might call 'the cross side' of Christianity. This is not a catchy praise chorus; it's a requiem. Jesus said that if any wanted to become his followers, they had to deny themselves, take up their cross and follow him (Mt 16:24). We think that this means discipleship is a hard road, with a heavy burden to bear. We turn 'taking up our cross' into something that we can take pride in. "Look at the crosses I've had to carry in my life! Look at all the challenges I've overcome!" we might think, even if we'd never boast like that out loud. If you've ever said—or thought—"Well, that's just my cross to bear," you've tragically underestimated what carrying a cross really means. We forget that people who carry crosses always end up in the same place: on them.

When Brad Pitt says, "First you have to give up. You have to know that someday, you're gonna die," he's describing the first step to freedom: to know that the road of the cross leads inexorably to Calvary. To understand that it is only a dead body that can be resurrected. He goes on: "It's only after we've lost everything that we're free to do anything." When Edward Norton is lying on the floor after this experience, basically in shock, Pitt's words to him are simple: "Congratulations. You're one step closer to hitting bottom."

But no one wants to hit bottom. Hitting bottom hurts too much.

We resist. "Lose everything? Deny myself?" we protest. "But that'll mean weakness...and death. That'll be the end of me!" Tyler Durden is right: The things we own end up owning us. In a tragic irony, it is the things that we imagine are giving us life—career success, well-adjusted children, good standing in our church—that consume our daily lives and threaten to destroy us.

Consider Malachi 3:2a, the half-verse *before* Doerksen begins quoting for his song: "But who can endure the day of his coming, and who can stand when he appears?" Though one would be understandably reluctant to put this sentence into a contemporary worship chorus, this is the truly profound part of the verse: God is not in the human improvement business. He's in the resurrection business. He doesn't burnish your edges a little bit and soap the dirt out from behind your ears. He burns you to the ground, making it impossible to claim that you can get this done on your own. He is an idol-destroyer, and he knows that your most beloved idol is your own self-sufficiency. Tyler Durden is right again: We are all polishing the brass on the *Titanic*, and it's all going down.

Refiner's fire, indeed. It's no wonder that—truly understood—the idea of God being like a refiner's fire or a fuller's soap is a terrifying one. Fear, though, is not the end of our story. This is not a path we must walk alone.

Ed Norton puts our greatest fear into words: "You don't know how this feels!" We cry out to God, "You rip my desires, my hopes, my dreams—my life!—away from me. You don't know how this feels!" Brad Pitt holds up his hand, showing his scar, proving to the faithless that he's been here before.

Our God has been here before, too. He is no stranger to "hitting bottom":

> He was despised and rejected by others; a man of suffering and acquainted with infirmity; and as one from whom others hide their faces he was despised, and we held him of no account. Surely he has borne our infirmities and carried our diseases; yet we accounted him stricken, struck down by God, and afflicted (Isa 53:3-4).

Like Thomas, converted by the wounds of the risen Christ, Norton is converted by Brad Pitt's wounds. Jesus Christ bore his cross so that death can be a beginning—rather than an end—for us. He died so that we might live. He died, and we died with him (Gal 2:20), so that now we can be free.

> But he was wounded for our transgressions, crushed for our iniquities; upon him was the punishment that made us whole, and by his bruises we are healed (Isa 53:5).

We have to know—not suspect—know, the reality of the cross. It is only then that we can really be.

Running on Empty

WITHOUT LIMITS

by

CJ Green

Without Limits reimagines the rise and fall of Steve Prefontaine, the mustachioed long-distance runner who set lasting national records and helped inspire the ascent of amateur running in America—essentially you have Pre to thank for the stream of runners puffing down the sidewalk, shaming you for how little you get out there. Infamous for both his charisma and his cockiness, Pre was known to look over his shoulder during races, sacrificing momentum in order to measure how far ahead he was, and at the height of his career, he competed in the 1972 Olympics in Munich. Once, after running neck-and-neck for three miles with competitor Frank Shorter, Pre bolted, crossing the line first. He later explained, "I was just thinking it wasn't that big a deal. Then something inside of me said, 'Hey, wait a minute, I want to beat him,' and I took off!"[32]

32. Moore, Kenny. "Transit and Sorrow." In *Bowerman and the Men of Oregon*, (2006) 320.

His can-do attitude made Pre a god. Packed-out stadiums chanted his name. His fans believed in him—and he believed in himself.

To be fair, it's important to separate movie version Pre from real-life Pre; I obviously never met Steve Prefontaine, but more than a handful of times I've watched my battered, paperback *Without Limits* DVD, which Warner Bros has branded with the subtitle: "Believe in yourself." Let the eye-rolling commence from *Orthodoxy* fans.[33] But, Mockingbird readers aside, who would actually watch a movie that advertises "Explore your limits"? Objectively speaking, the film doesn't command viewers to believe in anything; instead it *illustrates* belief, both in man and in God, and the irreconcilable tension between them becomes a central conflict.

Midway through the film, while Jefferson Airplane warbles in the background, Pre runs after his future girlfriend, Mary, and offers to carry her books. They chat for a bit, and Mary asks:

"Do you believe in God?"

"I believe in myself."

Cue smooching. This scene is tender and tense, and ridiculous, all at once. It is just one of the many moments when Pre sets himself opposite God, with whom he remains at odds throughout the entire film. God is Pre's biggest competitor, and we see that from the beginning. As the team squabbles about penis length, for example, Pre questions the value of arbitrary standards anyways, and his coach, Bill Bowerman, says off-handedly, "It's God's will, Pre." Visibly disgusted, Pre repeats, "*God's will?*" Later, when an AAU official prevents him from racing, Pre tries to attack him, repeatedly screaming, "You're not God! You're not God!" as if God was the real fun-sucker to be reckoned with. Pre's disdain for the almighty

33. From "Chapter 2: The Maniac" of G. K. Chesterton's *Orthodoxy*: "Complete self-confidence is not merely a sin; complete self-confidence is a weakness. Believing utterly in one's self is a hysterical and superstitious belief..."

stems from the implicit concession that the only one who could prevent him from running, winning, and becoming a god is God himself.

So it's a tender twist of events when, despite the line of girls outside his door, he falls in love with Mary Marckx, a practicing Catholic who refuses to sleep with him. Maybe it's her hard-to-get-ness that keeps his attention, but my hypothesis is that she represents a God foreign to Pre—one that's not a threat, but instead a gentle and left-handed invitation.[34] Entranced, Pre seems totally unaware that her God is the same one who threatens his sense of glory; he touches the crucifix on her necklace and whispers, "Oh, that's pretty."

While Pre tangles with God, *Without Limits* takes on another layer, meditating on the nature of man and his curious impulse to run. Christopher McDougall's bestselling research-memoir, *Born to Run*, explains:

> Running was mankind's first fine art, our original act of inspired creation. Way before we were scratching pictures on caves or beating rhythms on hollow trees, we were perfecting the art of combining our breath and mind and muscles into fluid self-propulsion over wild terrain...
>
> There's something so universal about that sensation, the way running unites our two most primal impulses: fear and pleasure. We run when we're scared, we run when we're ecstatic, we run away from our problems and run around for a good time.[35]

Running, as natural and human as it is, also requires effort—a no-no

34. The idea of left-handed power is propounded by Robert Farrar Capon in *Kingdom, Grace, Judgment*: "Left-handed power is guided by the more intuitive, open, and imaginative right-side of the brain. Left-handed power, in other words, is precisely paradoxical power: power that looks for all the world like weakness, intervention that seems indistinguishable from nonintervention" (19).

35. Christopher McDougall, *Born to Run* (2009), 92, 11.

word for grace enthusiasts. The movie suggests that, while Pre's effort is driven by the all-American pursuit of glory, it is also driven by fear: the constant need to be justified. His coach, Bill Bowerman, whose sloped eyebrows serve as a harbinger of sarcasm, has only gentle words for Pre, trying to nudge him down the right path.[36] Analyzing Pre's incurable need to run out front, Bowerman explains: "He couldn't stand a crowd—always wanted to race out front, from the start, like he was trying to get away from something."

Certainly running represents man's need to go, to escape the present state of things, but there's freedom in it too. Despite burning lungs and sore muscles, running remains rewarding and genuinely fun. A paradox. There's nothing quite like waking up early to hit the pavement, exploring new trails, and later, sitting in the same sweaty shorts, getting a whiff of those hardworking armpits while sipping a well-deserved fruit smoothie.

Ultimately long-distance running is a simple test to see how long you can handle discomfort. It's a test of will. Augustine is known for introducing the idea of the corrupt will into Western Christianity, emphasizing what Paul grieves in Romans 7:15: "I do not do what I want, but I do the very thing that I hate." In *City of God*, Augustine explains,

> [Man's] mind and his flesh do not obey his will…For in spite of himself his mind is both frequently disturbed, and his flesh suffers, and grows old, and dies; and in spite of ourselves we suffer whatever else we suffer, and which we would not suffer if our nature absolutely and in all its parts obeyed our will…By the just retribution of the sovereign God whom we refused to be subject to and serve, our flesh, which was subjected to us, now torments us by insubordination…

36. A couple of facts: Bill Bowerman was a co-founder of Nike, and Pre was Nike's first signature athlete. On a separate note, Donald Sutherland was nominated for a Golden Globe for his performance as Bowerman.

McDougall explains that the human body is a machine designed to run; the question then becomes why we don't do it more, and *better*. As Augustine reminds us, there's something internal that prevents us from doing what we know is good. *Without Limits*, however, shows Pre defying these expectations: He is different, and that's what we love about him. He wins races because he wants to. He obeys his will. Running along the beach with his sweetheart, they banter about his limits:

> MARY: You don't really believe you can do anything?
>
> PRE: Absolutely.
>
> MARY: Fly a plane?
>
> PRE: Well, sure, if I wanted to. You read the manual, get the best teacher, and take off.
>
> MARY: Steve, not everything can be learned, you know? I mean, some things take talent.

Offended, Pre grabs her shoulder and they slow to a halt. "Let me tell you something," he says. "Talent is a myth, Mary. There's a dozen guys on the team with more talent in their little finger."

"Then how come you can beat them?" she asks.

"A little secret I learned a long time ago, in Coos Bay, in the woods." He's talking about being bullied. "I can endure more pain than anyone you've ever met. That's why I can beat anyone I've ever met."

Even if Pre remains a theologian of glory, at least he understands that glory arrives only after excruciating pain. Still, he insists that he has earned this glory, because he has the will to endure the cross. St. Augustine, and Coach Bowerman, believe otherwise: It's not because of Pre's exceptionally strong will, but because his heart can pump more blood per minute than probably any other human on the planet—he possesses a gift given outside his control. Which suggests one thing: He has limits. "Be grateful for your limits, Pre," Coach Bowerman says, "because they're about as limitless as they get in this life." Pre seems nauseated; he will not accept that his fame and glory were given to him.

Nevertheless, the life formula—'Try your hardest and you will win'—proves toxic. His effort reaps rewards but none that save. Eventually, his exceptional will cannot place him in first. In the 1972 Olympics, against everyone's expectations, Pre crosses the finish line in fourth place. Thereafter everything seems violated—his identity, his worldview, his relationships. He can barely look his friends in the eye.

The truth is that the heart is fragile. Jean Vanier, in his 2015 Templeton Prize video, explains that humans are born weak, very small, and totally dependent on their mothers. "We were born in weakness," he says. "We will grow. We will die. So the story of each one of us is a story of accepting that we are fragile...The heart is a very fragile part of us." Vanier explains that a fragile heart is protected when it understands that it is important and loved; until that time, we are running. Famously, Augustine writes that our hearts are restless until they rest in God.

At the same time, it seems God gives us the freedom to continue running, blindly, in circles around him—and even so, all our shin splints and sprained toes aren't a total waste. Somewhere down the line we find that Pre was right. The purpose of running isn't to win a race; it's not even to experience the joy of doing it. Rather, it's to "test the limits of the human heart." And what's implicit in that is a paradox that's hard to hold in one sweaty fist: Running hard, with everything you've got, no matter how good you are, means pressing boundaries, testing limits, and ultimately acknowledging that you have them.

In the end, Pre crashes into God, who remains the only one who can threaten his sense of self. Tragically, he hits the ultimate limit: Flipping his car late one night, he dies young. In this moment we see that his awards are just that: awards. All that he earned "grows strangely dim," and we see clearly that whatever was valuable in Pre's life was given to him: loving memories with his friends, his coach, his girlfriend. We see that true glory could never be earned, not even by Steve Prefontaine. All glory has already been earned by someone else. Real-life Pre is famous for his one-liners, one of which goes something like, "Somebody may beat me, but they are going to have to bleed to do it." And bleed He did.

Jesus Christ in the

HAMMER HOUSE OF HORROR

by

PAUL F. M. ZAHL

There was the French 'New Wave.' There was Italian 'Neo-Realism.' There was Ingmar Bergman. There was Andrei Wajda. There was Mikail Kalatozov. There was American 'Film Noir.' There was the John Ford Western. There was *Lawrence of Arabia.*

There was Hammer House of Horror.

Hammer House of Horror refers to the Gothic horror movies produced in England by Hammer Studios from the late 1950s through the mid-1970s. Combining cleavage for teenage (and other) boys, lots of gore, and unexpectedly high production values—such as sumptuous sets and gorgeous costumes and romantic, unforgettable music—Hammer Studios hit a nerve and made a ton of money.

But there was something else to their lurid, luxurious horrors. And you don't have to look very close to find it.

With only a few exceptions, and notoriously their final film in the series, entitled *To the Devil a Daughter* (1976), the Gothic horror movies produced by Hammer Studios depicted a world in which the triumph of good over evil is assured. Good never fails and evil always does.

Moreover, the victory of good over evil is conveyed through the Cross of Jesus Christ in the hands of Christian practitioners, both likely ones (i.e., ministers and priests—and abbots, even—as well as anyone with the name 'Van Helsing') and unlikely ones (i.e., teenagers, housewives, doubting young people who still know the Lord's Prayer, even a few hypocrites and puritans).

For a Christian, if you want to see your faith affirmed and validated in a mainstream (uh...) movie, Hammer horror movies are a real encouragement. Right down the line.

How did this phenomenon, the explicit Christianity of Hammer horror movies, come to pass?

I'd like to try to answer that question, and then review the evidence. And before I do, let me commend my friend Paul Leggett's 2002 book entitled *Terence Fisher: Horror, Myth and Religion*, published by McFarland Books. This essay does not draw on Paul's book directly but agrees with his findings.

"WOULD IT HELP YOU IF I TOLD YOU I AM FIGHTING EVIL, FIGHTING IT AS SURELY AS YOU DO?" (THE HOUND OF THE BASKERVILLES, 1959)

Since I was a little boy, I have been living in the Hammer House of Horror. Before we were even teenagers, my friends and I used to spend our summer vacations making our own 8mm versions of Frankenstein and Dracula.

When we finally went downtown and saw our first *actual* Hammer horror movie in a movie theater—it was 1965, and until that fateful Saturday afternoon, we had relied entirely on photographs printed in *Famous Monsters of Filmland* magazine—we literally all exclaimed at the same time during the movie, "They stole that from us!"

I'm not kidding. Little Lloyd (Fonvielle) and Bill (Bowman) and Paul (Zahl) all believed immediately and without question that Hammer Studios had stolen their ideas about how to 'do' Dracula... from us.

As I said, I have been living in the world of Hammer horror since the early 1960s.

Later on, "when I became a man" (1 Cor 13:11), and especially when I entered the ministry, I saw there were other things going on in these movies, and specifically, their images of cruciform victory over the powers of darkness.

Now how did Hammer Studios get that way? What accounts for their almost Prayer-Book understanding of religion?

Well, I use that phrase intentionally: "Prayer-Book understanding of religion."

When I began to look again at Hammer horror movies in light of their explicit Christianity, what leapt out at first were the prayers spoken by non-believers and practitioners of evil. In particular, the Thuggee priest in *Stranglers of Bombay* (1959) and the Egyptian priest in *The Mummy* (1959), each played by the actor George Pastell. Those prayers gave me a clue, for the language was pure 1662 Book of Common Prayer, just adapted, shall we say, for a different use.

Then the answer came to me in a flash: prep school!

Whoever wrote these scripts or worked them over must have had early exposure to the Prayer Book of the Church of England. You see, if I wanted to compose a prayer and put it in the mouth of a priest—any priest—but didn't personally know any Thuggees, what would I do? I would go back to what I knew, or at least what I had heard.

In other words, these scripts were created by people who had some connection, probably a childhood connection, with the Church of England.

This would also help to explain the 'default position' of almost all the Hammer horror movies when it comes to the final conflict of good against evil. The form of the good is almost always a Christian form. There is one delightful exception, from 1974, and we'll get to that at the end.

I was not there when these movies were made. I was in the world, yes, sitting over in New York City and Washington, D.C., poring over *Famous Monsters of Filmland* and thinking about *Curse of the Werewolf* (1961). But I was learning my Prayer Book—the 1928 American version of it. And I could tell instinctively that George Pastell had been given words that he did not make up.

Later, too, when I found that Anthony Hinds, who produced many of these movies and wrote the scripts for a ton of them, sometimes under an alias, had gone to St. Paul's School in London—well, the traditional Christian tone of Hammer made sense.

Bottom line: Hammer horror movies of the classic period, and even later than that, and in some ways right through to the 'hinge' movie, *Twins of Evil* (1971), are saturated with the Church of England.

Don't you love this? The High Priest of Kharis, anointed caller-out to a 3000-year-old Egyptian mummy, sounding like the Archbishop of Canterbury! The inner sanctum of the Thuggee sect, suffused with Christian eucharistic symbols and rhetorically—without a trace of satire or cynicism—coming across like the chaplain at Winchester School! Not to mention the quaint but dear Bishop Frankland in *Hound of the Baskervilles*. Or the amazing Duc de Richleau with his invocation of the Coverdale Psalter that breaks up a Black Mass on Salisbury Plain in *The Devil Rides Out* (1968). Or the kindly vicar Dr. Blyss, who is actually a reformed pirate, in *Night Creatures* (1962). Or the thoroughly un-sentimental Monsignor, who gets the job done, in *Dracula Has Risen from the Grave* (1968).

The point is, Christianity, and most of its representatives, gets a big 'leg up' in the Hammer catalogue. And I think a big reason for this is that the 'powers behind the throne' had attended English public school!

Now it's time for a short inventory of the Hammer output, or, in Mockingbird terms, 'Jesus Christ in the House of Horror.'

"HE THAT DWELLETH IN THE SECRET PLACE OF THE MOST HIGH SHALL ABIDE IN THE SHADOW OF THE ALMIGHTY." (THE DEVIL RIDES OUT, 1968)

THE HOUND OF THE BASKERVILLES (1959)

This is Hammer's Sherlock Holmes. It portrays the great detective, played by Peter Cushing, as a man dedicated to fighting evil with conscious catholic intent—'catholic' in the sense of everywhere at all times. Not only does Sherlock Holmes completely 'one up' the Bishop/entomologist, played by a fuzzy but not unkindly Miles Malleson, but he communicates an extremely sharp insight into the revenge plan of the villainess, played by the eyes-flashing Marla Landi.

What I like about this movie is the fact that Sherlock Holmes is only one step removed from Abraham Van Helsing.

THE BRIDES OF DRACULA (1960)

Christianity, and the Mockingbird version in particular, connects a 'low' or realistic anthropology with a 'high' soteriology. That's theological language for saying that in order for Good News to make sense, there has to be a bad situation in relation to which the Good News does make sense. An old way of putting this was to frame it as a question: Why did Jesus Christ have to die? Could He maybe have just gotten sick? An extreme 'solution'—Christ's death— wouldn't make sense if the problem for which it was the answer were not extreme also. *The Brides of Dracula* is about this. It absolutely in no way underestimates the problems that people get themselves in to. To say the least.

Baron Meinster is all about his mother. His mother is all about him. And she is most concerned to 'protect' her son from the pretty young teacher who has come to teach in the local private school.

On the other hand, Baron Meinster likes Marianne, and persuades her to free him from his mother's literal shackles. Then he kills his mother—turning her into a vampire.

One thing leads to another, and it is not until Peter Cushing comes on the scene, as Doctor Van Helsing, that the proper cure can be found, for everyone.

Van Helsing throws holy water on Baron Meinster's face, thus disempowering him; and then, most Christianly, maneuvers both the Baron and the windmill in which they have been wrestling in such a way that the Baron is caught in the cruciform shadow of the arms of the windmill by the light of the silvery moon. Baron Meinster burns to death.

The Mockingbird quotient here is high: Incest and Freudian attractions/repulsions, lust and innocence and moth-to-the-flame, too. The local priest is more or less useless: he doesn't have enough faith! And the desperate reality of the situation comes to the point of but one way out: incineration by a giant improvised crucifix.

Hammer never quite equalled the combination of swashbuckling Christianity and earthy sensualism that seems to saturate every minute of *The Brides of Dracula.*

CURSE OF THE WEREWOLF (1961)

Although *Curse of the Werewolf* is also saturated with Christian images, it is not my favorite Hammer film.

Let's begin with the images: Leon the baby, who will grow up to be Leon the werewolf, is born on Christmas Day. He is the result of a sort of parthenogenesis, which is to say his mother, an innocent and sweet serving girl, is 'overshadowed' by a cruelly treated traveling minstrel, who has been so long in prison that he is utterly *non compos mentis.* When Leon is baptized—and please, let's hear it again for private baptisms on Saturday afternoons—public baptisms on Sunday morning are starting to get old—the water in the font is troubled. There is almost the feeling that Leon is an anti-Christ.

Later, between the power of the Cross, the sanctity of the church bell tower, and the silver bullet in his kindly uncle's rifle, Leon is killed; and the spell over his life, ended.

The problem with *Curse of the Werewolf* is its despairing ending. There is no good solution for Leon, played sympathetically by Oliver Reed, other than his violent death. Even the love of a good woman, played by Catherine Feller, whom Leon comes very close to murdering, is not enough.

I had to include *Curse of the Werewolf* in this Mockingbird guide, because if I didn't, someone would get up and say, "Wait, you've left out the most apparently Christian of them all."

But it's not.

You come out of the movie with a boulder in your stomach.

One important postscript, by the way: The musical score for *Curse of the Werewolf* was composed by Benjamin Frankel. It is usually described as 'serialist,' that is, as an example of the 12-Tone technique pioneered by Arnold Schoenberg. All my life I've heard this about Benjamin Frankel's score, which *is* wonderful. But I've also listened to some of Schoenberg, and can't quite grasp the connection between the two. I'm sure a connection is there, but remember, just because a critic says it's there, doesn't mean it is there.

KISS OF THE VAMPIRE (1963)

This one was known in America as *Kiss of Evil*, just as a few other great Hammers were given different titles for purposes of distribution in America. The alternate titles matter almost nothing today, because the DVD versions of these movies usually take the English title. What I am saying is that movie enthusiasts, and I am one, who like to make fine points in relation to the differing titles of these movies from fifty years ago, are only showing off when they do.

Kiss of the Vampire is an excellent movie.

For one thing, the villain, Dr. Ravna, is played by Noel Willman. Noel Willman was from Ulster, Londonderry, to be exact, so he should get our vote! (Gosh, I love the Northern Irish.)

Secondly, the climax of the movie is one of the Eight Wonders of the World. In it, the extremely Christian vampire hunter, Professor Zimmer, summons a colony of bats to destroy the vampire coven who are worshipping up in Dr. Ravna's castle. The bats are a little what we used to call 'fakey'—the Woolworth's kind, in other words. But with a little matte work, a nice model of the castle, and some modest animation over the matte, the saving and purging attack comes off.

The music for *Kiss of the Vampire*, which was composed by James Bernard, is outstanding. It includes one of the high points of all Hammer soundtracks, a Romantic and hypnotic sonata for piano that Bernard nicknamed "The Tooth Concerto."

CAPTAIN CLEGG/NIGHT CREATURES (1962)

Of all the Mockingbird Hammers, this one is the most friendly to the Christian Church as an institution. Or maybe I should say, it is the most friendly to the Church of England's official representatives.

Peter Cushing, who plays The Reverend Doctor Blyss, acts the very h___ out of this role. The idea is that Dr. Blyss, the vicar of Dymchurch on Romney Marsh, is really a reformed buccaneer who escaped execution years ago with the help of his trusty friend Mipps, played by the ubiquitous and always welcome Michael Ripper.

Not only has Dr. Blyss become the loved and admired pastor of his cure, Dymchurch village, but he uses his former skills to help his flock stay solvent during hard times. In other words, Dr. Blyss helps his people smuggle wine and fine liquor from France—but without violence. The vicar is a reformed criminal, about ninety-five percent. He is a marvelous, affectionate character, and Peter Cushing is perfect as Dr. Blyss.

The scenes that take place in church will warm the heart of any sincere churchman of almost any denomination. Dr. Blyss' kindness to all sufferers, and also the very deep affection in which he holds his daughter, who lives quietly and anonymously in the village and is also stunningly beautiful, makes him a most appealing and good man.

Dr. Blyss also knows to swing from a chandelier in church, from the pulpit, no less; and Peter Cushing did all the stunts himself.

When the vicar's past finally catches up with him, you want to say, "No, he's too good." And when Dr. Blyss is buried, in Captain

Clegg's grave, by the entire mass of his warmly affectioned parishioners, it is a pure expression of the pastoral bond that almost every sincere minister has known at least once in his or her years of service.

Jesus Christ is not exactly a character in *Captain Clegg/Night Creatures*. But one of his more human and sincere representatives is.

THE DEVIL RIDES OUT/THE DEVIL'S BRIDE (1968)

If there is a crown jewel in the Mockingbird list of Hammer horror favorites, it should be *The Devil Rides Out*.

This is because *The Devil Rides Out*, which is based on a novel by Dennis Wheatley, instantiates almost point for point the reality of what Christians sometimes call 'spiritual warfare,' and it leaves almost nothing out.

First, *The Devil Rides Out* understands that Satan works by deception, and hypnosis. With the exception of Mocata, the devil's high priest, played to wicked perfection by Charles Gray (of *Rocky Horror Picture Show* fame), all of Satan's 'adepts' are under a kind of acute spiritual hypnosis which prevents them ever from seeing where it is all leading, i.e., to their deaths. Mocata's sycophants, most particularly Simon Aron, a key figure in the book, whose hypnosis starts the story going, are entirely deluded. One by one, their delusions are unmasked, with the result that they die horribly. Wheatley obviously did not believe in 'free will' when it came to the power of Satan over the pliable human will. These people are not living; they are being lived.

Second, the movie (like the novel) understands that Satan is defeated by two wholly good conduit-objects: the Bible and the Cross. And I don't mean the Cross as a purely theological reality, but the Cross as a physical object that can be hurled at the Enemy. When the Duc de Richleau, together with his young (preppy)

American friend, Rex Van Ryn, charges into the Devil's Sabbat on Salisbury Plain, the Duc hurls the Cross at the devil incarnate; and the devil incarnate flees instantly away in a puff of smoke. (Something exactly like this happens in Stephen King's novel *The Shining*.) Dennis Wheatley, and also Christopher Lee, who plays the Duc de Richleau, have taught me how to throw a crucifix when you're in a tight spot. Dear reader, we all need to take lessons! See *The Devil Rides Out*.

Third, the movie depicts a humble and spiritually minded woman as the savior of the day. At the impressive climax of *The Devil Rides Out*, Marie, the mother of little Fleur, who is about to be sacrificed to Satan by Mocata, truly rises to the occasion. She remembers the inscription on her mother's pendant Cross. It goes like this: "He who loves without desire / Shall have power given in his darkest hour." In what might be the finest Christian moment in all of Hammer horror—but wait! I forgot about *Dracula Has Risen from the Grave*—the words spoken by Marie cause a bolt of lightning to come down and engulf the Satanists' space in consuming fire, as a huge golden Cross, etched into the wall of the room where they have gathered, appears. All are consumed, save Fleur, her mother, the Duc de Richleau, and their three friends.

The reason this movie is so outstandingly Christian, in what I think is the most noble way, is that it does not for a moment soften the power of the book. Richard Matheson, who was sympathetic to religion but not an orthodox Christian, adapted Dennis Wheatley's book for Hammer. It is the perfect adaptation.

Whenever I show this movie to friends—usually on Halloween when Turner Classic Movies seems to like to run a nice print of it—they are speechless. How did it ever get made? And in 1968? I close my eyes, put one finger to my lips, and say the *Benedicite*.

ROADS NOT TAKEN

I discern three 'hinge points' or forks in the road within a Christian trajectory of themes and substance in Hammer films. Whether these hinge points were a result of changing social attitudes, which is a common explanation, especially in relation to religion; or whether they reflected changing personnel as older craftsmen on the set began to retire or do other things; or whether they reflected exigencies related to the market or target audience, which were a function of changing attitudes in the surrounding culture, these hinge points exist between the films.

Parallel to shifts in the religious landscape of the ongoing Hammer universe would be shifts in the portrayal of sex and the portrayal of violence. There was more nudity and more sex in Hammer films as time passed; and the violence became more explicit—tho' the gore had always been explicit.

But in terms of a basically Christian view of the world, Hammer did not change fundamentally until their last film, *To the Devil a Daughter* (1976). That movie is a near 180-degree departure from almost all their earlier productions. Dennis Wheatley, the author of the source novel, became sick over it, and almost all of Hammer's traditional fan base left the theater sickened.

What I am saying is that the Christian 'narrative' in the Hammer output remained pretty constant until 1976, after which the project basically collapsed.

Here is the first hinge point, which ended up as a stunning and surprising reaffirmation of the positive role of Christianity in the struggle of everyday people against active, preying evil.

FIRST HINGE POINT:

DRACULA HAS RISEN FROM THE GRAVE (1968)

This was directed by Freddie Francis, and I don't find it as convincing as the earlier Terence Fisher Draculas. Is it the soft focus that seems to 'ring' the frame when Dracula comes on the screen? Is it the obvious attempt to portray a 'hippie' or rock-singer-type hero in the setting of nineteenth-century Transylvania? Is it the rather affect-less performance of the female lead? I just find this movie to be hard work.

But the *story* contains three jaw-dropping Christian elements. The first is the character of the gone-to-seed and entirely weakened parish priest, the one who looks like Larry of The Three Stooges, who becomes Dracula's bondservant. It is an unpleasant depiction of a priest who has not only lost his calling, but has taken on a conspiratorial role in service of the Prince of Darkness.

On the other hand, this priest, who is nameless in the film and played by an actor named Ewan Hooper, recants his recantation! At the end of the movie this priest "Turns the Beat Around" (Vicki Sue Robinson), and assists the somnambulant teenage couple to rebel against their Dark Lord. At the end of *Dracula Has Risen from the Grave* this priest recites The Lord's Prayer as the vampire count is staked by means of a crucifix and destroyed 'forever.' It is a powerful religious moment.

The second specifically Christian element in *Dracula Has Risen from the Grave* refers to the young 'hippie' hero's loss of, then recovery of, his Christian faith. Paul, played by Barry Andrews and looking like a member of The Who, is a devil-may-care lad who is sincerely in love with Maria, played by Veronica Carlson. But when it falls to Paul, and Paul alone, to hammer a stake through the heart of Count Dracula, he loses his nerve. He can't do it—or rather, he can't do it successfully. Why? Well, we learn that Paul is no longer a believer. He has become an agnostic, and is therefore unable to prevail against the vampire.

At the end of the film, when Dracula has been impaled upon the golden altar cross and Ewan Hooper is reciting the *Pater Noster* over the death of Death, Paul, restored to Maria, is moved. The last image of the movie shows Paul crossing himself. Wonderful religious music, by James Bernard, accompanies Paul's return to… well, I hope you don't mind me putting it this way: Paul's return to the Lord.

The third Christian element in *Dracula Has Risen from the Grave* is the unyielding and unbending character of the Monsignor, Maria's uncle, who defines the word 'steadfast.' At first you think, well, this Catholic priest is sure taking a hard line in relation to Maria's carefree boyfriend, Paul. But then you begin to see that the Monsignor, played by Rupert Davies, has his eyes open. He understands that Maria and Paul do not know what they are doing, and are quite vulnerable to whatever comes along. And it is Count Dracula who has come along.

When Maria is kidnapped by Dracula, Paul becomes worthless, and the Three-Stooges priest is a positive accomplice on the other side. It falls to Maria's priest-uncle to save the day. It is he who "saddles his ass" (Gen 22:3), shoulders the giant altar cross, and makes the long journey up the mountain to the castle. That man is someone whom you would want to have on your side.

In the end, the Monsignor of *Dracula Has Risen from the Grave* is an ideal priest.

The movie as a whole is an awesome affirmation of Christianity and its prime symbol. I call it a hinge point because it presents the possibility, in the character of Paul, of a person's losing their faith.

Moreover, it presents a Christian priest who, because he is spiritually asleep, ends up arming and re-arming the devilish foe. Thank God the priest recovers his nerve at the end and is able to turn back into what he is.

TASTE THE BLOOD OF DRACULA (1970)

In the same general sensibility as *Dracula Has Risen from the Grave*, *Taste the Blood of Dracula* plays off the younger generation's rebellion against the hypocritical Christianity of their parents, only to deploy Christianity, at the end, against the true enemy—which is not their parents, repellent as their parents, especially their fathers are, but, of course, Count Dracula.

What happens here is that we see Victorian or Edwardian fathers leading a double life, consisting of church on Sunday mornings and prostitution Sunday evenings. These are rather slimy characters who terrorize their wives and hold their children as hostages to their own guilt. It is a classic depiction of what is now called the 'religious right.'

However, there is also a devilish aristocrat at work, Lord Courtley by name, who succeeds in bringing Dracula back to life in a deconsecrated church. Dracula then attaches himself to the beset and addled young people, who live in big houses.

The only way out turns out to be the timely deployment of a gleaming Cross, with a little help from the sun and from a stained glass window through which the sun bursts through with triumphant purging light. James Bernard wrote some of his most poignant and also redemptive music for this movie. The teenagers are saved—hard to call them teenagers in their laced boots and layered corsets, but that's what they are—the fathers all pay for their sins, and the Prince of Darkness, "we tremble not for him." He is pulverized in the direct light of the Lamb.

SECOND HINGE POINT:

TWINS OF EVIL (1971)

Twins of Evil I would call the second hinge point in the slightly evolving attitude of the Hammer films in relation to Christianity. Here it is not the formalist lay hypocrites who are shown up by true religion, but the actual and sincere protagonists of religion. *Twins of Evil* is a frontal assault on Christian self-righteousness. It depicts the Puritans, in particular, as active agents of evil and mayhem. And yet...

Gustav Weil, played by Peter Cushing, is the worst sort of caricature of a Puritan. He leads a group of men called The Brotherhood in midnight rides around the countryside, hunting for young women who in The Brotherhood's opinion are possessed by the devil. In that country, being possessed by the devil means you have consorted with the depraved Count Karnstein. One poor farmer's daughter after another is dragged from her house and burned at the stake on the spot. The situation is horrible.

And yet...Gustav Weil is right about Count Karnstein. Weil understands instinctively that Count Karnstein is satanic mechanic for the whole region, and the true source of every evil.

Weil has two nieces who are identical twins living with him and his wife. These girls are young and nubile and therefore perfect objects for the attentions of Count Karnstein. One of the twins is (willingly, I am afraid) corrupted by the Count, and becomes a canker sore in the bosom of Gustav Weil's own house.

Weil, who is wrong about everything but also right about the main thing, leads The Brotherhood in an attack on Castle Karnstein. The problem is, one of his nieces is the vampire consort of the Count, but the other niece is pure and good. Which is which?

Twins of Evil is the second hinge point in this Christian trajectory within Hammer horror, because the appalling self-righteous villain, Gustav Weil, happens to be right about the nature of the evil he is fighting. Thus at the climax, Weil 'redeems himself' by giving his own life for his good niece, even crossing himself as he expires—having basically vanquished Count Karnstein. Gustav Weil was right in his core instincts about the evil influence, but he went about fighting it in the wrong way.

Never once does *Twins of Evil* 'relax' in its basic idea that Count Karnstein is wicked and must be destroyed. A more contemporary treatment might, while justly skewering the religious fanatic Weil, create some sympathy for Count Karnstein. He is, for example, handsome and apparently irresistible to women. But there is no "Sympathy for the Devil" in *Twins of Evil.* Weil and The Brotherhood are bad, but Count Karnstein is worse. So the movie is a hinge point, but not a reversal. By no means a reversal.

Whew!

DRACULA A.D. 1972 (1972)

This is a notorious movie because of its overly stylized attempt to sound hip. The supposedly cool 'brat pack' of twenty-somethings and younger who are the stars are continually using supposed hippie slang that makes you want to hide under your bed.

Curiously, *Dracula A.D. 1972* has aged well. Today, the movie is delightful, or at least something like that. It is gorgeously filmed and has some 'set pieces,' like the Black Mass in a deconsecrated church and the beginning chase out on Hampstead Heath, and the final confrontation of Dracula and Van Helsing, that are full of exactly the right kind of atmosphere, and conviction.

And when you realize who it is that is singing with the band during the 'high society' party near the beginning, it is impossible not to vote for *Dracula A.D. 1972.*

But again, all the hippies and occult dabblers in the world can't take away from the anchor world view of the movie, that Count Dracula is implacably evil and predatory, and that the only way to get rid of him is the old-fashioned way: the Cross and a solid stake through the heart, preferably accomplished in the shadow of a church.

Religious skepticism in this world is window-dressing and theater. It is not reality. Even the awful Johnny Alucard, Dracula's henchman, realizes this. He seduces would-be free-thinkers, taking full advantage of them.

Then he murders them.

P.S. I saw this movie, the first movie I ever actually saw in a movie theater in England, in 1973, during a visit to the most Gothic of all Church of England seminaries, the College of the Resurrection at Mirfield, Yorkshire. We were guests at High Mass, after which my friend took me to the movies. I'm surprised I am still alive to tell the story.

THE SATANIC RITES OF DRACULA (1973)

With the greater freedom and the license to show more nudity, to make the gore ever more up-close, and to bring into the script the person of Satan, Hammer studios seemed to be veering 'left' in their approach to the material.

But they hadn't, and they didn't.

The Satanic Rites of Dracula, with its supposedly accurate satanic sacrifice at the start, and its intense spirit of rebellion, especially in relation to boys and sex, that the heroine, played by Joanna Lumley, evinces to her own great cost, appears to be another container of contemporary permissiveness and revolt. But it's not. Far from it!

In fact, *The Satanic Rites* is a complete re-affirmation of an old and mighty Story. Count Dracula takes advantage of academics, cabinet ministers, and an army of para-military young men—not to mention the harem of female vampires who reside in the basement of his house, in their coffins.

There is only one way to kill him: let Professor Van Helsing loose to use his ancient Christian magic. Which he does: Van Helsing lures the Prince of Darkness (grim, we tremble not for him) to an open grave outside a(nother) deconsecrated church, entrapping him within a hawthorn bush, the symbol of Christ's Crown of Thorns. Van Helsing then rams a stake through Dracula's heart and he crumbles to dust.

Again, changes in the environment of the story are apparent. But there is no change in the substance of it.

THIRD HINGE POINT:

LEGEND OF THE 7 GOLDEN VAMPIRES/THE 7 BROTHERS MEET DRACULA (1974)

Many of us love this movie.

I took a trip to Hong Kong once in partial hopes of visiting the pagoda where the 7 Golden Vampires live. (It was part of movie set, in fact, and turned out to have been torn down long ago.) The movie is that good. (Uh…)

The premise of *Legend of the 7 Golden Vampires* is that a Chinese Buddhist priest went over to the dark side during a visit to Transylvania towards the end of the nineteenth century. He became actually possessed by the spirit of Count Dracula.

The priest then returned home, bringing Count Dracula with him, carrying Count Dracula inside him; and founded a vampire cult of seven 'Golden Vampires.' They all wear golden masks, and have golden bats attached to chains around their necks. Dracula, who looked like a Chinese priest on the outside but was the Hungarian vampire on the inside, succeeded in terrorizing a nearby village, especially the young girls of the village. He and his seven Golden Vampires used the young girls of the village for their supply of blood.

Fortunately, Dr. Van Helsing came to lecture at a Chinese university, and his lecture was heard by a young man who was from that village. The young man persuaded Van Helsing, together with Van Helsing's son and a pretty German woman, to accompany him to his village and try to free the village from the 7 Golden Vampires. They traveled in the company of six young Kung Fu experts—making a total on their side of '7 Brothers'—hence the American name for the movie, *The 7 Brothers Meet Dracula*. There is also one sister, who is herself skilled in karate.

Together, Van Helsing, his son, the 7 Brothers, and Miss Buren took on the 7 Golden Vampires and their high priest, which meant, ultimately, that they took on Count Dracula. But in China.

Daffy as it sounds, it is a wondrous movie in many ways, and is filled with several 'set pieces' that you can watch again and again, especially the initial attack on the village by the Golden Vampires and the courageous resistance of one man, the father of one of the unfortunate girls who has become part of the vampires' blood supply, who, with the help of a statue of The Buddha, manages to destroy one of the Golden Vampires.

As I write this, it sounds absurd. And it is absurd. But it's also wondrous.

The point for Mockingbird, the point for followers of a persistent Christian 'trope' in the Hammer output during its entire history, is that *Legend of the 7 Golden Vampires* manages to become a hinge point to a religious future for the vampire movie that is both universal and buoying. Let me explain:

During the journey to their remote village, Professor Van Helsing sits them all down, the 7 Brothers (and their one sister), and teaches them how they can destroy the vampires they will soon face. He says this: "In Europe, vampires are repelled by holy symbols like the Cross. Here," he says with emphasis, "it will be the symbol of the Lord Buddha."

I think this is one of the most benign and memorable lines in any vampire movie. What Van Helsing is saying is that the power of evil must be destroyed by the power of good, and that it can only be destroyed by the power of the good.

But the *symbol* for the wholly good is conditioned culturally. It is the Cross in the West, a statue of The Buddha in the East.

While an orthodox Christian, and I am one, would like to say that the Cross and only the Cross works against a vampire, Hammer Studios has sustained the central insight while broadening it out a little for the secular world. The director Roman Polanski did not believe this, and his entertaining parody of a Hammer film, entitled *The Fearless Vampire Killers* (1967), specifically rebuts it. That movie—and its ethos has triumphed in the despairing culture of the present day—contends that the power of evil is greater than the power of good; and that a thousand crosses, and garlands of garlic, are insufficient to keep the Count Krolocks of the world from taking over.

Yet as late as 1976, Hammer was contending for an older view. Instead of regretting Van Helsing's broadening out of the arsenal a little in *The Legend of the 7 Golden Vampires*, Christians should give that movie credit. After all, it was made in Hong Kong, funded by the Shaw Brothers, and was intended to provide a new vehicle, within Western distribution, for Kung Fu movies. Why shouldn't they have desired a little respect?

So 'we,' in the person of Professor Van Helsing, gave it to them. Yet the "Song Remains the Same" (Led Zeppelin): Only religion and the power of God can suffice against the flood of evils and Evil that forever invades the world.

CONCLUSION

There are always going to be a few hardcore fans who will now at this exact moment stand to attention and bring up *Scars of Dracula* (1970) and *Vampire Circus* (1972). And they will be right!

They will say that the opening 'church' sequence of *Scars* is by direct implication hostile to the Church, for all the unfortunates who take refuge in the parish church are attacked without mercy by vampire bats under the command of Count Dracula, and neither their faith nor their sanctuary is able to save a single one of them.

That hopeless passage at the beginning of *Scars of Dracula* is indelible. As a Christian fan, I offer no defense of it and no apology for it. It is a nihilistic and despairing moment in the *oeuvre* and I have no idea how it got made. I think it is almost in the same category as the birth of the devilish baby to the tied-and-bound (and willing) mother in *To the Devil a Daughter*.

Vampire Circus is another downbeat Hammer. It is one of my favorites, because of the music and the lurid 'eye candy' atmosphere of the whole. Yet almost everyone gets killed by Count Mitterhaus and his returned lover and minions. It is true the Cross still 'works,' but not well enough, or at least not often enough. *Vampire Circus* is good to look at, but there is a different sensibility in the creative team that made it.

And don't get me started on *Demons of the Mind* (1971). (Note that even *there*, at the fiery conclusion of *Demons of the Mind*, the mendicant fanatical priest was right! Like Gustav Weil.)

What I would like to say in conclusion is this: With a few exceptions, the conflict-structure of the world according to Hammer is a Christian one. Again and again, the power of goodness is locked in a struggle with the powers of evil. The powers of goodness always win.

Moreover, the form and physical symbol of the power of goodness is the Christian Cross. There is no dissonance in most Hammer films between that Cross and the arresting images of pulchritude that these movies glory in. There is also no sugarcoating of 'man's inhumanity to man.' In the world of Hammer, evil is not banal!

But nor is the Good just a good idea or a nice college try. Good is in direct encounter with the Crucifix of Jesus.

From *The Devil Rides Out*, which is the apogee of these movies, to *Twins of Evil*, which appears to be the end of the line but is not, the Illustrated Sacrifice of Christianity is the One Thing Needful when you have no other. Even in the farrago that is *Legend of the 7 Golden Vampires*, God and His messengers get the Last Word. They can't lose.

Mockingbirds everywhere should be on their knees tonight, giving thanks for the miracle, which we did not deserve, of Hammer Films.

Flavors of Failure in

THE BLOOD AND ICE CREAM TRILOGY

by

Jeremiah Lawson

Simon Pegg has summed up his career, saying, "You should always play losers because people love losers. The minute you threaten any kind of success, you're on the edge of being derided."

The losers in Edgar Wright and Simon Pegg's *Shaun of the Dead* (2004), *Hot Fuzz* (2007) and *The World's End* (2013) treat us to the various ways males in their twenties, thirties, and forties, respectively, can fail to grow up. The first movie features the 'kidult,' the physically adult male who never transitions into an emotionally and socially adult life. The second features self-righteous losers who are not completely outside a shot at redemption. And the third features failures who always find a way to disappoint. All together, this trilogy offers distinct flavors that are not merely the Three Flavors Cornetto.

SHAUN OF THE DEAD

So let's start with Shaun in 2004's *Shaun of the Dead.* Shaun is a twenty-nine-year old man who has never truly begun to embrace the ambitions and goals of adult life. His girlfriend Liz feels stuck in a boring, ritualized relationship that doesn't seem to go anywhere. Her proposed solution is to vary the rhythm of life, while her friends simply think Shaun is unworthy of her. Shaun's friends also tell him that his friendship with Ed (Nick Frost) is a tether tying him down and preventing him from ever properly growing up. Ed's lazy lifestyle of video-game-playing only makes Shaun look fully adult by comparison.

In every other respect Shaun's life is marked by a failure to achieve anything. He works at a dead-end job, puts up with his girlfriend's quotidian complaints about their inert relationship, and is largely estranged from his mother, who remarried in the wake of his father's death. As the first act shows in detail, Shaun's existence is a living death. It takes a full-scale zombie invasion for Shaun to realize how dead his life has been and how much he has to lose.

Shaun, foolish and incompetent though he is, springs into action as best he can, enlisting the help of his friends to survive the zombie outbreak. His master plan, even facing a zombie apocalypse, is to revert to his old habits and comforts, taking refuge in his favorite drinking spot, the Winchester Pub.

The only difference is, now, Shaun has become a man who knows for what, and whom, he is willing to fight. In failure, he realizes that he loves his new stepfather far more than he had cared to admit. He discovers the truth of his friends' rebukes about Ed. And despite Shaun's continued shortcomings as a man, Liz has seen that when push comes to shove, he is desperate to be with her. As billed, the film is indeed a romantic comedy. . . with zombies. Shaun and

Liz resign themselves to death before the day is miraculously saved (this is a comedy after all) by Ed, sacrificing himself. Shaun just barely survives his twenties, but at last he grows up.

But, of course, it's possible to learn about adult responsibility *too* well.

HOT FUZZ

In *Hot Fuzz*, Simon Pegg plays Nicholas Angel, a workaholic so responsible and righteous that he's already lost his girlfriend. He may be a supercop but he's almost completely out of touch with reality. Flatly declaring that Sergeant Angel makes them all look bad, his precinct gleefully dispatches Angel to a town in the middle of nowhere whose only distinction is winning a pretty village contest year after year. If failing to be a man in one's twenties means not grasping adult responsibilities, the man in his thirties can fail by so disappearing into those adult responsibilities that he loses his identity.

As we know from countless horror and action movies, evil tends to lurk in the quaintest, quietest, and prettiest villages. Before long, Angel discovers that murders are occurring but that the incompetent, lazy police force is completely uninterested, taking no notice of the phenomenal "accident" rate in their town. The only cop willing to give any credence to Angel's conspiracy theory is Nick Frost's Danny Butterman, the laziest and least engaged officer on the force. But what Danny lacks in initiative (or a realistic understanding of police work), he makes up for in his intimate knowledge of everyone in the village. While in the first film Nick Frost's character held Simon Pegg's back, in *Hot Fuzz* the two literally can't survive without each other.

When Angel discovers the true nature of the murders in the

village, he confronts the fathers and mothers who are behind it all. They justify murdering everyone who falls short of perfection by their need to present the image of a perfect little community. The villagers' behavior forces Angel to confront the dark manifestation of his own perfectionism and selfishness, and he sees that his commitment to proper appearance and procedure has come at the expense of empathy and humanity.

THE WORLD'S END

Nearly every cinematic trilogy ends with at least some disappointment. Perhaps the anticipation of this end-of-trilogy letdown inspired Wright and Pegg to make disappointment the overarching theme: that the inevitability and pervasiveness of failure is the hallmark of humanity. In *The World's End*, Simon Pegg plays Gary King, a man who has gone beyond merely failing to integrate into 'normal' adult life: He's an alcoholic who willfully tumbles off the wagon in a last desperate effort to relive the glory days of his drunken teen years.

An alcoholic entering his forties, Gary reminisces about an epic pub-crawl he attempted with high school friends twenty years earlier. All of his mates have since gone on to be bankers, real estate agents, and generally successful men. But in Gary's mind, he's still king—the undisputed leader of the pack. He determines to go back with his four friends to complete The Golden Mile, the dozen-pub juggernaut of drink he failed to finish decades earlier. Though all his friends, especially the estranged Andy (Nick Frost, again), think the idea is terrible, they reluctantly consent out of pity and sentiment.

Having failed to get more than halfway through the crawl in their raging and healthier twenties, all the men besides Gary seriously doubt it's possible to finish the same foolhardy project decades later. As they humor Gary and drink, he reminds them that although they have their wives and jobs, he still has his freedom. Rather than concede that he is enslaved to alcohol, Gary has convinced himself he is freer than his friends.

When the men enter the pub-crawl, they discover they literally and figuratively can't go home again—the pubs have been taken over by robots. A few pubs in, Gary and friends run into a homicidal robot that attempts to kill them. A network of replicant robots has replaced nearly all the citizens of Newton Haven. The robots look and talk and act more or less the same as their flesh and blood forebears and are even improved—yet they all categorically deny that they are robots, mirroring Gary's own refusal to look at himself as he truly is.

As the night moves on, Gary discovers too late that a couple of the men he thought were his friends on the crawl have turned out to be robot replicants. In a village full of blank robot replicas of those who once lived, how can you tell who is truly human?

The answer is in the wounds and scars and character flaws that simply don't improve with age. As Gary and his friend Andy get closer to the truth about the robot army and its master, they confront The Network behind the robot assimilation of Earth. The Network offers all of humanity a chance to evolve into a new glorified state of consciousness: eternal robotic existence free of the shackles of flesh and blood. Gary and Andy are invited to join this Network, but they refuse. Gary, the remorseless drunk, turns into the great preacher of human potential. He rants that changing into an immortal robot would take away his ability to change and evolve. He goes further, arguing that the irreversibly stupid decisions and ineradicable weaknesses we never completely overcome are what make us truly human. *This* is what real humanity is, not the robotic fleshless perfection promised by The Network. Thus humanity as we know it is saved by a drunken rant.

The capstone of the Cornetto trilogy's exploration of male failure reveals that it's not just men who fail, but the whole human race. Our fallibility is what makes us who we are. We inevitably disappoint each other and ourselves. Wright and Pegg shrewdly anticipated that the third film in their trilogy might be a letdown, and make disappointment their theme. Of course by now we've been able to see that disappointment and failure have been their themes all along. Gary inadvertently saves the world and stays away from alcohol by the end of the film, a shift achieved primarily through confession. Humans may be failures, but each flavor of failure is unique, and the things we fail at show us who we really are.

'The Shape' of Revelation and the Formulation of Evil in

HALLOWEEN

by

Blake Collier

> It was all to make a new legend. There's something really creepy about the fact that evil never dies. It can't be killed. If, as in the movie, he really is just a force of evil, he's like nature. Well, in the end, he's back up again. — John Carpenter on Michael Myers

> He walked out in the gray light and stood and he saw for a brief moment the absolute truth of the world. The cold relentless circling of the intestate earth. Darkness implacable. The blind dogs of the sun in their running. The crushing black vacuum of the universe. And somewhere two hunted animals trembling like groundfoxes in their cover. Borrowed time and borrowed world and borrowed eyes with which to sorrow it. — Cormac McCarthy, *The Road*

October 31, 1978 was "The Night *He* Came Home." The "he" in the tagline of the 1978 horror classic, *Halloween*, spoke of the first appearance of Michael Myers in horror cinema mythology. Myers reaches an intimidating stature both in the film and in the horror canon. He stands across the street, leering in our direction, in his mechanic's jumpsuit and emotionless white mask—which was developed from a poorly likened Star Trek mask of William Shatner. *Halloween* effectively jumpstarted a new subgenre of horror: the slasher flick. But, much like Myers' physical presence in the film, subsequent slashers stood in the shadow of Carpenter's creation, never quite able to maintain the menace and dread.

Halloween is a testament to the power of a simple narrative, effectively paced without gratuitous exposition. The death knell of horror is always exposition. Horror cinema is most effective when it refuses to provide easy explanations to the visuals and narrative it projects onto the screen. John Carpenter is arguably one of the greatest horror directors simply because he puts the audience in the midst of a horrific event, lets us witness the terror, and refuses to explain away the evil inherent in the event. Instead, he lets it burrow under our skin, throbbing from beneath with more questions than answers. John Kenneth Muir, in his essay "The Tao of Michael Myers? Or the Hidden 'Shapes' of John Carpenter's *Halloween* (1978)," delivers the central question that sets *Halloween* apart from the slashers that followed:

> Specifically, as percipients of *Halloween*, we gaze intently at that blank, white, featureless mask of "The Shape," Michael Myers, and then immediately recognize, at least subconsciously, that *we are missing some crucial aspect of understanding* [emphasis mine].

BEHIND THE MASK, BEHIND THE VEIL

What is that crucial aspect of understanding hidden within *Halloween*'s cinematic landscape? Michael Myers is a being who is both *like* us (human) but *other* than us (not exactly what we recognize as 'human'). Unlike in other slashers, Michael Myers' presence—and continual return in the sequels—doesn't feel incidental or like a consequence of the bottom dollar of the box office. The deluge of slashers in *Halloween*'s wake featured villains that were human and sought to kill people out of a recognizable human distortion of justice: *vengeance*. Something cruel and unjust had been done to them and, in their view, they were *righting the wrongs*. Throughout the first film, and its sequels, Myers never has a *human* motivation for killing the teenagers of Haddonfield and beyond. This is what makes Myers the first and most intriguing slasher villain. We can comprehend his 'shape' and some of his actions, but he is void of traits that characterize even the worst of us.

Eugene Thacker, author of *In the Dust of This Planet: Horror of Philosophy, Vol. 1*, explores the origins of human fear from various sources, but he repeatedly comes back to H. P. Lovecraft, and other authors like him. Lovecraft, one of the early writers of horror fiction, might be the most helpful voice in further drawing out the idea of the "missing understanding" identified by Muir. Thacker states:

> Herein lies the basis of what Lovecraft called "cosmic horror"—the paradoxical realization of the world's hiddenness as an absolute hiddenness. It is a sentiment frequently found in Lovecraft's many letters...When we cross the line to the boundless and hideous unknown—the shadow-haunted *Outside*—we must remember to leave our humanity and terrestrialism at the threshold.

Lovecraft seems to have hit upon humanity's limitations and how revelation actually works. Revelation, both in the realm of Lovecraft and the Bible, is not something that can be sought out wholly by the human mind. No, revelation is an invasion into the realm of the human will, mind, and reality. It shows itself to us, and we are forced to contend with news that we are ill-equipped to process comprehensively on our own.

We can use our intellect, instruments, and various forms of

research to find the order that undergirds our world, but we always find that with each answer, there are more questions. It seems that the micro- and macrocosms of our world are endless. Lovecraft would say that there is always something *other* about the world that humans can never quite master or quantify *until it is revealed to us*. It is that revelation from beyond the void that, in Lovecraft's stories, is something that does not fully fit within our constructs of reality. We find this to be the case in scripture as well. Revelation always illuminates and blinds humanity.

What Carpenter does in *Halloween*—whether intentional or not—is to show the otherness of that revelation—the being of Michael Myers. An otherness that is foreign to our constructions of a human being. It looks familiar, but there's that crucial aspect to our understanding that is missing. Myers' actions are not uncommon to us: We live in a world of hatred, violence, and death. But the part that escapes us is *the why*. Myers is given no psychological motivation. From the first scene in the film, when he murders his sister, throughout the rest of the film, we are given nothing of why Myers is the way he is. We are just told that he *is*. Dr. Loomis (played by the classic Donald Pleasance) describes Myers' state:

> I met him, fifteen years ago. I was told there was nothing left. No reason, no conscience, no understanding; even the most rudimentary sense of life or death, good or evil, right or wrong. I met this six-year-old child, with this blank, pale, emotionless face and, the blackest eyes...the devil's eyes. I spent eight years trying to reach him, and then another seven trying to keep him locked up because I realized what was living behind that boy's eyes was purely and simply...evil.

Human conceptions of evil ultimately find an origin in a why, a motivation, a desire. No such safety is given to the audience in *Halloween*. Michael Myers is other...outside of any human likeness we can place upon him. Behind the mask is something *other* that has revealed itself to us.

It seems Michael Myers is much more than a serial killer; he is anathema. His being only reveals judgment to the audience. In all of the 'kill scenes,' Myers' judgment is based on a loss of sexual purity. Myers' sister, in the beginning—it is implied—consummates her relationship with her boyfriend, and Michael kills her. He picks off each of Laurie Strode's friends as they consummate or are setting out to consummate their relationships. This is made very clear in one of the most famous scenes of the film, when Lynda and her boyfriend are separately dispatched immediately following sexual intercourse. The deaths are Myers' judgment on their 'impure' character.

Not even Laurie Strode can escape the pursuit of Myers' judgment, even though she is shown to be the quintessential 'good girl,' pure and virginal. But when she talks to Annie—who is also killed by Myers—about one of the boys at her school, there is a sense that her purity is at risk by her mere interest. But what does Myers' judgment mean? What does his motiveless dispatch of these sexually impure teenagers tell us about the substance that his presence represents within the scope of the film? Is there something in his being and action that finds an analogy in our world?

HADDONFIELD: LIVING IN THE LAND OF DEAD TEENAGERS

Michael Myers personifies the curse—the judgment—that the Old Testament Law brings down on those unable to live up to its demands. *Halloween* brings the audience into an unknown world where Law rules and grace, if not totally non-existent, is ineffective. He is not *the Law*, but the *effect of the Law*. In the world of the slasher, everyone has transgressed, and all must pay. Adam Rockoff, in his seminal text on the history of slasher flicks, *Going to Pieces: The Rise and Fall of the Slasher Film, 1978-1986*, describes Michael Myers as void of any noticeable trace of humanity. He has absolutely no emotions, no care, and no *mercy*. He is a precision machine, not human, and his 'justice' is never quenched—simply because people are repetitive creatures, especially concerning their inability to live according to the good and right order that the Law pronounces.

Within this framework, Michael can be a rather dark and sinister expression of the effect of the Law. He does not understand forgiveness; instead he wants propitiation, aka *dead teenagers*. And no one and nothing is able to live up to the code of righteousness.

We who live in a land of Law *and* grace recognize how heavy the illustration of the slasher film really is. We know that, under the rule of an unforgiving and condemning Law, we would all be *dead teenagers* dispatched by Myers' swift knife. Every transgression, minor or major, would warrant death according to the Law. In the New Testament, Paul's letter to the Galatians alludes to the reality created for humanity by the Law as presented in Deuteronomy 27:26 when it states:

> All who rely on observing the law are under a curse, for it is written: "Cursed is everyone who does not continue to do everything written in the Book of the Law."[37]

The slasher villain is simply a manifestation of the curse of the Law in popular horror cinema.

Within a Christian framework, the ultimate revelation of God was in the being of Christ, the God-man. He was wholly human—something known and relatable to us—and wholly *other*, or, in

37. Gal 3:10

Christian parlance, *holy*—something not fully knowable by us. It is in this perfect revelation of God that we see both the Law (embodied and fulfilled) and grace—Christ becoming the scapegoat, analogically dying from the swift blade of Myers' anathema. Christ fulfilled the Law, and yet died the death of one who couldn't fulfill the Law, so that all who couldn't would be free from the condemnation of the Law's curse, free from death at the hands of Myers.

Where Christ is the perfect revelation, Myers is an imperfect revelation, almost an inversion of revelation. The Law is a revelation of God's goodness and order for his created world and creatures. But even the Law points beyond itself to the one that would fulfill it, the final revelation of God in Christ. Myers is a revelation detached, within the scope and world of the film, from the Law and from the one who would embody and fulfill that Law. Myers is curse—anathema—only. He is the swift blade of judgment without reference to the code of righteousness he is upholding and without any foreshadowing of escape from his judgment. He is evil because he is *other* only, separated from goodness and mercy.

John Carpenter's creation fits nicely within the realm of Lovecraft's absolute and indifferent hiddenness of the world. There is no escape and there is no mercy from its relentless pursuit.

The slasher subgenre *should* provoke a response from viewers because they are forced into a world that is, to a large extent, unknown to them. This should create a dissonance within the viewer who lives within the excesses of God's grace in the world we all experience (and take for granted). Slasher films should be a stark reminder to us all of the realities of a world left to the unforgiving nature of the Law. And much like the Law, the slasher should point out that there is nothing we can do, in and of ourselves, that will save us from the blade. Grace could only enter Haddonfield, IL if Michael Myers fell on his own butcher knife in place of his victims. Fat chance.

EPILOGUE: MICHAEL MYERS AND LAURIE STRODE: WHEN TWO BECOME ONE

2015's *It Follows* takes the Michael Myers narrative and bends it into itself. David Robert Mitchell removes the figure of Michael Myers from his existential version of *Halloween* and creates a tense marriage of Michael Myers and Laurie Strode in the character of Jay (Maika Monroe). The curse is transferred to Jay through a supernatural sexual transmission—think of it as the metaphorical plunging of Myers knife into Laurie Strode if Laurie hadn't survived in *Halloween*. Jay not only suffers the consequence of the curse but also *becomes* the curse. She is both *dead teenager* and *executioner*.

There are many uncanny similarities between *Halloween* and *It Follows*, but, within the scope of my above argument, *It Follows* ultimately creates a fuller picture of human reality. We no longer have to view Michael Myers as the metaphorical harbinger of the curse of the Law, but instead we view ourselves as both the judge and the judged—in the world of the slasher and in real life.

Grace is no more present in the world of *It Follows* than in *Halloween*; however, *It Follows* takes the next narrative step towards finding a representation of the curse in our reality. We are all passive victims of the Law and active executioners of the laws we create for others and ourselves. Curse begets curse. Only Jesus could vanquish the vicious cycle that we began back in the garden. He is the only one who, while victim of the curse, imparts grace and forgiveness to us.

POST-APOCALYPTO

compiled by

David Zahl

It used to be preachers who told us we were living in the end times. Today it is Hollywood. You don't have to be a pop culture junkie to have noticed the ballooning number of end-of-the-world fantasies on offer, not just at the multiplex but on our bookshelves and televisions. The Eschaton is everywhere. What accounts for the uptick? The most common theory is that these stories tap into mounting collective anxieties over political tumult and environmental decline, compounded by post-Christian spiritual vacuity.

Of course, the end of the world has always fueled human imagination. It has proven particularly alluring to those seeking to underline and extrapolate on social ills. There's no better backdrop for a cautionary tale about moral decay, after all, than a nuclear wasteland.

In recent years the tone of the genre has shifted to a more cynical footing. Projects are less interested in exploring the potential cause(s) of collapse than in looking at what it might take for the individual to survive in an environment where the triumph of cruelty over compassion is a foregone conclusion. In other words, as our narrative imagination has flourished, our moral imagination has all but atrophied. Some would go so far as to chalk the current glut of apocalyptic material up to a deep-seated despair at the heart of secularism. Perhaps when you take away the essential prophetic component of apocalyptic fiction, all you have left is the fetishization of death in which hope can take only the most asinine of forms. Or become an endless parody of itself.

To theorize further, it could be that such films grant the viewer permission to drop the inflated anthropology that goes along with most forms of nonbelief—while also remaining entertaining enough to divert us from our own limitations and pain. It never quite works, though. And thus the further we get away from honest belief in anything larger (and better) than ourselves, the more nagging that feeling of emptiness grows, and the louder we have to turn the volume on our fantasies. No sooner have the credits rolled on one, than we're queuing up the next.

Writing for *The New York Times*, Steve Almond couldn't help but point out how the proliferation of such films almost confirms their content. Or at least their implicit understanding of human fallibility:

> Imagine, if you will, that a race of superior beings discovers Earth 10,000 years from now, or even 10 centuries, a world no longer inhabited by humans. In surveying the remains of our civilization, what would they make of a species so intellectually advanced as to understand the precise threats posed to its survival and yet so immature as to ignore these threats? And what of the vast troves they would find containing elaborate and childish simulations of our destruction?[38]

38. Almond, Steve. "The Apocalypse Market is Booming." *New York Times*. 2013.

If these visitors were able to locate a New Testament amongst the rubble, they might find that Romans 7 sheds some light.

Despite the pessimistic bent, however, most of these movies start from a religiously resonant point, at least in so far as they reveal a collective sense of impending judgment, and appeal to a universally fervent desire for mercy and deliverance. The notion that the human race will destroy itself—that the human race *is* destroying itself—on its own or via divine retribution may sound cynical, but it is not foreign to Christian thinking. Given the biblical estimation of humanity, self-annihilation might almost be considered an inevitability—barring the Second Coming of course. Nothing illustrates that we are our own worst enemies better than, well, nuclear Armageddon.

On the other hand, a careful viewer will notice that these films are rarely one hundred percent nihilistic; there is almost always a redemptive story being told. Which should not surprise us, at least not if we have Calvary in mind. In its distinctive light, we see that the death of all things does not necessarily spell the end of all things. It might even spell the beginning.

This is not to suggest that their distinctive subject matter necessarily vindicates these films on an aesthetic level. Post-apocalyptic movies are notoriously difficult propositions: elaborate productions that rarely make much money. The genre has often served as an outlet for directors to realize their most ambitious and eccentric visions. As such, the end product tends to be either amazing or awful, and nowhere in between. So the more of these films that get made, the more fiascos there are. Of course, even when they are awful (*The Postman*), they're fascinating. An introductory list is clearly in order.

Note: As irresistible as sci-fi dystopias are (*Brazil*, *Gattaca*, etc.), this list concerns itself primarily with last-man-on-earth fables.

TEN POST-APOCALYPTIC MOVIES

1) THE ROAD WARRIOR (1981)

The gold standard, and very much still the reigning champ. Not a false move in the entire two hours, and Mel Gibson remains utterly iconic. This is where director George Miller took the old-meets-new makeshift aesthetic of L.Q. Jones's *A Boy and His Dog* and perfected it. Apparently, the end of the world produces an abundance of elegantly "distressed" clothing, unorthodox hairstyles, and inventive weaponry.

2) CHILDREN OF MEN (2006)

The ultimate post-apocalyptic Christmas film, in which light shines into a very darkened world in the form of a miracle child. The final scene, where the presence of the long awaited babe stops everyone in their tracks, crowns director Alfonso Cuarón's wondrous achievement. Moreover, the self-sacrifice of Clive Owen's character lends the perilously hopeful ending real gravitas.

3) 12 MONKEYS (1996)

Sure, much of the action takes place before doomsday, but the time travel conceit—executed perfectly—puts this one over the edge. Taking Chris Marker's 1962 short *La Jetée* as his source material, cult director Terry Gilliam wrung the single greatest performance out of Bruce Willis. Of course, even Gilliam's pre-apocalyptic films have that post-vibe/look. No one does steam-punk detritus better.

4) 28 DAYS LATER (2002)

Zombies are a genre unto themselves at this point, but Danny Boyle's shiver-inducing picture of a desolated England paved the way for countless knockoffs (*The Walking Dead*), and works beautifully as a post-apocalyptic yarn. It also includes what has to be the most stunning use of the Anglican hymn "Abide With Me" in modern cinema. Those who have watched the DVD need to ask themselves: Which ending would *you* choose?

5) WALL*E (2008)

Pixar's entry reclaimed the prophetic heft missing from many of its non-animated peers, yet without sacrificing any of the studio's ingenuity or heart. Parables of one-way love (and strength in weakness) are seldom more charming.

6) DELICATESSEN (1991)

Pitch-black humor and continental whimsy abound in this gem from Jean Piere-Jeunet and Marc Caro, known primarily for their work on *Amelié*. Who knew the end of the world would be so... tasty?

7) MAD MAX: FURY ROAD (2015)

The long-awaited fourth installment of the *Max* trilogy, and Miller somehow did not miss a beat. It's almost impossible to believe this hyper-kinetic free-for-all was directed by a seventy-year old—one who hadn't touched an action film in almost thirty years. Don't let the non-stop action fool you; this one brims with engaging subtext and careful details. A master class in world-building *sans* dialogue.

8) THE BOOK OF ELI (2010)

Derided at the time of its release as an assembly line Denzel Washington vehicle (and transparent *Mad Max* pastiche), the Hughes brothers' tale of a mysterious loner negotiating a blighted landscape is better than you remember, not the least because of its biblical themes—a surprisingly underutilized element in the genre. In fact, given how much violence and grime the brothers pile on, it is sad that the religious establishment missed this one almost completely. Gary Oldman hams it up as the creepy villain.

9) SNOWPIERCER (2013)

A Korean director adapts a French graphic novel with an Anglo cast, and the results are stunning. After a climate change experiment kills nearly all life on planet Earth, the few remaining humans hustle for survival on a high-speed train. Nearly all post-apocalyptic films envision a scorched Earth; this one is frozen. At its heart lies the same question posed by lesser exercises in the genre, namely, is humankind even worth saving? If they're capable of the brilliance Tilda Swinton exudes in this film, then perhaps so.

10) ESCAPE FROM NEW YORK (1981)

It may not have dated terribly well, but John Carpenter's nightmare blockbuster about a Manhattan that has been turned into a *Lord of the Flies*-like prison still strikes a chord. Plus, Harry Dean Stanton is Harry Dean Stanton.

BONUS TRACK: THE STAND [TV MINI-SERIES](1994)

Television introduces countless other contenders, but *The Stand* will inevitably be filmed, and regardless of how effective the adaptation is, we can't not include it, given its stature in the genre. Based on arguably the greatest work of post-apocalyptic storytelling (and one of David Foster Wallace's all-time favorite books), Stephen King's masterpiece is also the most profoundly religious.

HONORABLE MENTIONS

Dawn of the Dead (1978), *The Road* (2009), *The Day After* (1983), *Planet of the Apes* (1968), and *The Omega Man* (1971)/*I Am Legend* (2007).

THE DARK KNIGHT (DIES AND) RISES

Sacrifice and Freedom in Gotham

by

William McDavid

"All their days are full of pain, and their work is a vexation; even at night their minds do not rest." — Ecclesiastes 2:23

"Put your sword back in its place, for all who take the sword will perish by the sword." — Matthew 26:52

Christopher Nolan's Dark Knight Trilogy traced Bruce Wayne's journey from street fighter to hero, from hero to villain, and from villain to…recluse. *The Dark Knight Rises* begins with Bruce dead to the world, only holding on to the shadow-life of mourning for his love interest, Rachel. We see different forms of death that *look* like life and different forms of life that look like death: "A Death blow is a Life blow to Some," as Dickinson had it.

LIFE, DEATH, AND THE FAILURE OF FORCE

While Bruce laments Rachel's death from the previous film, Alfred shatters him with the revelation that Rachel had preferred former Gotham DA Harvey Dent anyway. This severs their friendship, but Alfred reminds him that the only thing worse than being hated by and estranged from Bruce would be the thought of Bruce's reckless death. Alfred offers his vision of Bruce learning how to live as a civilian with a wife and kids, his bat-days behind him. And yet a potent mixture of personal anger and the hero's call to deal with Bane persuade Bruce to again live through his persona as the Caped Crusader, now a reckless vigilante with no fear of death or, as Alfred would say, with an eerie attraction towards it. Alfred's use of the 'law' to kill Bruce disabuses him of his obsession with what could have been, but it doesn't make him fully alive. For that, he needs the true death of brutality and failure, the kind that only lived experience and the failure of self-reliance preach effectively.

Enter Bane, a vicious mercenary and agent of the genocidal League of Shadows, which our hero spent most of *Batman Begins* destroying. As Alfred reminds Bruce, Bane is younger than he is, and far stronger, tougher, faster, and trained in Batman's same fighting style. While Heath Ledger's Joker questioned all of the hero's values—parodying, complicating, and negating them—Tom Hardy's Bane is devoted to his own ideals: savagery, mastery by force. If the Joker was the perfect counterpoint to *The Dark Knight*'s Batman, Bane fits perfectly with a vengeful and disaffected Bruce, intent on using sheer force, as he did when he was younger, to fight crime. The end of sin is death, and the end of Wayne's devotion to self-reliance and force is literally being broken, his back in two. He has tried sheer force...and it didn't work. His self-destructive orientation has, as Alfred predicted, killed him—he lies on the floor of a dark pit "where the worm never dies and the fire is not quenched." Sounding familiar? It becomes even more so with the Rising.

FEAR AND HUMILITY

The first movie started with Bruce Wayne overcoming all of his fears—especially of bats and death—and *Rises* comes full circle when a wise man in the Pit tells Bruce he must relearn the fear of death and use it. But first Bruce must have something real to live for. Bane ends up giving Batman exactly what he needs: death to victory by sheer individual force, and then the will to live. Only by entering a living hell of death does Bruce realize that he wants to live for something outside of the Pit and outside of himself. He realizes his calling is to help Gotham. Thus Bruce again transcends himself for the city he loves; his humiliating death to self opens the space in his heart for renewed devotion to Gotham. And so he rises out of the prison, making the final leap without the customary safety rope. Now that his fall has renewed his desire to live, he becomes afraid of death again; this fear, in turn, propels him. Bruce has moved from reliance on his own power to humility, and he's concomitantly shed the fearlessness of nihilism for the bravery of one who feeds off of fear because there is so much to lose. The character development is astounding.

A few critics were concerned that *Rises* didn't have enough Batman; that is, Bruce's character wasn't as prominent. Indeed, the side characters take up a massive amount of screen time, and yet this is appropriate for an aging Batman who has, at last, met someone too powerful for him to deal with. Paradoxically, Bane's very use of force to break Batman teaches Bruce that force doesn't always work. To this end, he relies on Fox, a brilliantly acted Detective

Blake, along with Miranda Tate, Gordon, and Catwoman.

Catwoman is a smart and resourceful thief (played by Anne Hathaway) who only desires to clear her record and get a fresh start. Batman's knowledge of his inadequacy against Bane, as well as Catwoman's inability to escape her involvement with Bane's thugs, force the two into a beautiful relationship. Catwoman grudgingly gives up her independence and Bruce, in turn, must trust someone who betrayed him into his first death at Bane's hands. Batman's honest reckoning with a world in which the good-evil fault line runs through every human heart finds its highest expression in Catwoman. He trusts that there's "more to [her] than that," meaning deceit and self-preservation. The ending will prove his judgment correct and/or his imputation effective: If Batman does have a superpower, it's anthropological insight into a crippled yet redeemable human nature.

NO NEW WINE IN OLD WINESKINS—ALFRED'S VISION AND THE ENDING

Now that Bruce has experienced the same death as Bane in the Pit, he's prepared to face him again. Batman doesn't defeat Bane because he's been working out more; instead his secret weapon is humility. Knowing that he cannot defeat Bane in some idealized contest of physical prowess, he more humbly targets Bane's mask, taking slashes (aka 'cheapshots') at its valves. With Bane finally defeated, however, Batman finds again that he cannot attain victory on his own: He is still the quintessentially human superhero, and this time his wits and judgment have failed him. Miranda reveals her leading role in the League of Shadows and stabs the Caped Crusader. Again, however, Batman's humility (you could even say 'desperation') saves him: His dependence on Catwoman pays off, and she promptly destroys Bane with the Bat Bike's cannons.

Some may complain that Batman never quite 'gets the best of' his enemy, and yet none of us ever do—that would be more appropriate to more superhuman heroes. Nolan's Batman must open himself to the world to find victory and redemption, and it's a victory which happens despite his prior arrogant and self-destructive attempts to take on Bane's entire army by himself. The side characters are so prominent because that's their natural role in any remotely honest story of human heroism. And so Batman's victory finally costs him his life: As he fails to account for all the contingencies (i.e. Miranda's treachery and flooding of the reactor), he must give up his last resource to stop the bomb.

Or so we think. He survives through the banal, down-to-earth magic of autopilot, so again his humanity is affirmed. He doesn't survive through heroics, but rather through a painfully obvious software patch. He can now begin to live Alfred's vision for him as a normal human being; both his victory over Bane and its attendant humility allow him to do this. Evil is not, of course, naively eradicated; instead, Nolan gently reminds us that others are capable of taking up Batman's mantle for Gotham. His death hidden in Batman's, Bruce has now been freed to be...drum roll...a mere human! He died to bodily self-preservation in the form of fear in *Begins*, he died to self-justifying moral high ground in *The Dark Knight*, and now in *Rises* he dies to being any kind of hero at all. And this is why Nolan concludes the trilogy perfectly: Evil isn't vanquished permanently, Gotham's era of heroes isn't over (as we see from Robin's spelunking scene), but age and humility have finally freed Bruce.

As befits Batman, the closing scenes are not the epic rebuilding of Gotham or the punishment of evil. Instead, we see one man's delight in simple human life (after dying to the hero's burden) and a woman's freedom now that her record has been cleared. To paraphrase Gerhard Forde, life isn't about being a godlike hero; it's about learning how to live as a creature. And so Bruce Wayne does. Nolan's final frame, however, resonates even more than Bruce's and Catwoman's 'normal lives.' If there's any symbol for God in the movie, it's Alfred, the one who adopts Bruce, who bears Bruce's hatred to save his life when telling him about Rachel's letter. And it's Alfred we see in the final scene, a benevolent smile on his face, reveling in Bruce's liberty and rest.

The Seven Sacraments of

HARRY POTTER

by

Ethan Richardson

Before anyone calls bluff on a *Harry Potter* essay found in a book about movies, let us first consider a fact about the *Harry Potter* movie franchise. As of July 2015, total movie sales for the eight *Harry Potter* films had almost surpassed total *Harry Potter* book sales, a ridiculous feat when you consider how much money that is (over $7 billion). And when you consider that its box office gross beats out the total tenure of the 50-year, 25-film James Bond empire, it certainly lends some cred to "the boy who lived."

Of course, numbers hardly ever justify the cinematic quality of a film, but they do say something about us: Blockbuster films give us characters and plots with which we resonate or with which we would *like* to resonate (looking at you, 007). It goes without saying that readers very much resonated with *Harry Potter*, so much so that they took their obsessions into the theaters with them.

Why, though? What is it about Harry? Is it his lowly upbringing in the cupboard under the stairs, and his unknown superstar status? Is it the magical world of Quidditch and Thestrals and Wandmakers that we get to discover alongside him? Lord knows we'd all want a wand to choose us!

Above all, what is baffling to me is the fact that, in many churchgoing circles, the books were not read and the movies were not watched. For fear of flying brooms and werewolves, many parents forbade their children the opportunity to go to Hogwarts with Harry. Such scorn is to be expected, I suppose, especially when the themes found within the books (and not the magical feats) are the real threat. Themes like love resurrecting the dead, strength proving itself in weakness, hope shining through immense suffering—these messages will get you killed, after all.

It certainly didn't keep the kids from reading the books or watching the movies, though. It instead offered them the mischievous lot of reading the books by flashlight under the covers and watching the DVDs at sleepovers. From these hidden places, with flying cars and live chocolate frogs, they found the wisdom hidden since the foundation of the earth. For muggles and wizards alike.

If sacraments are 'outward signs' of God's hidden wisdom, these are the seven sacraments of Harry Potter.

I: THE SCAR

It has become the brand: the focal, jagged-tail P that's emblazoned on X-Box games and bathmats and amusement park merchandise. Harry's lightning-bolt scar is his Superman 'S'. It is an ironic mark for a hero, though, because it also represents, for Harry and the rest of wizarding world, an event of immense devastation. But it is just the first hallmark of a recurring theme within the Potter chronicles: of living with one's wounds, that only through the experience and confrontation of suffering can one ever truly live.

The origin is well known by now. When Harry was only a year old, his parents were killed by the evil Lord Voldemort. But when Voldemort tried to kill Harry, the killing curse backfired unexpectedly; Voldemort was undone. It turned out Harry had been protected by a charm Voldemort could not understand—love. All that remained of the failed curse was a lightning bolt scar on his forehead. As Dumbledore explains, "He'll have that scar forever... Scars can come in handy. I have one myself above my left knee that is a perfect map of the London Underground."

Dumbledore foreshadows a thread that will weave from the opening of the first film through to the final scene of the last film: A scar does mark suffering, but it may also act as an avenue through which something useful happens.

Harry grows to find that his scar is much more than a bragging right; it is a physical and mental connection to Voldemort. Harry is, despite himself, in a living communion of pain with his darkest foe, inseparably linked to him. He can sometimes see what Voldemort sees, feel what Voldemort feels. As Harry grows older, and Voldemort's powers grow stronger, this link intensifies. Rowling portrays this wound as Harry's cross to bear, a life inside of him that is not his own, the force of which is nearly impossible to oppose. Harry finds the link to be useful, but this proximity is also intolerable. The pain of this connection is tempered only by the very thing that also saved Harry as a child: *love*.

At the end of the first movie, Dumbledore explains to Harry the power that has been stamped beneath his skin—the love of his mother. Regardless of Harry's own strength, the strength of the love he inherited is what stands in for him. To Dumbledore, Harry's scar is also subject to the power of *imputed love*: "[Your mother] sacrificed herself for you, and that kind of act leaves a mark...This kind of mark cannot be seen. It lives in your very skin...Love, Harry. Love."

Throughout the entirety of the *Potter* series, we find that love is Harry's only antidote to the immense suffering brought on by his union to the darkness. Part One of the *Deathly Hallows* film ends with the burial of the house elf Dobby, who died to save Harry. It also ends with Voldemort's acquisition of the Elder Wand, or the Deathstick. That these moments come together, like the night that produced Harry's scar, demonstrates the ineffable power of death meeting the unlikely power of love. Harry finds that his mark of imputed love stands victorious, even here. Rowling writes:

> [Voldemort's] rage was dreadful and yet Harry's grief for Dobby seemed to diminish it, so that it became a distant storm that reached Harry from across a vast, silent ocean...His scar burned, but he was master of the pain; he felt it, yet was apart of it...Grief, it seemed, drove Voldemort out...though Dumbledore, of course, would have said it was love...

II: THE MIRROR OF ERISED

Harry, in his nighttime wanderings of Hogwarts School, stumbles upon a room completely empty and unused save for an enormous mirror, the reflection of which startles him. In it, Harry glimpses his parents whom he'd never known and always longed to know.

It is no coincidence that 'Erised' backwards spells 'Desire,' the basis of the magical mirror's enchantment. Entranced, he takes Ron the next night to show him his parents. Ron does not see Harry's parents, though. He sees himself, older, good-looking, successful: "Do you think this mirror shows the future?" he asks. Harry responds, "How can it? All my family are dead."

Despite Ron's concern for Harry's fixation with the mirror,

Harry goes back a third time on the third night, only to find that this time he's not in the room alone. Dumbledore is there, and, understanding the boy's fascination, explains its function:

> It shows us nothing more or less than the deepest, most desperate desires of our hearts...However this mirror will give us neither knowledge nor truth. Men have wasted away before it, entranced by what they have seen, or been driven mad, not knowing if what it shows is real or even possible.

The mirror, in fact, does what all mirrors do, albeit on the deepest level: The Mirror of Erised reflects the heart's desire. In the same way that an average mirror reflects to the viewer a self constrained by its external appearances, this magical mirror makes manifest those invisible deities which lie below the surface. It reveals those idols upon which we'd hang our hat every time, giving us the glory story we wish we had.

Rowling betrays a low anthropology here, observing that human beings are incurable escapists. No one wants to accept things as they are, and the deepest-set 'if only...' can easily arrest anyone's ability to live the lives they've actually been given. Harry and Ron are drawn into their custom-made fantasy worlds. The Mirror does not reveal a desire to live for others, a desire to love compassionately, to seek truth. Instead, it shows us that the desires of the heart are always self-oriented. Rather than some external Odyssean temptation to the courageous and pure-hearted, this mirror conveys, as Dumbledore explains to Harry, what lies precisely *within* us.

Dumbledore tells Harry that only a truly happy man could look into the Mirror of Erised and see himself as he is. The Mirror of Erised is powerless over a person who has confronted the givens and accepted them. In Rowling's universe, then, true contentment—if it is possible—cannot bypass self-knowledge. True happiness means leaving our "private hall of flattering mirrors" (Franzen) and seeing first the person we're not so proud to see. At this juncture, we are left to wonder, is happiness even possible if it requires the stamina to see the worst in ourselves?

It seems that if it was ever possible, Dumbledore would be the virtuous example. Yet, in the *Deathly Hallows*, Harry discovers that Dumbledore, too, could not escape his own desire for power. He understood Harry's addiction because he, too, had similar susceptibilities. More on this later.

It is for this reason, the Mirror's lustrous allure to the addict human heart, that Dumbledore must remove the mirror from young Harry, knowing that a slap on the wrist or word of caution would only bring him back for more. He doesn't want Harry maddened by a reality that is unreality, paralyzed by his own picture of life. Dumbledore says it best in his hospital visitation at the end of *The Sorcerer's Stone*. Harry is befuddled that Dumbledore would have destroyed the Sorcerer's Stone, with its abilities to give eternal life and endless riches, to which Dumbledore replies, with delightful wit:

> You know, the Stone was really not such a wonderful thing. As much money and life as you could want! The two things most human beings would choose above all—the trouble is, humans do have a knack of choosing precisely those things that are worst for them.

III: THE DEMENTOR

Harry first meets a dementor on a train to Hogwarts School in *The Prisoner of Azkaban*, in his third year at Hogwarts. The famed mass murderer Sirius Black (whose innocence is undisclosed until the end of the film) has escaped Azkaban Prison—something unheard of in the magical world—with the apparent intent of finding Harry and killing him. As Harry's new professor, Lupin, informs him, dementors are the soulless guards of the Prison, "set on a tiny island, way out to sea, but they don't need walls or water to keep the prisoners in, not when they're all trapped inside their own heads, incapable of a single cheerful thought." During Harry's first experience with the dementor on the train, a rush of cold enters his body, and before he loses consciousness, he hears the scream of his murdered mother. Harry is ashamed he can't seem to 'handle' their presence as well as his peers, until Lupin explains that "Dementors are among the foulest creatures to walk this earth. They feed on every good feeling, every happy memory until a person is left with nothing but his worst experiences."

It is not Harry's lack of courage or fortitude that weakens him before the dementor but the anguish of his past. Feeding on happy moments, the dementor leaves its victims in a pit of depression, with only their worst memories, robbed also of the ability to pull themselves out of hopelessness. Ron notes that he "felt like [he] would never be cheerful again." Such defenselessness and hopelessness points to the world of depression. Rowling herself mentioned that the dementor concept came from a time when she was throttled by severe depression, where she felt "that very deadened feeling, which is so very different from feeling sad."[39]

The Dementor's Kiss, its final blow, is one in which the victim's soul is literally sucked out. This, according to Professor Lupin, is worse than death.

The only charm which can defend someone from the dementor is the Patronus Charm. Rather than battling the dementor on one's

39. "J. K. Rowling, the Interview," *The Times* (UK), June 30, 2000.

own, the wizard who conjures the Patronus Charm is summoning a power greater than they are, which will stand before the dementor and defend them. It is a complicated spell—one must connect with and focus upon a memory that is powerful enough to protect. If one's picture of happiness is not rooted in love but in exhilaration or excitement, the Patronus founders. In other words, the strength of the Patronus is as strong as the love that generates it.

The Patronus is a positive force that stands between the dementor and the wizard. In Latin, the charm's incantation (*Expecto Patronum*) means 'I await a protector.' The Patronus charm works as a stand-in for the wizard, a spiritual force that acts as substitute prey for the dementors to feed on. The reason that Harry attracts the attention of dementors is also the same reason that he is one of the youngest wizards to have ever conjured a Patronus: He is stamped (imputed) by the powerful love of his parents. The murder of his parents is more than an eternal stain upon his memory—it signifies the power of sacrifice that gave him life. Through it, Harry has a protector, who communes with him in the deepest depths of grief.

IV: THE PENSIEVE

Dumbledore's Pensieve is a shallow stone basin of milky, ethereal liquid—like a birdbath—wherein one drops the hair-thin substance of one's memory. Once dropped into the Pensieve, the wizard is transported to the scene of the memory from the perspective of the memory's beholder. The 'visiting' wizard cannot participate in the memory, but can behold it to better understand why things are the way they are:

> I sometimes find, and I am sure you know the feeling, that I simply have too many thoughts and memories crammed into my mind...At these times I use the Pensieve. One simply si-

> phons the excess thoughts from one's mind, pours them into the basin, and examines them at one's leisure. It becomes easier to spot patterns and links, you understand, when they are in this form.

The Pensieve, in short, helps make sense of things. It acts as a record book of the shaping elements of one's personal history, a proper understanding of what one has dealt with and what one carries. In the sixth installment of the saga, *Harry Potter and the Half-Blood Prince*, Harry and Dumbledore use it precisely to examine the memories and experiences that transformed the infamous Hogwarts student, Tom Riddle, into Lord Voldemort. Harry doesn't understand why such archaeology is necessary, but Dumbledore seems to treasure the memories as vital clues in knowing their enemy. Here Dumbledore invites Harry into his first memory of Tom, a troubled and friendless orphan with a penchant for pain.

After this particular trip into the Pensieve, Dumbledore notes key features of Tom's psychology: Tom seeks self-sufficiency and isolation at every turn. He has no friends, and has never wanted them. And, above all else, he seeks power.

The Pensieve shows Harry and Dumbledore that humans are inheritors and effectors of a condition. The Pensieve, in allowing one to peer into what makes people who they are, shows that humans do not exist and act *ex nihilo* (out of nothing), but through the "marshes of memory and experience."

Moreover, though, the Pensieve is an instrument which allows a wizard to confront his or her offenders/enemies by understanding their heritage. A conjunction of 'sieve' (sift, sort) and 'pensive' (thoughtful, reflective), the Pensieve is a weapon that first listens to and receives counsel from the past, that seeks to reconcile the present by coming to grips with, as the church confession describes, "things done and left undone."

V: THE MUDBLOOD

"No one asked *your* opinion, you filthy little Mudblood," Malfoy spits in the second movie. It's not just any wizard bad word, and it's not a catchall insult any one person can use to offend another—even worse, it is about something true. In this case, the first time Harry Potter hears the word 'mudblood,' Draco Malfoy is hurling it at Hermione Granger. It instantaneously incites violence. Ron, defending Hermione, casts a curse on Draco that backfires on himself, leaving him barfing up slugs—a kid-friendly diffusion of the gravity of the moment—but Harry, being new to the wizarding world, needs an explanation. "Dirty blood, see. Common blood. It's ridiculous," Ron says. "Most wizards these days are half-blood anyway. If we hadn't married Muggles we'd've died out."

Rowling is, of course, drawing some anthropological continuity between our two worlds. The incredibility of Harry's world can be off-putting, and yet throughout the series, we find the inner lives of wizards to be no different than our very own. Wizards are humans, just as love-hungry and power-hungry, compassion-seeking and conniving. 'Mudblood' is poignant because, although the reader is finding out its meaning alongside Harry and Hermione, it turns the reader back on his or her own world of bigots and pharisees, outcasts and ingrates. It takes the potentially unbelievable world of *Wingardium Leviosa* and Crumple-Horned Snorkacks and grounds it in the weight of the human rift. Exclusion is not new to Harry, of course—he spent his first twelve years in the closet under the stairs—but he had also heard such distinctions from Draco before his first year at Hogwarts:

> I really don't think they should let the other sort in, do you? They're just not the same, they've never been brought up to know our ways. Some of them have never even heard of Hogwarts until they get the letter, imagine. I think they should keep

> it in the old wizarding families.

Little did Draco know that Harry *is* one of those kids, who didn't know about Hogwarts until he was taken. Ironically, Harry is the meshing of the two worlds. He is in the "old wizarding families"—far more famous than the Malfoys and the Longbottoms—but any credit bestowed by being a 'pureblood' is lost on him. He knows nothing about it.

'Mudblood,' like the law, marks distinction. It is ironic because Hermione, who is far more distinguished than her peers in *actual* wizarding talent, finds herself excluded by a worthiness she can't prove or earn. A daughter of two Muggles, she is—to the Slytherins, the Malfoys, the purebloods—an outsider. Despite Harry's and Ron's words of comfort, the place that had once been a celebration of her peculiar gifts now represents, just like any other place, the confusing rift between the haves and have-nots.

If the question is, "Magic, who really has it, who doesn't?" then 'Mudblood' exposes the schism that will later be exemplified in the final battle. On one side, there are those pure-bloods who make the distinctions, and use them to seek control. Led by Lord Voldemort (who is not pureblood, as it happens), they intend to 'cleanse' the magical world with a rigorous reinterpretation of who is worthy. They do so by upending the Ministry of Magic, by interrogating those with questionable blood heritage, and by refusing Muggle-borns admission to Hogwarts. It goes without saying, though, that there are no friends on this side; there is instead perpetual suspicion and surveillance. Once one *claims* to be 'pureblood,' he or she has only begun the ordeal of having to prove oneself, or pretending to act like one, as Hermione suspects: "The Death Eaters can't all be pureblood, there aren't enough pureblood wizards left. I expect most of them are half-bloods, pretending to be pure."

On the other side of the final battle are the Mudbloods, the Half-Bloods, and the 'Blood-Traitors,' purebloods like the Weasleys, who see no distinction, who believe in the magic over the heritage. In this sense, it is some Spirit of Magic that operates universally ("The wand chooses the wizard!" says Ollivander) and not the blood. This side, where Dumbledore stands at the helm, believes in magic as a great leveler, where all are equally chosen. Wizards and witches are magical because magic has been given—magic chose *them*! Hermione, in this sense, is righteous. On this side, then, the magic—which sounds a lot like the Holy Spirit—will do the fighting for them. There is nothing to fear. It for this reason that Hermione, in *The Deathly Hallows*, is able to say:

> "I'm hunted quite as much as any goblin or elf, Griphook! I'm a Mudblood!"
>
> Ron started, "Don't call yourself—"
>
> "Why shouldn't I? Mudblood, and proud of it!"

VI: THE HORCRUX

> SLUGHORN: You must understand that the soul is supposed to remain intact and whole. Splitting it is an act of violation, it is against nature.
>
> RIDDLE: But how do you do it?
>
> SLUGHORN: By an act of evil—the supreme act of evil. By committing murder. Killing rips the soul apart. The wizard intent upon creating a Horcrux would use the damage to his advantage: He would encase the torn portion—There is a spell, do not ask me, I don't know!...Do I look as though I have tried it—do I look like a killer?

A Horcrux is an item within which a wizard has stored a portion of his soul, thus allowing a portion of himself to live on if his body is destroyed. As a student, Tom Riddle (Voldemort) learned about Horcruxes through his (and later Harry's) Dark Arts professor, Horace Slughorn. The process of creating a Horcrux is extremely gruesome, as it requires the murder of another, and repudiates one's selfhood by fracturing it. Very few dark wizards have attempted the process even once. In the pursuit and study of Voldemort, Dumbledore slowly discovers that the situation "is beyond anything I imagined":

> The careless way in which Voldemort regarded this (first) Horcrux seemed most ominous to me. It suggested that he must have made—or been planning to make—more Horcruxes, so that the loss of his first would not be so detrimental. I did not wish to believe it, but nothing else seemed to make sense.

Voldemort has, in fact, created *seven* Horcruxes, strewing himself into seven hidden compartments, including his own living body, thus living as long as these portions of his soul remain intact. This division, however unstable it renders the soul (the wizard becomes, as Dumbledore tells Harry, "most unhuman"), provides eternity for the wizard willing to kill. This eternity is cursory, though, in that one's soul dwells in a substitute that is not its true home. Thus, the Horcrux is a noteworthy if perverse example of Paul's inversion of "strength as weakness." A Horcrux may promise eternity, but it is an eternally unstable, soulless strength, deposited in fragile foundations. This is why, when Harry asks whether or not Voldemort feels a part of himself destroyed when a Horcrux is destroyed, Dumbledore responds, "I believe that Voldemort is so immersed in evil, and these crucial parts of himself have been detached for so long, he does not feel as we do. Perhaps, at the point of death, he might be aware of loss..."

In a theological sense, a Horcrux is an inverted representation of substitutionary atonement. Voldemort's suffering as a human—his loveless childhood, his estrangement in an orphanage, his defensive arrogance and solitude—created a fierce desire for substitution, for someone (something) to stand in for his pain. Much like Dorian Gray's portrait, his sins and sufferings are transferred onto (and within) a façade. While he is given life superficially, the cost of this substitution is profound. According to Hermione's reading, the splitting of one's soul in such a way leaves one with only the hope of healing through repentance:

> RON: Isn't there any way of putting yourself back together?
> HERMIONE: Yes, but it would be excruciatingly painful...Remorse. You've got to really feel what you've done. There's a footnote. Apparently the pain of it can destroy you. I can't see Voldemort attempting it somehow, can you?

Like most villains, Voldemort has chosen the path that will ultimately lead to his demise. And, like most villains, that demise is rooted in his will to power. Voldemort's pursuit of immortality has also made him strangely unwieldy. He is, in his immense strength, vulnerable and out of control. In his greed for standalone power, the wreckage required to get him there has involuntarily broken his strength.

There is also a power Voldemort cannot understand. The love of Harry's mother, a love that unequivocally surrenders one's life for the life of another (*proper* substitutionary atonement!) is a power too furtive to be noticed by the Dark Lord. Like Calvary, it is a power that makes itself known through death, something Voldemort would never have the notion to see. This love is also what unwittingly ties him to his fate. His will to power is cursed by love. Dumbledore explains it to Harry:

> You were the seventh Horcrux, Harry, the Horcrux he nev-

> er meant to make...He left part of himself latched to you, the would-be victim who had survived...He took your blood believing it would strengthen him. He took into his body a tiny part of the enchantment your mother laid upon you when she died for you. His body keeps her sacrifice alive, and while that enchantment survives, so do you and so does Voldemort's one last hope for himself.

VII: THE DEATHLY HALLOWS

> Three objects, or Hallows, which, if united, will make the possessor master of Death...Master...Conquerer...Vanquisher... The last enemy that shall be destroyed is death...

The myth of the Deathly Hallows is only sparsely known throughout the wizarding world, though the very old story from which it is derived is as well-known as a child's nursery rhyme. "The Tale of the Three Brothers" introduces the Hallows, though not explicitly, as Xenophilus Lovegood explains to Harry, Ron, and Hermione:

> That (tale) is a children's tale, told to amuse rather than to instruct. Those of us who understand these matters, however, recognize that the ancient story refers to three objects, or Hallows, which, if united, will make the possessor the master of Death.

It is not a subtle hint that a children's story would contain the key to the magical universe, and that such wisdom would be foolishness to Voldemort. Nonetheless, the Deathly Hallows are: the Cloak of Invisibility, the Resurrection Stone, and the Elder Wand. Historically speaking, they are the original relics of the three Peverell Brothers, incredibly talented wizards who each crafted an instrument of magic that could make them death-proof.

Each brother used his particular Hallow to respond to the reality of death. The fashioner of the Elder Wand sought the power to kill his enemies; the brother with the Resurrection Stone sought the power to bring life back to those who are dead; and the brother with the Cloak of Invisibility wished merely to avoid death until the time was right. As the tale illustrates, the first two brothers—who essentially wished to appropriate the powers of Death—found their new gifts unfitting, the use of them resulting in a strange lifelessness. In identifying themselves with powers that were not theirs, they die. The third brother, on the other hand, wanted no power but to be left to grow old on his own—his Hallow (the Invisibility Cloak, now owned by Harry) represents an acceptance of mortality. Because he surrenders to impending death, he lives long and "greets death as an old friend."

The possession of the Hallows, then, provides a second, equally dangerous route to everlasting life alongside the Horcrux. While the creation of the Horcrux gives the creator eternity at the expense of his soul, the Hallows provide their master with powers too tempting to refuse, and consequences too heavy to carry. Both the Hallows and the Horcruxes whet the appetite for the strongest human delusion: power. For this reason Harry's ethereal reunion with Dumbledore presents him with an old man's confession, "Real, and dangerous, and a lure for fools...And I was such a fool...Master of Death, Harry, Master of Death! Was I better, ultimately, than Voldemort? No...I too sought a way to conquer death, Harry."

Dumbledore had been so allured by the power of the Deathly Hallows that he had tried on the ring of the Resurrection Stone, despite his knowledge that Voldemort had made it a Horcrux. Dumbledore's motive was to atone for the guilt of the mysterious death of his sister, Ariana. While it was a kind of self-atonement, a different kind of power hunger, it was still his folly: His use of the

Stone meant his death.

It becomes obvious to Harry that Voldemort does not know about the Deathly Hallows, mainly because Voldemort had turned the ring upon which the Resurrection Stone was placed into a Horcrux. Voldemort's chief interest is in the only Hallow that would matter to him, the Elder Wand, or the Deathstick. It is more publicly known because "the bloody trail of the Elder Wand is splattered across the pages of Wizarding history." As Dumbledore says to Harry later:

> [Voldemort] would not think that he needed the Cloak, and as for the stone, whom would he want to bring back from the dead? He fears the dead. He does not love... Voldemort, instead of asking himself what quality it was in you that had made your wand so strong, what gift you possessed that he did not, naturally set out to find the one wand that, they said, would beat any other. For him, the Elder Wand has become an obsession to rival his obsession with you. He believes that the Elder Wand removes his last weakness and makes him truly invincible.

Just as with the other two Peverell brothers, it is this flaw in Voldemort's logic that will undo him. His quest for power has left him looking for a tool which will *make* him eternal, rather than seeing in Harry the eternal quality that makes him supreme. That quality, more penetrating than the power of a wand or a life-giving stone, is love. Harry, marked by the love of life lain down, carries it and is compelled to do the same. Harry, in the name of love, lays down his life so that his friends might live. And, because Harry has given up his life, he is given a proper resurrection.

This self-sacrificing love is what leads Harry into his encounter with Dumbledore, in an empty King's Cross Station. There he recognizes that he is the unlikely Master of Death, the bespectacled descendant of the third Peverell brother and, more importantly, because he has died to death: "You are the true master of death, because the true master does not seek to run away from Death. He accepts that he must die, and understands that there are far, far worse things in the living world than dying." It is in this faith, which looks to all the world like death, that the real magic happens. And it is the hope upon which all of us—Muggle or magic—rely.

Can Anything Good Come Out of Endor?

RETURN OF THE JEDI

by

DAVID ZAHL

Poor *Return of the Jedi*. Somehow it has become the Rodney Dangerfield of the original *Star Wars* trilogy ("no respect!"), routinely ranked as the least favored installment. In lists that include the prequels, it sometimes falls below *Revenge of the Sith*. Those who have been subjected to *ROTS* more than once know this is not a minor slight.

I would like to believe that there is something in my Christian DNA that compels me to defend the indefensible, love the loveless, and stick up for the marginalized, even in an ostensibly silly way. Alas, my affinity for the film probably has more to do with a sentimental attachment to it being the first non-animated movie I saw in theaters and to the spell that experience cast. Of course, if I truly cared about least *qua* least, I would be writing about *Attack of the Clones*. Some sand is too coarse.

There are plenty of tacks a theological defense of *Return of the*

Jedi could take. We could zero in on the single most profound ten seconds of the six films, the climatic moment in the throne room when Vader *silently* casts his lot with his son.[40] We could examine the redemption of Lando Calrissian, especially the leap of faith he takes vis-à-vis his friend and forgiver, Han Solo ("He'll have that shield down in time"). We could even dive into Yoda's deathbed soliloquy, surprisingly resonant all these years later.

Ultimately, though, you can not defend *Return of the Jedi* from any point of view unless you tackle the Wompa in the room. I'm referring to the Ewoks, the target of most of the derision lodged at *Jedi*. The line goes like this: The Ewoks are the first indication of the infantilizing tendencies that George Lucas would let bloom in the prequels, a cuddly toxin that would come to all but destroy our beloved galaxy. Or worse, they are evidence of a prioritization of licensing over story, revenue over content. Then you hear rumors that Lucas had originally intended to populate the Forest Moon with Wookies and you wonder what might have been. (A bit like when you hear that David Lynch was in the running to direct *Jedi*.)

While tonally the introduction of the Ewoks may indeed be a bit jarring, especially so late in the game, they are far from a liability. They may even represent the theological lynchpin to the saga's conclusion. If nothing else, Wicket and co. provide an object lesson—on numerous levels—in what we might call the Nazareth Principle.

The Nazareth Principle refers to the place in the New Testament where Nathanael scoffs at Jesus by asking, "Can anything good come out of Nazareth?" (Jn 1:46). The implication was that Nazareth was a city in the region of Galilee known for its 'mixed-

40. As disconcerting as the Greedo-shoots-first revision was, Lucas's gravest latter-day sin has got to be the "Nooooo!" he added to this scene.

blood' and therefore suspect practice of Judaism. Because our favorite carpenter came from there, didn't that disqualify him from being the real thing? Obviously not. In fact, the Bible sets a powerful precedent for good things—the best things even—coming from unlikely places, or blindspots. Out of trouble and wounds, disappointments and closed doors, the actual breakthroughs of life often arrive. When we talk about 'strength in weakness' we are talking about the Nazareth Principle (2 Cor 12:9).

The original trilogy is rife with the Nazareth Principle. Tatooine has a distinctly Nazarean quality—it's a backwater barely able to support life, a far cry from the Jerusalem of Coruscant, yet subject to imperial authority. The rebel alliance itself is a ragtag group, non-glamorous to the max, comprised predominantly of misfits and their refurbished weaponry, the galactic equivalents of fishermen and tax collectors. Han Solo is a smuggler. Luke Skywalker is the 'son' of humble moisture farmers. Yet next to the wooden, hand-sewn arsenal of the Ewoks, the motley rebels and their junky starships look pretty impressive.

Anyway, if *Jedi* is the Nazareth of the original trilogy, then the derided Ewoks are the Nazareth of *Jedi*. What I mean is that the key to the Empire's defeat comes from the least likely place imaginable. Not at the hands of pristine, well-trained soldiers but from an unorganized group of primitive goofballs, essentially Lucasized hobbits. To invoke more Tolkien imagery, the battle of Endor would have felt like far less of a eucatastrophe had it been Wookies trying to take control of the shield generator. To paraphrase Han Solo, short help proves to be much better than no help at all.

What's more, the Ewoks prove themselves to be much-needed agents of grace in a universe filled with struggle. Think about it: No character suffers more abuse in the original trilogy than C3PO.

Only the Ewoks treat the irritating, anxious protocol droid with respect. They go so far as to venerate him as a god! In fact, they flip the entire hierarchy on its head, relegating Luke and Han to dinner ingredients. The first shall be last, indeed.

There is one final aspect of Ewok brilliance that warrants a mention. Just before the closing battle begins, in a scene that lesser filmmakers might have left on the cutting room floor, C3PO recounts the rebels' adventures to an audience of their furry friends. The Ewoks listen with utter delight, like the wide-eyed children they are. It turns out they find the whole tale just as wondrous and enveloping as we do. For a split second, the Ewoks are us, recipients of a gift beyond their wildest imagination. Their part in the story may be small, maybe even unnecessary—it may even seem to detract from the greater glory—but perhaps that is what makes it so precious.

All this to say, the denizens of Endor may not be so different from those of Nazareth. Unpopular and even offensive, their power runs against the grain of human instinct, inseparable from humility and abounding in foolishness. At least, until it blows the doors off your bunker and lowers your defensive shields. Which is good enough news to make even the fiercest bounty hunter say "amen"—or "yub nub," as the case may be.

John Ford and

THE SEARCHERS

by

Paul F. M. Zahl

I heard from someone who knows the Manhattan art world that there have been at least four exhibitions recently in New York City art galleries that were devoted to John Ford's famous Western movie *The Searchers* (1956). *The Searchers* has penetrated so deeply into popular culture and cool-awareness, that you should rightly ask whether there is anything left to say about it.

I ask myself that question.

What I can offer by way of a response to it is my own experience. I saw *The Searchers* when it was first becoming cool, after the New York premiere of *Star Wars* in 1977. Since then, I have seen it twenty times, and several times in a real movie theater. It hit me between the eyes on first seeing it, and I still honor it. Later, through the DVD revolution—DVDs actually didn't exist at one time—I also had the chance to see every movie John Ford ever made that one could get hold of.[41]

Moreover, from a Mockingbird perspective, *The Searchers*, as well as many of his other movies, deals with the number one issue of human living: the conscious sacrifice of one person for another, one person's giving everything—his or her all—for the sake of another person: the nature and essence, in other words, of love.

To some degree or another, John Ford's movies almost all deal with redemptive pictures and redemptive situations—and all that in a pictorial, or what John Ford himself called a "painterly" package that was memorable and indelible.

I have been thinking about John Ford for thirty-eight years.

I have also been thinking about John Ford for thirty-eight years in the *company* of someone else. That person was Lloyd Fonvielle, my childhood friend and later Hollywood script-writer and director. Lloyd died a year ago, and it is to him that this essay is dedicated.

DON'T GO FURTHER THAN THE EVIDENCE

Can we talk for a minute about the *auteur* theory of the cinema?

The *auteur* theory is the idea, very deeply entrenched now and widely accepted, that the *director* of a movie is the real author of it. This theory, which originated with a Frenchman named André Bazin, wants to say that the director stamps the movie with his or her own artistic personality and inclinations, and that the final product is a singular effort on the part of this one controlling artist, rather than a team or collaborative effort.

The *auteur* theory is not true, or rather, it's not true in most cases. All you have to do is look at *Gone with the Wind* or *The Wizard*

41. And all this while preaching and teaching in churches, week in and week out, for over thirty years. John Ford became a part of my life in the ministry. I talked about him all the time, at least until...I discovered Mizoguchi.

of Oz or almost any movie directed by Henry Koster, and you'll see that the final product is the result of many artistic personalities and also circumstances of the moment.

What the *auteur* theory does have going for it is that when a personality like John Ford, who was an extremely strong personality, is in charge, and has some real freedom to do what he wants, then there are some elements that he brings to the work which come from him individually and in particular.

John Ford's movies are in general a good instance of what one artist can do, or how one artist can impress the result of what is still a team-effort. Thus, Ford's Westerns were mostly shot in the same location, Monument Valley. And his script-writers, with whom he usually worked on several movies, knew his interests, and also his core beliefs, as well as subjects he didn't like. And his cameramen, with most of whom he worked again and again, developed a feeling for how Ford liked to compose a group, or more than one group, in the shot. And his actors, the ones who could put up with his drinking and his almost violent way of dealing with creative resistance, kept coming back and doing again and again what they had done once. The same is true of the composers, such as Alfred Newman, who wrote the music for his movies.

John Ford was an intimidating man, and he seemed to be able to scare even Hollywood studio executives who controlled the money. Ford was also wily, and could do a kind of dance in relation to the commercial success of his movies. Thus, when one of his movies made a lot of money, as *The Quiet Man* did in 1952, he realized he had the temporary freedom to go out and make a cheaper movie, but on his own time and in his own way. In other words, he kept 'borrowing' artistically on his big successes, such as *Fort Apache* (1948), in order to make smaller movies, such as *Wagonmaster* (1950) and

The Sun Shines Bright (1953).

A result of Ford's wiliness, coupled with his intimidating personality—the outward manifestations of which were connected, in my opinion, to his drinking—was that he lasted, professionally, for a very long time. His career in the movies lasted fifty years!

So the French theory of authorship, if it applies to anybody, applies to John Ford. Yet even so, he could not have done what he did—absolutely could not have done it—without the gifts of actors like Henry Fonda, cameramen like Winton Hoch, and writers like Dudley Nichols.

And parenthetically, please don't forget what I said about directors such as Victor Fleming and Henry Koster. They constitute an instant objection to a conceptual categorization like the *auteur* theory of the cinema.

HIS "PAINTERLY" EYE

When Peter Bogdanovich asked John Ford what he had brought to his movies, in other words, what was the most specifically or particularly 'John Ford' element in his work, John Ford replied that he had had an eye for composition, by which he meant the way he arranged space, objects, and people in individual camera set-ups.

This is a feature of Ford's work—his conscious, actual contribution—that is unmistakable. It is as clear in sequences within a silent movie such as *Cameo Kirby* (1923) as it is, say, in *The Searchers*. The spatial values of individual actors and groups of actors, and their interactive (or static) relationships within the frame of the shot, are carefully ordered.

Historians of the movies sometimes say that John Ford was influenced by German Expressionism, which refers to a group of films that were exceptionally 'stagey' in the lighting and the sets.

Words are invoked like 'chiarascuro' to describe Ford's visual approach, for example, in *The Informer* (1935). Painters are referenced such as Caravaggio, who placed his light sources on his subjects with exceptional care.

There are definitely a number of John Ford films that look a little 'arty'. The most famous example of a stylized or self-conscious visual approach is *The Fugitive* (1947). I myself think that that movie goes a little *far* in this direction. Ford himself 'blamed'/credited the highly controlled look of *The Fugitive* on its Mexican cameraman, Gabriel Figueroa.

My point is that while three or four of Ford's movies, *Tobacco Road* (1941) being one and *The Long Voyage Home* (1940) being another, are 'over the top' in terms of closely controlled lighting and static ordering of clusters of people and objects, almost all of his movies are visually compelling. Almost all of them are lovely to look at, right from the beginning of his career through to the end, the end being *Seven Women* (1966). Even at the end, when John Ford seems to have taken a rather 'flat' TV-style approach to what you see on the screen, there are moments of great beauty. The closing shot of *Seven Women* is one of them.

So yes, if you want to know the essence of John Ford, focus on the way his movies look.

WHAT YOU SEE IS WHAT YOU GET

I don't remember who said that where a director points their camera, that's where their interest lies. It was certainly Lloyd Fonvielle who first quoted it to me. A way of saying this in relation to John Ford would be that wherever and whenever he moved the camera in for a close-up, *that's* what he wanted us to see.

A perfect example of this occurs in *The Searchers*. Ethan

Edwards, played by John Wayne, has just been interviewing white captives of the Indians, who have been rescued by the Cavalry. Each of these captives, from a completely disoriented old lady to blonde teenaged twins who are clearly in post-traumatic stress, can offer him no information regarding the object of his search, his niece Debbie. As he turns to leave this sorry group of traumatized people, Ethan turns around and looks at them. The camera moves right in, to a complete close-up. What you see on Ethan's face is utter agony! That is what Ford wants you to see.

Another 'classic' example of this camera work occurs in *The Sun Shines Bright*. Judge Priest, played by Charles Winninger, is presiding in his court room, and the clerk announces that the case of Mallie Cramp will now be heard. Mallie Cramp is the local madam, but also a person for whom the movie has sympathy. Mallie Cramp is a compassionate person whose life has sadly placed her in the position for which she is now in court. Not only will Judge Priest treat her with respect and kindness, but later in the story she will appear at his house on an errand of particular mercy.

This is what John Ford's camera does:

As Mallie's case is announced by the clerk, the camera moves from the level of the judge, from his vantage point overlooking the court room, down to the level of Mallie Cramp and then over the benches straight towards her face. The camera takes an 'object'—the accused in a county courtroom—and turns her into a subject, a real person.

Because John Ford generally moved his camera very little in comparison with the more 'fluid' approaches of directors like Alfred Hitchcock, whenever he *does* move the camera, you have to take note. That's when you can best 'hear' what he is trying to say.

This is all to say that John Ford was a visual director. He liked beautiful or majestic settings, he wanted what the viewer sees to look good, and he took pains to achieve this. He used to say that he didn't do a lot of 're-takes,' nor a lot of alternate angles—especially not a lot of alternate angles once he had made up his mind how a scene should look—because if he did, an editor later, or, worse, an interfering studio executive, could cut the film in a way other than Ford intended. I think that this is one of the reasons why many 'takes' in John Ford movies are quite long and appear visually static. They aren't static, because dramatic exchanges are happening in the scene, but there aren't cuts that interpret what's happening in ways other than what is actually happening in front of you. Good examples of this 'long take-' or seemingly static style occur in *Young Mr. Lincoln* (1939) and, much later, in *Two Rode Together* (1961).

A GOOD REP AND REDEMPTIVE SACRIFICE

Much has been written about repeating themes in the movies of John Ford. I think the best book on the subject is still *The John Ford Movie Mystery* (1983) by Andrew Sarris. The reason I say that—and there are many excellent books about and biographies of this artist—is that Sarris picks up directly on the Christian theme of sacrifice, which is conscious and in many of Ford's films. Ford 'meant it that way,' in other words.

John Ford was a practicing Catholic and referred to his Catholicism in several of his interviews. He was a cagey subject for any interviewer, as he was a cagey subject period! But he often asked that a Catholic priest be on the set, and said that he would never make a movie that conflicted with his beliefs as a Catholic. Even in his lifetime, John Ford was considered a very conservative and traditional person in his beliefs. This came out in his patriotism, too.

Because so many of his films were either Westerns or took place in small town America of the nineteenth or early twentieth centuries, the stories concerned Protestant people. Ford liked faith, and sincere expressions of it; and included many kindly religious characters, even eccentric kindly religious characters, in his movies. Some examples are Reverend (Captain) Clayton, played by Ward Bond, in *The Searchers*; the Church of Ireland (Protestant) minister, Mr. Playfair, in *The Quiet Man*; Judge Priest himself, in *The Sun Shines Bright*, who preaches a short and brilliant Christian sermon at the end of the movie; Elder Wiggs, played by Ward Bond, in *Wagonmaster*; The Rev. Ashby Brand, Confederate war hero and Episcopal minister in *Judge Priest* (1934), played by Henry Walthall—the list goes on and on, and I have barely started.

The bottom line is this: Sincere and humble Christianity, both Protestant and Catholic, gets a good 'rep' in John Ford's movies. Incidentally, I could also list the good Roman Catholics and good Roman Catholic priests who appear in Ford's work. Henry Fond's character in *The Fugitive* and Ward Bond's character in *The Quiet Man* come to mind immediately. (There are many more.)

But there's more to this than a friendly sympathetic attitude to Christian pastors.

The heart of John Ford's thematic, the one that makes a connection instantaneously to the concerns of Mockingbird, is *the theme of redemptive sacrifice*.

Many years ago my wife and I were sitting in a lake cottage in Central Florida on a Sunday afternoon at the end of a much needed vacation. One of our three sons, who were all little boys, was taking a nap in the next room. The other two were with their grandparents 'in town.' I turned on the television and we found ourselves in the second half of *The Man Who Shot Liberty Valance* (1962). Although we were both tired, neither of us could stop watching. At the end, I turned to Mary and said, "Is that about what I think it was about?"

What we had each noticed was that *The Man Who Shot Liberty Valance* is about substitutionary sacrifice. One character, Tom Doniphon, played by John Wayne, gives his life, or better, his whole life's hopes, in order that another character, Ransom Stoddard, played by Jimmy Stewart, can survive and thrive.

Moreover, the beneficiary of Tom Doniphon's sacrifice is not only Ransom Stoddard, but a woman named Hallie Ericson, whom Doniphon himself truly loved but who married Stoddard. And beyond that, the beneficiary of Tom Doniphon's sacrifice is the flowering of an entire community, a whole 'land' that has turned from being a wilderness into a garden. Those are the words that are used at the end of the movie.

It is all explicit. You don't have to manufacture or import a Christian sensibility to understand the story. *The Man Who Shot Liberty Valance* concerns the positive after-effects wrought by a good man's entire (and unrecognized, even unknown) gift of his entire self for the sake of the woman he loves and the man to whom she is married.

This theme, of the fruits wrought by sacrifice, occurs again and again (and again) in the films of John Ford. "Let me count the ways": *Wee Willie Winkie, Pilgrimage, Judge Priest, The Informer, The Prisoner of Shark Island, Young Mr. Lincoln, The Long Voyage Home, How Green Was My Valley, They Were Expendable, The Fugitive, My Darling Clementine, Fort Apache, She Wore a Yellow Ribbon, Rio Grande, The Sun Shines Bright, The Quiet Man, 3 Godfathers, Mogambo, The Long Gray Line, The Searchers, Mr. Roberts, The Wings of Eagles, Donovan's Reef, Cheyenne Autumn,* and *Seven Women.* And that's not all; there are even more.

Each of these movies carries within it in one way or another the theme of love's sacrifice on behalf of another person, or group of persons. This is what is rightly called 'a persistence of vision.'

CATHARSIS, ABREACTION, AND PEACE

I think it was Orson Welles who said that John Ford was close to the earth. What he meant is that Ford's movies are about primal relationships and primal realities.

Take *How Green Was My Valley* (1941). *How Green Was My Valley*, which is based on a moving novel by Richard Llewellyn, tells the story of the collapse, over about a five year period, of a Welsh working-class family. Every member of this loving and faithful family loses just about everything, either through unfortunate, unhappy marriage, emigration to another country, physical illness, or finally, as the result of a mining accident, the death of the family patriarch.

This movie has you crying—and I mean, *crying*—about once every ten minutes from the beginning to the end. The emotional music and choral singing; the spatial relationships of the characters to one another in absolutely every picture that you see; the body language of the older characters in relation to the younger, of the men in relation to the women, of the children, even the adult children, in relation to their parents, of the church elders in relation to the minister, and of the minister in relation to the people; and, probably most important, of lovers and prospective lovers in relation to each other: The combination of what you hear and what you see creates the emotional wallop of what you feel.

But what *is* it that you feel? What is it about *How Green Was My Valley* that creates this tremendous impression that stays with you?

I think the answer is loss, and mourning.

How Green Was My Valley concerns physical and therefore emotional loss. You cry because it makes you identify with your own losses; and everyone has them. When Angharad is separated from her family forever because of her marriage to the rich man on the hill, and when she is separated from her true love, the minister, Mr. Gruffydd, forever because of that marriage, and when she is separated by death from her father, who dies in the mine as she is hastening to the mine in order to stand watch: When these separations happen, we tune into our own separations. Everyone loses people they love. It is the universal common ground, and will never change.

Thus when Orson Welles said that John Ford was working from the earth, he meant this. He meant that Ford was instinctually in touch with the most raw emotions of the world: grieving, mourning, aloneness, "Moscow Does Not Believe in Tears," the cutting and sundering that death inflicts upon life.

Fortunately, when you cry in a John Ford movie—and don't miss *My Darling Clementine* (1946) if you want to cry, and don't miss *Tobacco Road* (1941) if you want to cry and truly not understand why you are crying—you feel better. You almost always feel better. It's just like in life. When you 'abreact,' that is, when you allow your emotions to be felt (by you) and not suppressed anymore, you almost always feel relief. You might even feel elation. That's why crying is a good thing.

To sum up this thought, I would say that John Ford's psychic proximity, through his movies, to deep-seated human emotions that are too easily suppressed or displaced—denied, in other words—make his movies a natural field for positive emotional engagement with what sufferers go through. I think that the key to understanding the enduring appeal of John Ford's movies, an appeal which will probably outlast us all, is this way they seem to have of unearthing buried feelings inside people.

They are, in other words, cathartic, and have the high possibility of creating peace where there was conflict, and hope where there was no hope.

THERE IS ONE FAIL, THOUGH

John Ford was blind, in my opinion, to one feature of many of his films, which is at times almost terminally disruptive, trivializing some of his greatest effects and mulcting them of their proper value.

I am talking about Ford's liking for slapstick humor.

Now I think I know what he was trying for: John Ford understood that he was telling stories visually that were extremely emotional and 'core.' He was usually talking about the most important emotions and disruptions that you can have in life. And he knew instinctively that you don't want to get *too* serious. Or rather, people need a little relief when they're watching stories about lonely widowers going into battle (Nathan Brittles), husbands whose wives really love somebody else (Ransom Stoddard), ex-cavalry officers who love their brother's wife but she has just been tortured and murdered by a Comanche raiding party (Ethan Edwards), a benign judge who lost his wife and baby girls in an influenza epidemic thirty years ago and who lives alone in a big falling-down house, doing good to the living out of affection for the dead (William Pittman Priest), etc. People need relief, right?

But what Ford provides the audience by way of relief is rarely funny. Rather, it is almost always wincingly over-played. Thus *She Wore a Yellow Ribbon*, which is one of Ford's most emotional films, has, stuck in the middle of it, a sequence involving Victor McLaglen's supposed retirement from the Cavalry and a kind of brawl related to it that is so colossally un-funny as to make you literally want to leave the room.

The same goes for the knock-your-block-off scene towards the end of *The Searchers*, in which two suitors vie for Vera Miles in her bridal gown. It doesn't work.

The same goes for another knock-your-block-off scene in the middle of *Two Rode Together*. It is stupid and silly; and rather than being a way to rally your forces for the next phase of Jimmy Stewart's fruitless bargaining for Quanah Parker's captives, it makes you want to turn off your DVD player and read Richard Rohr.

The same goes for scenes in *The Informer*, *Cheyenne Autumn* (1964) —a very long scene in that one—and *Tobacco Road;* and don't even talk about *What Price Glory* (1952) or *When Willie Comes Marching Home* (1950).

There is just no reasonable excuse for it. These scenes are repetitive and over-long and terrible.

I'm all for comic relief, and especially when you need it or if it prepares you for the next moment of cathartic abreaction. *Or*, if it's funny! In the cinema of John Ford, the main chronic problem is that he didn't know funny.

ON THE DOCKET: THE SEARCHERS

Let's spend a few minutes now applying this summation of John Ford's over all 'values' as a film-maker and artist to one celebrated film of his, *The Searchers*.

First of all, *The Searchers* is a visual tour de force. I don't think there is a more beautiful-to-look-at Western that has ever been made. The Monument Valley scenes are breathtaking. The kind of primal inward psychic landscape that the outward mystic landscape of Monument Valley connotes is mirrored perfectly in the story of Ethan Edwards' search both for his niece Debbie and for himself. Because that is what *The Searchers* is really about: Ethan Edwards' search for himself. And he finds himself, at the end, in a famous scene in which he murderously pursues Debbie right into a cave but then changes his mind.

Second, and as a result, *The Searchers* is a psychological and emotional tour de force. Ethan is a tortured man and he has only just returned to Texas from Mexico, in any event, after going South of the Border as an un-surrendered Confederate soldier. Now he has to confront his racism in the most physical situation possible, and his sexual jealousy—it's really there, in the story—and the demon of revenge. Ethan 'breaks through,' though! That's evident at the end when he changes his mind about Debbie, and instead of killing her, takes her up tenderly in his arms and says, "I'll take you home, Debbie."

The viewer has broken through, too. You feel better, and ready to re-join your life. Only Ethan himself, who is still alone in life without love, has to stay back. He has done very well, you could almost say he has saved his soul, but he can't quite join in the rejoicing of everyone else. *He* is the hostage, you might say, for the viewer's relief and successfully abreacted loss.

Third, *The Searchers* is a tale of redemptive suffering and its fruitful after-effects. Ethan has changed after a journey of self-discovery—the hyphenated word sounds awfully 'modern.'

Let's say, rather, that Ethan has found peace where there was an almost savage bitterness.

He has given three years of his life in search of Debbie, and has not only brought her home, but has, reluctantly but successfully, helped an immature and needy young man, Martin Pawley, become an adult. When I see—for the fiftieth time—the last shot of *The Searchers*, it makes me think of The Rev. Sam Shoemaker's poem "I Stand at the Door." In that poem, Sam Shoemaker understood himself as one who helped others enter the Kingdom of God but he could not enter it himself.

This is like the hero's ending in *The Searchers*. Ethan has given everything, his whole self; and he has everything to show for it, in terms of others' happiness and rewards. In his person, however, he remains outside the situation, possibly forever.

CONCLUSION

John Ford was an artist possessing an instinctive understanding, moreover a *visual* understanding, of what takes place between people, especially in the forms of loss and separation. He also understood the process of growing up and self-discovery, again in visual terms, as well as any popular artist—any person—probably can.

Because he was a convinced Catholic Christian, John Ford was sympathetic to ministers and pastors, and sincere Christian people in general. (Of course he had no time for religious hypocrites and 'time servers,' and he's got a few of them in his movies, too, as, for example, 'Mr. Parry' in *How Green Was My Valley*.) John Ford appreciated the Church, and that's uncommon for a major Hollywood director in almost any period. (D.W. Griffith was a convinced Christian, by the way.)

But "More Than This" (Roxy Music), John Ford had a strong feeling for what Andrew Sarris once called, when I interviewed him in his office at Columbia University, "the Christian myth of redemption." That picture of sacrifice, grace and redemption comes over again and again and again, with the astonishing persistence of vision I talked about, from his early silent movies to...well, the last movie he ever made, *Seven Women*.

Finally, a personal word: I said that I have been studying John

Ford and his movies since 1977. That's a long time, and during the same period I have tried to study a lot of other film-makers, especially film-makers who don't avoid the subject of religion, from Leo McCarey to Woody Allen to Roberto Rossellini to Frank Tashlin to Akira Kurosawa to Robert Bresson to Frank Capra to Eric Rohmer to Ingmar Bergman to Terence Fisher to Andrei Tarkovsky to, well, there are some others, too. All of these film-makers made some movies with religion at the center and with a sympathetic attitude to it. I would even say that Tashlin (*Say One for Me*) and Bresson (*Diary of a Country Priest*) and Capra (*Meet John Doe*) and Rohmer (*A Winter's Tale*) and Fisher (*The Devil Rides Out*) and Tarkovsky (*Mirror*) all made at least one movie that is unambiguously or rather, unambivalently, Christian.

Yet for all that, the most Christian of all major Hollywood directors would be, for me, John Ford.

The Gospel According to

HOOSIERS

by

MATT PATRICK

THE BRUTALITY OF JUDGMENTAND THE END OF CHASING

There's no question in my mind that *Hoosiers* is the best sports movie ever made, period. While I'm slightly biased, the film actually appears on most sports movie 'top ten' or 'greatest' lists. The incredible soundtrack and Gene Hackman's sweet leather jacket are not the only reasons I adore the film. The ways in which the enduring themes of judgment and grace are made manifest are what really hit home in this hardwood classic.

The film's protagonist, Norman Dale (Gene Hackman) is the newly hired varsity basketball coach at Hickory High School in Hickory, Indiana. Coach Dale is hired seemingly as a merciful favor by Hickory High's principal, his long-time friend. The Hickory community receives Coach Dale with suspicion, wondering why the former college coach would take a job at a tiny high school in the middle of nowhere. Leaving the college ranks to coach at Hickory isn't exactly upward mobility. One local citizen, who had been serving as the interim head coach, ferociously tells Coach Dale in the middle of practice, "I don't know why Cletus [the principal] drug your tired old bones in here. He musta owed you somethin' fierce." What a fitting avowal of the town's skepticism towards their new coach. Hickory's distrust of Coach Dale is similar to Dillon's suspicion of Coach Taylor in *Friday Night Lights*. The morale of both communities rises and falls with the success of their athletic teams.

The character that most suitably personifies Hickory's anxiety toward Coach Dale is Ms. Myra Fleener, a teacher at Hickory High. From the get-go, Fleener stands in direct opposition to the coach. When she greets Dale on his first day on the job, her words, along with her intrusive glare, are anything but welcoming. She doesn't trust Coach Dale a bit, and her scheme to crush him controls her every move. Though she seems to genuinely care about the students at Hickory High, her proclivity to control others (namely Jimmy Chitwood) only makes things worse. My take on Fleener is that she is more concerned with Coach Dale because he serves as a threat to her sense of comfort and control. In any case, Fleener is absolutely committed to finding out exactly why coach Dale has come to Hickory.

During a later scene in the film, in which Coach Dale and Ms. Fleener are taking a walk, the truth comes out. Fleener pulls an old newspaper article from her coat, which reveals that at his previous job as a college coach Dale was fired for physically assaulting one of his players. This scene is excruciating to watch. Fleener was right about Dale's "ulterior motives" in coming to Hickory—trying to escape his past and start over in the small town.

The fact that Fleener's judgment is true is exactly why the scene is so brutal. Indeed, the law is unfailingly accurate in exposing failure. The law has certainly had its way with Coach Dale.

Meanwhile, the team struggles, losing a game or two. Things are going downhill, and according to the Hickory community, it's all due to Coach Dale's unconventional coaching methods (e.g. infamously playing with only four players during a game). Eventually, a town meeting is demanded by the angry Hickory community in order to decide, once and for all, whether Coach Dale is to remain the coach of Hickory High.

A tense, courtroom-drama aura pervades the scene as Coach Dale spills his heart out. He confesses that he coached the team in an honest and diligent manner. When the gentleman officiating the meeting opens the floor for comments concerning Coach Dale, Ms. Law herself, Ms. Fleener, volunteers to speak. I still remember the first time I saw the film. I cringed watching her walk up to the podium, anticipating the hammer of Myra Fleener to finish him off, to kick him while he's good and vulnerable.

As she arrives at the podium, Ms. Fleener opens a piece of paper. She is prepared to share the incriminating newspaper clipping that would ensure Dale's dismissal. Everyone is expecting the hammer, *but* she decides against what she thought was "fair."[42] Midsentence she has a change of heart, and with tears in her eyes she says with a shaky voice: "I think, in order to be fair…I think it would be a big mistake to let Coach Dale go. *Give him a chance*." This is the last thing you expect from Ms. Fleener, who hasn't shown an ounce of sympathy for Coach Dale the entire film. Fleener is the ultimate t-crosser and i-dotter, yet she vouches for the hothead

42. "But God, who is rich in mercy, out of the great love with which he loved us even when we were dead through our trespasses, made us alive together with Christ—by grace you have been saved" (Eph 2:4).

coach—thereby being an agent of grace. "Giv[ing] him a chance," for Fleener, translates as, "I know he doesn't deserve it…I *know* he has a past, but give him a break." This is huge. Mrs. Fleener, like all lawgivers (i.e. everyone) has the potential to squash her subject with ample demands and expectations. Yet the lawgiver of the narrative proves to be the agent of compassion. She knows his transgressions and forgives them publicly.

HICKORY'S LEPER AND THE LOVE THAT TAKES NO ACCOUNT

Hickory has a town drunk named 'Shooter' Flatch, who is also the father of one of Coach Dale's players. Not only is Shooter an impossible alcoholic, he loves the game of basketball with endearing zeal, and has impressive insight into the sport. Coach Dale and Shooter have a very interesting (and hilarious) relationship. The suspicious town of Hickory gets extremely angry at Coach Dale's "unconventional coaching methods"—Shooter does not. In fact, he's one of the only Hickory citizens who isn't suspicious of the new coach. Shooter seems to recognize Coach Dale's knowledge of the game, as well as the ways in which he is helpful to the players, on and off the court.

Coach Dale and Shooter's relationship consists of a few things: Shooter randomly showing up at the wee hours of the night to talk basketball strategy with Coach, Coach counseling Shooter's son down from being upset with his drunk father, and Coach shoving Shooter's face into a sink, telling him to sober up (all of which, again, are reminiscent of Eric Taylor). Coach's friendship toward Shooter might seem 'conditional' on the surface ('I'm your friend, only if you sober up,' etc.), but it's not—just wait. Coach Dale has an undeniable 'soft spot' when it comes to Shooter.

Compassion comes to the forefront when Coach Dale approaches Shooter at his home, asking him to be his assistant coach. Shooter responds with reluctance, and seems offended. Shooter's not fooling anyone—his pride and fear is on full display in the exchange. Later on, Shooter arrives at a game in his suit, which he calls his "wing-dinger"—and Coach Dale introduces his "new assistant" to the team.

Coach Dale—being quite the hothead—is known for his technical fouls and frequent ejections. Shooter knows this, pleading with Coach Dale: "You have to promise me you won't get thrown out of no games." Clearly, Shooter is afraid of coaching by himself, if and when in fact Coach Dale was to get ejected. With the town of Hickory's insanely high expectations, who wouldn't be?

A few scenes later, Coach Dale intentionally gets ejected from a game in order to give Shooter a chance to coach by himself. Shooter is initially terrified, of course. You can feel the tension in the air when Coach Dale tells Shooter, "It's up to you now."

As the game carries on, Shooter seems to believe in himself or, rather, in whom Coach Dale has named him to be: the *coach*. Shooter bends down and tells the guys to run the fabled 'picket fence' play, and it works—Shooter coaches the team and they win by following his own strategy.

But this moment isn't about glory. The beauty of this scene is not in 'winning' the game; it's in the power of imputation—the power of giving someone another name—and its life-altering effects. Coach Dale didn't say to his team: "Hey guys, Shooter here is an alcoholic. He might even be drunk right now for all we know, but he's all we got. Now do what he says." Coach doesn't call him an alcoholic, or a bad father, or a dead-beat jobless bum. Dale calls him *coach*—and treats him as such throughout the story.

Maybe Coach Dale reaches out to Shooter because he sympathizes with him. Maybe knowing the consequences of his own past mistakes, Coach feared it was only a matter of time before the Hickory community would cast Shooter off as a leper. Nevertheless, his befriending Shooter is remarkably spontaneous. There isn't an ulterior motive in being kind to Shooter. Shooter's got nothing to offer back. There are plenty of more reliable candidates for the assistant coaching spot in Hickory. But Coach picked the drunk.

In his treatise, *On Christian Liberty*, Martin Luther elaborated on the nature of love to one's neighbor, which sheds some light on Coach Dale's posture toward Shooter:

> Behold, from faith thus flow forth love and joy in the Lord, and from love a joyful, willing, and free mind that serves one's neighbor willingly and *takes no account of gratitude or ingratitude, of praise or blame, of gain or loss. For a man does not serve that he may put men under obligations.* He does not distinguish between friends and enemies or anticipate their thankfulness or unthankfulness.

Toward the end of the film, Shooter has a Romans 7 moment—another drunken escapade—and ends up in the hospital. Other than his son, Coach Dale is the only member of the Hickory community that comes to visit him.

There's just something about the kind of love that isn't concerned with feedback or return policies, and there's certainly something to be said for the effect(s) this kind of love has on people. Just look at Shooter's facial expression at the end of this scene!

And remember, don't get caught watchin' the paint dry!

FIVE SPORTS FILMS

You May Have Missed

compiled by

HOWIE ESPENSHIED

Regarding sports-related movies, *Field of Dreams*, *Chariots of Fire*, *The Natural*, *Remember the Titans*, *Rocky*, *Raging Bull*, etc. have been seen widely and met with universal esteem, for good reason. Here are a few sports films that fly a bit more under detection but that can absolutely go toe-to-toe with the heavyweights.

5. HEAVEN CAN WAIT (1978)

A lot of films from the 70s don't hold up to repeat viewing in the new millennium, as those who have tried to make it through *Three Days of the Condor* (1975) know full well. As a sports fantasy/romantic comedy, *Heaven Can Wait* is an exception. Beatty plays Joe Pendleton, the star quarterback of the Los Angeles Rams whose 'person' is taken from his body by an overzealous angel just before impact in a fatal crash. This 'mistake' results in Joe getting a second chance at life when his person is put into the body of recently murdered millionaire, Leo Farnsworth. The endings of films like *A.I.* (think David and the Blue Fairy) and *The Family Man* (think snow falling in the background at the airport coffee shop) owe a bit of their magic to the ending of *Heaven Can Wait*. It's brimming with hope and possibilities for even the smallest chance of a lasting connection, allowing the viewer to speculate about where things go next...even if the liver-and-whey shake never caught on as a health craze.

4. SECRETARIAT (2010)

If a horse (this side of Mr. Ed) could talk, it would be Secretariat, and he would channel Eric Liddell (*Chariots of Fire*): "... God also made me fast, and when I run, I feel his pleasure." If you see only the re-creation of the last thirty lengths of the 1973 Belmont Stakes (the third race in the Triple Crown), you've seen enough to warrant a full price movie ticket at the theater. I sat on my couch and cried like a baby watching that horse run. I hadn't cried over an animal in a movie since Timmy buried Lassie's toys, figuring her for dead. *Seabiscuit* doubled the box office take of *Secretariat*, but the latter is the better film, and the better horse. (Sorry all you fans of downward trajectories for horses.) Secretariat, the character, is a stunning picture of what it might look like to live as if justification has truly "set us free."[43]

3. WIN WIN (2011)

Welcome to the wonderful world of Thomas McCarthy (writer/director of *Up*, *The Station Agent*, *The Visitor*, and *Win Win*). McCarthy writes and directs in the style of Alexander Payne (*Sideways*, *About Schmidt*) and Jame L. Brooks (*As Good as It Gets*).

43. Gal 5:1

Meaning, McCarthy wants to say something about how human connection and beauty emerge alongside dysfunction, injustice, and regret. Giamatti plays Mike Flaherty, a small town lawyer trying to make ends meet. He's also the wrestling coach at the local high school. Flaherty and his wife (Amy Ryan) take in a runaway teen who joins the wrestling team. There are some supercharged redemptive moments that sneak up on the viewer throughout the film. If you enjoy *Win Win*, you'll love McCarthy's other films.

2. WARRIOR (2011)

Warrior is the *Rocky* for the new millennium. It contains all of the underdog themes, and has a more tragic back story. One doesn't have to have seen a minute of an Ultimate Fighting match (let alone know the sport) in order to love this film. If you have the Jacob and Esau sibling rivalry in the back of your mind going into this film, it helps. The central relationship certainly plays out that way. *Warrior* has been described as a maddening film by some who feel like so much is left unresolved. In the final scene, however, the camera zooms in and fades out on a Jacobian 'wound of grace' that answers every question.

1. SEARCHING FOR BOBBY FISCHER (1993)

Is chess a sport? ESPN thinks so, listing *Searching for Bobby Fischer* in its 2004 list of the Top 25 sports films. The reason *Searching for Bobby Fischer* is the best sports film ever (in my opinion) is that it contains all of the elements—mentors and coaches that err on the side of developing the heart over the mind (and vice versa), well-meaning parents who nevertheless struggle not to live their sports fantasies vicariously through their child prodigies, and best of all, a tremendously rootable protagonist. Sprinkled throughout the film are narrated black-and-white flashbacks of the life of Bobby Fischer, the enigmatic, aloof U.S. chess champion from the 1970s. His story of self-sacrifice at the altar of winning serves as the perfect backdrop for this film about a normal nine-year-old kid with a special gift. I'm amazed at how many people have not seen this film. It cannot be recommended more highly for a family with kids ten and up.

Killing and Then

SAVING PRIVATE RYAN

by

NICK LANNON

A sun-bleached American flag flaps over an American cemetery in France. An old man walks along a path amongst the gravestones, looking for one in particular. He reaches his objective and crumbles to his knees. This is James Ryan. We zoom in on his face, and are transported back in time to Normandy Beach on D-Day, June 6, 1944.

Saving Private Ryan, written by Robert Rodat and directed by Steven Spielberg, won five Academy Awards in 1998. Though deemed Oscar-worthy for things like cinematography, sound, and film editing, *Saving Private Ryan* ought to win something for being a more accurate picture of the effect of the law on a life than any other piece of media in recent memory.

The film follows Captain John Miller (Tom Hanks) from his approach to the beach at Normandy on June 6 through the grueling next few days as he receives new orders and completes that mission.

Shortly after he and his squad have successfully cleared an exit for the invading troops from Normandy, Miller is told that a certain Pvt. James Ryan (Matt Damon) has lost three brothers in the last few weeks of the war, and is therefore being sent home. The only problem is that in all of the confusion of the D-Day invasion, no one knows exactly where Ryan is.

Miller and his squad set off in the direction of Ryan's intended drop zone (Ryan was Airborne), ordered to find Ryan and bring him back. Miller clearly considers this a dubious order, but is bound to follow it. On their several-day search for Private Ryan, Miller's squad loses several men in various engagements, and the remaining soldiers begin to question the logic of their orders. Why send eight men to rescue just one? The men's resentment of Ryan is palpable.

Miller doesn't share verbally in the griping, but the viewer can tell that he is sympathetic to his troops. This is evident when, for example, Private Reiben (Edward Burns) wonders aloud how Miller feels.

"I don't gripe to you. I don't gripe in front of you. You should know that," says Miller. Reiben responds: "Sorry, sir, but let's say you weren't a Captain, or maybe I was a Major. What would you say then?" In a voice dripping with sarcasm, Miller says, "In that case, I'd say this is an excellent mission, *sir*, with an extremely valuable objective, *sir*, and worthy of my best efforts, *sir*. Moreover, I feel heartfelt sorrow for the mother of Private James Ryan and am willing to lay down the lives of me and my men—especially you, Reiben—to ease her suffering."

Later in the film, Miller lets his guard down a little bit, and lets some of his real feeling slip out to a trusted sergeant: "He better be worth it. He better go home and cure a disease, or invent a longer-lasting light bulb."

The filmmakers' desire is clearly for the viewer to question the orders right along with the troops. When, at great expense to their numbers and to their relationships, the squad finally successfully locates Ryan, he's guarding a bridge that can't be abandoned. The unit decides to stay *with* Ryan, if only to salvage something good from what they consider a 'FUBAR' situation.

In the climactic battle, every man of Miller's original squad who came on the trip to 'save Private Ryan' dies, including Miller himself. Just before he dies, though, he's able to grit his teeth and say two words to Ryan, who is—in short order—rescued by an Allied bombing run. Miller's words to Ryan are killers of a different stripe, however: "Earn this."

As the sounds of the battle fade in the background, we return to the coast of France in the present day. James Ryan is slumped in front of a gravestone bearing the name "Captain John H. Miller." He speaks: "To be honest with you, I wasn't sure how I'd feel coming back here. Every day, I think about what you said to me that day on the bridge. I've tried to live my life the best I could. I hope that was enough. I hope that, at least in your eyes, I've earned what... all of you...have...done for me." At this point, Ryan's wife comes up behind him, and curiously reads the name from the headstone.

Turning to her, Ryan begs: "Tell me I've led a good life...Tell me I'm a good man." She responds simply, "You are."

THE SCENE OF THE CRIME

James Ryan is clearly totally and completely crushed by John Miller's words on the bridge. At the time, he probably thought he could "go home and cure a disease, or invent a longer-lasting light bulb"—something to retroactively deserve the sacrifice of Miller and his men. However, no matter what he actually did when he got home, even if it was to cure a disease or to invent some product that dramatically improved the quality of life on Earth, even if *everybody on earth* would have agreed that he had earned the sacrifice that those eight men had made for his sake, Ryan himself could *never* have felt satisfied. In the same way that everyone in an alcoholic's life can see that he has a problem except the alcoholic himself, Ryan would have been blind to his own worthiness even if it was acknowledged by all of those around him.

The film itself proves that this is true. He clearly *has* lived a good life. His wife says so. We, as the audience, are at least meant to think so. The minor indiscretions that mar every man's life are swept under the rug here. Ryan's wife does not say, "Yes, with a few minor exceptions." She reports an unequivocal yes.

Ryan's own reservation about his life's living up to the standard set for him by Captain Miller is his reluctance to return to France, and specifically to visit the grave of the man who gave his life so that Ryan might live. Ryan is worried that, confronted by Miller's grave, the inadequacy of his life will be brought into stark relief. "Captain Miller was such a selfless, giving man," he surely thinks. "He gave his life so that I could have mine. I have not lived up to the standard that he set." All too often, such heightened standards keep sinful men and women from coming to church. Their experience with church has been law-based, and they know that if they go back there, to the 'scene of the crime,' they too will be revealed as not good enough.

If people feel like they have to 'earn' what Jesus has done for them, then they will be reticent to come to a place where they know they will be reminded of Jesus' deeds. The Church will be their cemetery in France, and they, like Ryan, won't be sure how they feel about coming, if indeed they ever come at all.

HE WHO SHALL NOT BE NAMED

The second intriguing thing about the final exchange between Ryan and wife is the fact that in all their years together, Ryan has never breathed a word to his wife about Captain Miller and what happened between them during the war. When Ryan's wife comes up behind him, she reads the name off of the tombstone in such a way that it is clear it is unfamiliar to her. Then, when Ryan asks her if he has lived a good life, she is flabbergasted by the question. If Ryan had told her the story, even if he had left out Miller's final exhortation, she would have known the significance of the grave to her husband and known the power of his question.

If people associate Christianity solely with the law and its preaching, the evangelistic task of Christians will be stifled. The bridge rescue during World War II and the sacrifice of the eight men who wrought it was undoubtedly (for how could it be otherwise?) the most seismic event in James Ryan's life. Even if he had gone on to become the first man to walk on the moon, Captain John Miller would have occupied his mind every second. Ryan says so: "Every day, I think about what you said to me that day on the bridge." The fact that he has not shared this part of himself with his closest human relation speaks volumes. It must be Miller's final words to Ryan that prevent him from sharing the story. Without those words, he could present Miller as his hero, a brave and gallant man who saved his life. With the words, though, the quality of his life since its salvation is immediately called into question. Clearly, Ryan cannot bear to have the actual life he has lived examined in light of such a powerful sacrifice, and so has kept his life's most crucial event a secret ever since.

When Christians are burdened by the law—when they feel that they have to earn what Christ did for them—Jesus becomes a dirty word. All these poor sinners can think about is what that "earn this" says about the lives they have lived since they heard it. Any talking they do about the man who spoke thus will inevitably turn the spotlight on the life that was supposed to earn it, and that must be avoided at all costs. Indeed, though law-driven Christians will *say* that Jesus is a priority, they will not, under *any* circumstances, speak of the man who gave his life for theirs. They, like James Ryan, will speak only of what they've tried to do for him.

THERE IS NO GOOD ENOUGH

The third fascinating thing about this exchange is Ryan's paralyzing need for affirmation. Ryan's wife is clearly a sweet, loving woman, who is undoubtedly a model wife to Ryan and model mother to their children. Ryan's children are healthy and strong, and his grandchildren are beautiful. All are blonde, blue-eyed poster children for the American Dream. Ryan seems to have twin granddaughters who are destined to be models. In short, his life has, in the movie-world, been perfect. His nuclear and extended family loves him and each other. It just doesn't get any better than this, in movie terms.

Unfortunately for Ryan, all of that doesn't seem to be enough. He is brought to tears by the gravestone of Captain Miller, and has to ask his wife if he has lived a good life and been a good man. Turn around, man! Look at the legacy of perfection you're leaving! But it's not enough for Ryan. Nothing would be. Miller's words have put Ryan in a losing battle with destiny. There is literally nothing that he could do to reassure himself that Miller's enjoinder was fulfilled.

People will react the way that Ryan did upon hearing that Christ demands that they earn his actions on their behalf. No amount of feeding the hungry, providing drink to the thirsty, welcoming the stranger, clothing the naked, caring for the sick, or visiting the prisoners will assure anyone of their inclusion among the 'righteous.' No amount of altruism or quality parenting can assure James Ryan that Captain Miller is satisfied. He says, "I've tried to live my life the best I could. I hope that was enough." He's not fooling anyone, least of all himself. His hopefulness is based on some imaginary standard that he has self-applied...and he knows it. The hesitation in his voice when he says, "I hope that, at least in your eyes, I've earned what...all of you...have...done for me" betrays the fact that Ryan is sure that he has not. He wouldn't be kneeling in front of Miller's gravestone if he had.

LOVE FOR THE UNLOVABLE

Finally, after a life of being beaten over the head with *The Law According to John Miller*, James Ryan is offered a bit of a respite. When Ryan asks his wife if he's been a good man, she says simply, "Yes." This is the Gospel—good news for a weary sinner. In contrast to Miller, who requires something of Ryan, Ryan's wife requires nothing. She *declares* him to be a good man. The power of this is that *Ryan does not consider himself a good man*. As we have seen, Ryan, under the weight of Captain Miller's exhortation, has never considered his life worthy of Miller's sacrifice. He asks his wife if he's been a good man because he doesn't think he has been. If he thought he'd been a good man, he wouldn't need affirmation from another party.

The power of her "yes" is in its lack of qualification. There is no, "Yes, except for that time you were short with me when I wanted my own way," or "Yes, but not all those times when you thought of yourself first," or even "Yes, but not including that time you slept with your secretary." The fact that she issues the blanket statement,

"You are a good man," means that she is declaring him to be good, period. In other words, to be satisfactory, *even for Miller.*

The parallels between this situation and the Gospel of Christ are clear. God requires of us (Law). God offers eternity with himself, but we have to earn it—"Be ye therefore perfect, even as your father in heaven is perfect" (Mt 5:48). But then, God makes us into the thing that He requires (Gospel). Miller requires perfection. He says that Ryan "had better be worth it." He gives examples of how Ryan might be worth it: by going home and curing a disease or inventing the longer-lasting light bulb. For Ryan, though, the examples are tantalizing illustrations of his unworthiness. If he were to cure a disease, he would no doubt feel the need to cure a more fatal one. If he were to invent a longer-lasting light bulb, how long would the bulb have to last to satisfy him?

So Miller's required perfection is unattainable, as is God's. Ryan has no way out. Neither do we. It takes a declaration to make Ryan righteous. But good news is there for James Ryan. His wife declares him to be a good man, and so he is. All standards are satisfied. In the Christian world, the paradigm is that the same God that requires righteousness also pronounces us—on account of Christ—righteous.

Through the blood of the Christ, shed on the cross, we are cleansed of unrighteousness. The law of God still exists, as Miller's command to "earn this" still exists for Ryan. However, it is the pronouncement of Ryan's wife that satisfies the demand of Miller's law. Its sting is no more (1 Cor 15:55). In the same way, it is the pronouncement of God through Christ that satisfies the demand of God's law.

Saving Private Ryan is a great movie. The performances are powerful, the action is intense, and the soundtrack is moving.

Unfortunately though, too many people see their Christian 'walk' as a parallel to Ryan's life after Miller's command and before his wife's declaration. Christians think they hear "earn this" on Jesus' lips as he hangs on the cross. They live their lives under the paralyzing and intolerable weight of that command. They do everything they can to earn it, but never feel like they have. The Gospel though, is more like Ryan's wife, who in the face of what could not have been a perfect life, declares Ryan a good man, which means, in movie terms, "a perfectly good man, and worthy of the sacrifice Miller and his men made." It is by the declaration of God himself, in Christ, and not by any attempts to "earn," that we are judged as righteous in the eyes of a Holy God. It is finished. The end. Fade to black.

Art Beyond Art: Terrence Malick's

THE TREE OF LIFE

by

Zach Williams

"Imperfection is our paradise."
Wallace Stevens

A play of scarlet light beams wrapping around one another in a dark space. A girl with hair the color of flame inside a barn, staring in wonder outside through the top of a stable door; then standing outside among the woods, holding a baby goat, head the color of milk chocolate. A choral sings Tavener's "Funeral Canticle": "What earthy sweetness remains unmixed with grief? / What glory stands immutable on earth?" A field of sunflowers. "The nuns taught us there are two ways through life. The way of nature and the way of grace. You have to choose which one you will follow."

To write about it faithfully. That is the difficulty.

Writing about Terrence Malick's *The Tree of Life* is a kind of transgression against the film's central ethic. Thinking about the film analytically (as we invariably do), manipulating it into a dramatic structure (as we invariably do)—exposition, rising action, climax, *denouement*—does violence to the film's intentional and careful non-structure. We find it difficult not to so manipulate the film. This compulsion is our Nature.

But *The Tree of Life* resists our attempts to impose upon it. It is a work of numerous layers, coalesced into a singularity after three decades of gestation, but fundamentally a work of art that exists beyond the boundaries of its art in a way that few works of art have ever done. On the one hand, one can imagine a film attempting to distill all of human Life into a single work, as *The Tree of Life* attempts to do. And on the other, many films have portrayed traditional narratives with stylistic ingenuity—in particular, ingenuity that casts doubt on our reliance on traditional dramatic structures. Such was the story of Malick's feature-film resume through *The New World*; there are thousands of other examples from the past century, in all artistic media, from *avant-garde* to low-brow. In *The Tree of Life*, Malick does both: The film lays bare all of human existence, both the enigma of individual lives and Life, both in the present moment and through all Time, aided by—or rather, necessitated by—the rejection of traditional storytelling. The result is at once vitalizing and saddening. This revelation is the film's Grace.

Cows grazing, tails whisking in the summer light peaking through the oak tree branches.

To determine what this film *is*—an endeavor, mind you, of nature imposing on grace—it helps to state what *The Tree of Life* is *not*. It is not a pastoral story about a family in Waco, Texas: three playful adolescent boys and a soulful mother, along with an Australian Shepherd, all under the thumb of a dictatorial father, Mr. O'Brien, who visits upon his family his frustration born of failure to achieve a classical musician's career. It is not a bildungsroman about the eldest son's growth from infancy to pubescent rebellion against his stifling father. It is not a tragedy about two parents' grief over the sudden death of their nineteen-year-old son. It is not modern drama about an architect in Dallas struggling to come to terms with his brother's death in the past and his own imminent death in the future. It is not an epic about the creation of the universe. It is not a postmodern fable about every human individual's uncertain destiny.

The Tree of Life is none of those stories. *The Tree of Life* is all of those stories. And more.

The girl's father holds her close.

The Tree of Life is the film about being human—the film that films being human, the film that attempts to be human being. The film evokes the full texture of human life, both the 'small' events, like a family playing in its yard, and the 'big' events, like a son's suicide, and discloses their unity within the same seamless garment. The film certainly records some events of one Texan family, but it embeds those events within a wider Event: Life's beginning through its end, elevating the significance of life's 'small' or seemingly illusory events—the thought a person thinks to herself, an interaction between two dinosaurs, children running in the front yard, a mother imagining herself flying—and proposing a relation of equal weight between the 'small' events and the 'big' events. *The Tree of Life* achieves this 'content' through its 'style,' eschewing reliance on dialogue and plot clues that are staples of film storytelling, and relying instead on images and score alone.

The Tree of Life has no plot, as we understand the concept. Malick had to reject the dramatic structure to make *The Tree of Life* the film that films being. He could not have grounded *The Tree of Life* in a plot, on beginning-middle-end, on exposition-rising-climax-*denouement*, on established genre. A plot as we know it reveals characteristics about human beings, but it hides the experience of being human.

Plots create phenomena that we describe as *events*. Any occurrence is an event—maybe you scratch your arm, or a leaf falls, or a car honks. These occurrences are literal events, but they are not *events*, which is what we speak of when we use the word 'event.' The Latin root *evenire* can mean 'to happen' but also 'to result'; an implicit reference is to *outcome*, hence one definition is 'to come out.' We are shaped by the conventions of plot, a fact our language reflects.[44] We think of an occurrence as an *event* only in its relation to a story's end—the result of its *events*, their outcome, the resolution. In the basic dramatic structure, an occurrence is only invested with *event*-ness, earning its mention, because it affects the story's outcome. Malick is hardly the first artist to play with the weight we attach to *events* in observing stories and living our lives. But we remain wedded to dramatic structures: Next time you argue with your boss, meditate on the way you resolve the disagreement in your mind.[45] In the main, our reliance on stories is no defect, but rather a simple fact.

But we forget that the plot of a story—be it *Gone with the Wind* (film) or *All the King's Men* (novel) or *Phantom of the Opera* (musi-

44. "We knew for long the mansion's look / And what we said of it became / A part of what it is." Wallace Stevens, "A Postcard from the Volcano."

45. Recall Joan Didion's famous, sententious words: "We tell ourselves stories in order to live... We look for the sermon in the suicide, for the social or moral lesson in the murder of five. We interpret what we see, select the most workable of the multiple choices. We live entirely...by the imposition of a narrative line upon disparate images, by the 'ideas' with which we have learned to freeze the shifting phantasmagoria which is our actual experience." Joan Didion, *The White Album*.

cal) or *Les Miserables* (all three) or *Red-Headed Stranger* (album) or *Rime of the Ancient Mariner* (poem) or *Return of the Prodigal Son* (painting) or the *Peita* (sculpture)—exists in parallel from life, cleaved from it. That is not to say a plot is an illusion, for every plot is its own occurrence in life: The plot is "the figure and not / An evading metaphor."[46] But in a plot, any non-*event*—an occurrence that bears no obvious relation to the plot's outcome—is ignored, dispensed with in the service of the plot's outcome. Which is to say that very many occurrences of human life, including many quite important occurrences, are omitted, concealed by the plot. Plot's conceit is its feigned ignorance about the importance of certain occurrences. The plot is insouciant: It would act surprised if told of all the important occurrences it omitted. Plot acts like a republican; in fact, plot is an autocrat, proceeding with unshakeable prioritization of *events* over occurrences.

"Grace doesn't try to please itself. It accepts being slighted, forgotten, disliked. It accepts insults and injuries."

Malick dispenses with plot. Throughout his career, plot as an entity has dwindled further and further. *Badlands* has a plot, though Malick seems to taunt the plot's presumptions with every statement from Kit and the infusion of classical score into scenes from the barren Midwest. In *Days of Heaven*, one sees more conscious effort to use voice-over from young Linda to disjoin, rather than to marry, the plot on one hand and the film's sights and sounds on the other. In crucial moments of *The Thin Red Line*—ostensibly a portrayal of the Guadalcanal Campaign—the camera's focus turns to an injured insect, birds scattering from the trees, soldiers babbling at one another in different languages. By *The Tree of Life*, this dis-

46. Wallace Stevens, "Add This to Rhetoric."

juncture is complete. Malick has no interest in carving out a specific problem from that great, big Problem that governs all of Life and guiding the little problem to an outcome.

Malick displays events that are not *events* by the logic of dramatic structure—adolescent boys playfully chasing their mother down the street; a father coercing affection from his son; a woman attempting to console her daughter-in-law, the mother of a nineteen-year-old just deceased, with platitudes; rays of light expanding into the universe and the earth we inhabit; dinosaurs roaming the primeval earth; a middle-aged man muttering words of apology on a telephone call with his father. None of these occurrences are *events* by logic of the plot, but all of these occurrences are significant in their occurrence in a fleeting life.

Chief among these significant non-*events* is what Roger Ebert called the characters' "parallel commentary," which are manifested as deceptively simple voice-overs.[47] These voices are not narrators. Since *Badlands*, Malick has featured characters' voices speaking over the images on the screen. These voices have been addressed—one surmises—to another person, to the speakers themselves, to no one perhaps, and to God, whether real or sought. In *The Thin Red Line*, as the Americans harrowingly overrun a Japanese outpost, we hear Private Witt ask, *This great evil—where'd it come from? How'd it steal into the world? What seed, what root did it grow from? Who's doin' this? Who's killin' us?* These voices are more than interior monologues. They are more than thoughts. They are not the interwoven narratives we constantly spin in "the motion of thought / And its restless iteration" in "the place of the solitaires."[48] They are more like the creation, each characters' portion in it, groaning in

47. Roger Ebert, *The Tree of Life* (Review).

48. Wallace Stevens, "The Place of Solitaires."

the pains of childbirth. In *The Tree of Life*, Mrs. O'Brien learns that her son has unexpectedly died; while she hustles down the block at nothing in particular, we hear her exclaim breathlessly, desperately, *My son. My hope. My God, what did you gain?*

It is easy enough to think of non-*events* like these commentaries, or the film's 'impressionistic' images of family life, or the sight of an exuberant mother taking flight in air, as plot devices. But plot devices are exactly what they are not.

Here is an irony: A dramatic structure tries to arouse an experience and thus shields the viewer from experience. *The petulant and childish woman cheats on her husband, a doctor. The doctor takes his wife to a remote region in China to treat patients suffering from a cholera outbreak. She watches her husband, and a group of nuns, treat the sufferers, causing her to see her selfishness and pettiness.* Stories like *The Painted Veil* are good. They will always be with us, for the better. But the dramatic structure has no time for types of experience external to its range of interests, for simply experiencing experience. Awe, sympathy, anger, etc.—all part of experience, but individually narrower than the full experience of being, the difference between drinking a glass of water and plunging into a lake.

Which is where Malick would like to take us. Malick's art is more than art; it is art beyond art, an art that seeks not to arouse in us a feeling but allure us into all feeling.

Malick's approach evidently did not sit well with many people who bought tickets to see *The Tree of Life*. Much was made about the lack of a plot, and what in the world is going on with those voice-overs? The reaction was hardly unexpected. As interpreters of life occurrences, we have taught ourselves to mistrust even demonstrable facts when reported by a disagreeable source; facts about human psychology are used to create unanswerable questions about biases and motives, all to avoid the difficult and humbling exercise of thinking critically and participating in an ever-imperfect world. And yet: Popular news sources are filled with stories about the personal lives of celebrities and the real-life travails of reality television stars. Having an email account from a provider other than Google is a sign of social atrophy. In this country, our schools, churches, and neighborhoods are more racially segregated than ever, and to the racial segregation we have added ideological segregation. These are just some of our methods for allowing our own immersion in plots cleaved from life experience.

Just so, by all accounts, the rate of walk-outs at showings of *The Tree of Life* was extremely high. One theater in Connecticut posted a sign announcing that requests for ticket refunds would not be honored.

A flame-haired woman in a plaid dress twirls on a rope swing hanging from a front-yard tree over a lawn of live-and-dead, green-and-grey grass and almond-colored leaves. Two boys play with an Australian Shepherd.

Films with plots beget commentaries with plots. The commentator makes a silent pact with the filmmaker, even in a negative review: The commentary provides some background details (exposition), then offers some reflections, then lets the reader in on the problem the film raises (rising action), then some more reflections, then The Judgment. Many fine reviews are written in this form. Many reviews of *The Tree of Life* have taken this form, many of them quite good.[49]

49. *The Tree of Life* has inspired quite a lot of thoughtful and lyrical commentary, which should be a signal to those walk-outs about what they're missing. The best I've seen come from Niles Schwarz and, unsurprisingly, Roger Ebert. (Niles Schwarz, "Terrence Malick's Song of Himself," *The Point Magazine*; Ebert, Roger, *The Tree of Life* (Review), June 2, 2011; Roger Ebert, "A Prayer Beneath the Tree of Life," May 17, 2011.) Not long before his death, Ebert put *The Tree of Life* on his list of the ten best

But attempting to be faithful to the film, to write a commentary with no plot about a film with no plot, risks pure senselessness. The faithful writer is forced into clunky phrases like 'what transpires' because a phrase like 'the film's events' grafts onto the film the expectations of a plot. The film is often described as 'impressionistic,' but that label is as ill-fitting on *The Tree of Life* as it is for the *Water Lilies* or *Olympia*: Every film is composed mainly of impressions, and every film is itself an impression, just like every painting is an impression drawn from impressions. I have described Malick's technique as 'imagistic,' but, again: not new. This description is rooted in the different manner that Malick treats images—as ends unto themselves, rather than as means to a narrative end—but, still, the language sounds silly, like eating soup with a fork. Malick, like Joyce and Eliot and Picasso and Stevens and Mozart and so on and so on, renders everything that came before, including our very descriptions, insubstantial, ill-fitting, inadequate, disappointing.

A father sits down to the lunch table as two boys run toward the open window, white shears billowing in the wind.

Writing faithfully about *The Tree of Life* is challenging because the film itself speaks in challenging ways. There is some of what we might think of as dialogue—one character speaking to or at or toward another character, that character hearing, maybe listening, perhaps responding with verbal speech. (Inasmuch as film characters listen to what other characters say, films are unrealistic representations of real life.) There is some of that, but not much.

Malick does not record conversations so much as he eavesdrops on them, picking up only little bits and pieces. Neighborhood boys pressuring Jack to hurl rocks and bust the windows of an

films. (Roger Ebert, "The Greatest Films of All Time," Apr. 26, 2012.)

abandoned house. Jack yelling at his father and hustling away. A mother-in-law badly failing at consoling the mother with an inventory of religious-sounding shibboleths ("Life goes on. The Lord gives and the Lord takes away. Nothing stays the same. You still got the other two. He sends flies to wound that he should heal."). In the lingual desert that is *The Tree of Life*, the moral dirtiness of the elder Ms. O'Brien's bilious consolations is disclosed for all to see. Anyone who has been the wrong end of a cliché—or been in a conversation, really—can appreciate Malick's decidedly pessimistic view of interpersonal speech.

More notable is the film's second kind of speech, the parallel commentary. This commentary is an oft-cited point of consternation for those with no patience for Malick. But why should these voices seem so unusual to us? As if Malick is portraying some imagined conduct foreign to human experience. Most of the speech expressed in the world, past and present and surely future, never leaves our mouths audibly. And yet we are thrown—for some, only a momentary pause; for others, leaving the theater—by a director human being's most common type of speech. We squirm when speech does not have 'a point,' does not further the 'outcome' or 'resolution' of the 'story.' Which is to say we are uncomfortable, and feel like our time is being wasted, when the simple experience of being, of having thoughts, is portrayed.

For viewers who have patience and ears to hear, the film's silent speech is powerful. Still: Why should the portrayal of our second-most-frequent activity be so affecting? For each of us, the running commentary in our minds is our second-most frequent activity, after breathing. So that it should be revolutionary, confusing, boring, and upsetting for a filmmaker to portray this activity on film—that is, for him to place a mirror up to ourselves—is an indictment. The intensity of your boredom or irritation by Malick's method correlates to the intensity of your despair, in Kierkegaard's formulation, the intensity of your attempt to rid yourself of the relating relating to yourself. Experiencing can be difficult, grinding work. Simply being is hard for us, even painful, like exercising an atrophied muscle. If you find yourself bored, impatient, or irritated, you probably spend lots of time watching sports on your smartphone. Like me.

So perhaps this is genius: the vision to portray the obvious; to unencumber; the courage to observe experience in its fundamentals; not of building-up, but of reduction; not to find the new, but to disclose the old, exhume the buried, remind of the forgetful of the forgotten.

"Nature wants only to please itself, get others to please it, too; likes to lord it over them; to have its own way. It finds reasons to be unhappy, when all the world is shining around it, and love is smiling through all things." In the dusk, three boys play with their father and mother in the front yard, tossing a ball with the sheepdog, running after their mother wearing a baby-blue dress on a dirt road.

Another kind of speech is heard in all the images that make up the film—the young Mrs. O'Brien staring at the sky in wonder; the middle-aged Mrs. O'Brien mourning her son; the vision of the universe's beginning, the spreading of the stars and planets, the formation of the earth, a show of mercy from one dinosaur to another; Jack's birth, both in realist vision and poetic rendering of Ms. O'Brien flying and the opening door of an underwater bedroom; the poignant scenes of three boys rambling about the neighborhood, wrestling with their dog, growing up; family tension revolving around the simmering Mr. O'Brien; middle-aged Jack O'Brien's malaise; the world's end.

Speech is present, even in lieu of words, as all these images pass gracefully to one another, like air bubbles in water, embracing, merging, floating as one, cleaving, with no exertion, no will, only being a bubble, like a grain in wind. Images of stillness: grieving Ms. O'Brien, staring at her husband, sullenly, he regretting shaming J. L. for turning the pages of the piano songbook wrongly; young Jack, gazing at his father, frustrated, gazing at the crowd of boys about the neighborhood, gazing at the world, thinking, studying, organizing, writing his story in his mind. Images of movement: In the kitchen, Ms. O'Brien tells J. L. that his father is "gone on a trip," J. L. turns and grins, the boys prance gleefully around the house, they bring a lizard from outside, chase their mother with it, through rooms, her dainty figure almost falling over as she speedily turns from hall to living room, now *The Mysterious Barricades* drowns out the boys' shouts and their mothers' screams, they run into the bathroom, *Barricades* recedes under the boys' shouts, the four children dash outside, into the front yard, creaky wooden screen door crashes as if it, too, is in on the fun, *Barricades* again, compact sing-song notes rising and falling, arraying the free verse of the children's play into rhyme and meter.

Even amidst the sound—the lush and often searing score, the yells of young boys, the growl of volcano fire—the film's dominant mode of speech is silence. The fleeting, decontextualized dialogue, overlaid with the characters' ruminations, creates a fissure in the viewer's perception; it *disjoins* the film's sights and sounds from our expectations of how sight and sound on a screen should function. The result is a spiritual silence: We can only watch, hear, recollect, experience. Not a portrayal of experience, but experience. We feel the range of emotions we feel in life. Cancer-ridden Jenny Diski recounted a similar sensation when she suffered a panic attack:

"Without a doubt, I was dying of suffocation. It wasn't a metaphor, it was an inability to breathe, to take in air."[50] As our expectations of a dramatic structure recede, we do not watch fictional characters act out lives but rather we live, we experience—we experience and nothing else, which is everything.

"They taught us that no one who loves the way of grace ever comes to a bad end." A river spumes down a waterfall, thrushes of mist puffing like clouds.

Brad Pitt described Malick's direction as a "freeform, butterfly-net kind of way of catching moments ... On a normal set it's very loud," Pitt explained, "generators going, over one hundred crew members. There was none of that on this. There's one guy with a camera on his back, no lights, and we're free to roam wherever we want to roam."[51] This for a film three decades in gestation. Douglas Trumbull, the film's special effects supervisor who became famous for his work on *2001: A Space Odyssey*, said that Malick consciously "didn't want to use a very stringent design process, he wanted the unexpected phenomena to occur—and [to] use that."[52] Perhaps all those years, all the shifting and shaping of his vision while experiencing a brother's suicide and two failed long-term relationships, Malick came to see something of 'the way of nature' in planning, aesthetic discipline, storytelling, and something of 'the way of grace' in spontaneity, simple presence, things as they are.

This relentless physicality, of sight and sound. An unyielding participation with things—by filmmaker, viewer, and things themselves. And often things—human bodies, clouds, water, trees, dogs,

50. Jenny Diski, "Spray it Silver," *London Review of Books*, July 2, 2015.

51. Steve Rose, "Brad Pitt talks about Terrence Malick and *The Tree of Life*," *The Guardian*, June 30, 2011.

52. Phelim O'Neill, "The genius of Douglas Trumbull," *The Guardian*, July 8, 2011.

leaves, sand, stars—not doing anything in particular, not doing anything of note more than breathing or skipping or swinging. Malick's philosophical realism recalls Chesterton's letter to his wife: "I like Cyclostyle ink; it's so inky. I do not think there is anyone who takes quite such a fierce pleasure in things being themselves as I do. The startling wetness of water excites and intoxicates me: the fieriness of fire, the steeliness of steel, the unutterable muddiness of mud."

Another irony: The greater the attention to things—the more sustained the attention, the steelier the commitment, the more unthinking the approach—the more we awaken to the spirit of the world in which the thing exists. One would think a greater attention to tree leaves would beget knowledge of chloroplasts and chlorophyll. In fact, gazing at the leaf, watching it sway in the wind and dance in and out of shadows, discloses a fleeting, bittersweet beauty. Perhaps that sense of beauty is the disclosure of your relation to the leaf—you watch the leaf, begin to care for it, to see it as a valuable leaf, and that realization changes you. Or perhaps there is something else at work, some force connecting you to the leaf.[53] You are open, exposed, uncertain, vulnerable—if those words, or

53. *The Tree of Life* seems to act as a mirror for each commentator's own convictions about providence. In a typical turn, Schwarz describes Malick's conception of the Divine "God is that You within," and religion as "linking back" to one's childhood; Ebert wrote that the film "stands free from conventional theologies" but granted that "at its end it has images that will evoke them for some people." (*See* n. 4 & 6.) On the ledger's other side, Damon Linker argues that *The Tree of Life* and Malick's next film, *To the Wonder*, "are deeply Christian in outlook and inspiration" and chides critics for failing to acknowledge, whether positively or negatively, the films' theological grounding. (Damon Linker, "Terrence Malick's moving Christian message—and film critics' failure to engage with it," *The Week*, Apr. 26, 2013.) Brad Pitt describes Malick as a person who "sees God in science and science in God," and Martin Sheen has disclosed that conversations with Malick in Paris during the early 1980s led Sheen to return to the Catholic Church. (*See* n. 8; David Kupfer, "Martin Sheen Interview," *The Progressive*, July 2003.) Ultimately, though, no one knows the convictions of the exceedingly private Terrence Malick.

any words, can describe the experience. A more controlled storytelling would not lead us to this point. Just as Malick's forebears Kierkegaard and Heidegger take a pickaxe to well-worn language, Malick must invent his own artistic mode.

Perhaps our reliance on plots reflects the basic fear underlying human life. For thinking about first things inevitably leads to thinking about last things.

"I will be true to you, whatever comes."

A young postman delivers a yellow letter to the red-haired woman opening the door. She walks back in side, slipping the letter open, stops, drops the letter, begins to shake, trips over herself in a convulsing cry shouted from her stomach.

It begins with a death.

A moment of beauty. Childbirth. A field of sunflowers bathed in sunlight on a warm day. Dogs wrestling. A marriage. A show of humility. Tree branches swaying in the charcoal-tinted sky. Love. A suit cut like an extension of your skin. The sound of water in a brook eddying over stones. You are not separate from beauty. You are luminous. You are not 'an observer.' The heart is roused. You are in the beautiful experience—it changes you, and your adoration preserves it.

But there is something else. The heart feels it. Rather, the heart feels what it is not. There is no word for it. Incompleteness. Fleetingness. A keyhole through which is seen the going-away of the experience of beauty. The experience is temporary.

Or perhaps a waiting. Amidst the radiance, a still-greater radiance is outstanding, waiting to manifest. And it is felt. The cusp. "To be outstanding means that what belongs together is not yet together."[54] Month four comes and there is a little less infatuation. While chewing filet mignon, you admit to yourself it is just a piece of meat.

And what comes next? "[T]he terror of death," writes Diski, "has been soothed to the fear of blank nothingness into eternity. A nonsensical fear as soon as you stop to think about it. Though think about it I certainly do."

The third kind of speech—silence, terrible silence. Felt in the heart as an assurance, the certainty that this experience will pass away, a portend of This Experience passing away. A cold, non-negotiable assurance.

This is part of what gives the Beautiful its spiritually distended effect, its sense of fullness. A dollar has greater value than a scrap of paper because it is desired and it is scarce. Like so in the spirit of Life. But Life is scarce. This is the terrible fact for us. *Ms. O'Brien prancing with her son points to the sky and says, That is where God lives*. But what kind of god is God? He speaks, but in what kind of speech? In moments of beauty, there is a terrible silence. Terrible enough in its simple assurance. And that is a fact, a terrible fact, even notwithstanding the kinds of deaths the unfortunates among us can die—beheading, self-asphyxiation, cancer eating the body, immolation, plane crash, etc.

J. L. O'Brien, nineteen years old, dies. Possibly Vietnam. Possibly J. L. is Malick's older brother, Larry, breaking his own hands out of frustration over perceived deficiency in his guitar-playing, and later committing suicide. (Recall Mr. O'Brien's lamentation about punishing his son for how he turned the pages of a songbook.) But it may be something else altogether—a fatal accident, an overdose, a murder. In the vacuum lies the purpose. And in

54. Martin Heidegger, *Being and Time* § 48.

any other life, it could be something else. This is a Malick film; our expectations about the impact of a particular fact are not likely to be met; we are enticed to think differently about the deserved loci of our attention.

But J. L.'s death is not altogether unexpected. The film lurches forward in time to adult Jack waking up in his modern home—cold in its clean lines and lack of color, like a Le Corbusier idyll—out of sorts, depressed, uncomfortable at work, still grieving his brother. Then, lurching backward in time, to, it seems, the Beginning. The enigmatic play of scarlet light—the ground of being, maybe God, a distant presence that draws the mysteries of the universe into itself. The light recedes; then, light, refracted through darkness, like smoke: the genesis of the universe. Light slips through vapors, crimson, then bright white. Expanding, enveloping, falling like shards of glass, like bands of light refracting through diamonds, stretching into a single band, taking shape into a spiral. It takes form. It begins.

But then, a strange feature: the score, Zbigniew Preisner's "Lacrimosa," from *Requiem for My Friend*:

> *Ah! that day of tears and mourning!*
> *From the dust of earth returning*
> *Man for judgment must prepare him*
> *Spare, oh God, in mercy spare him!*

"For dust though art, and unto dust thou shalt return"[55]: the grief of Death at the beginning of Life. The death the film begins with. The death the world begins with. The death each human life begins with. During the passing images of Jack's birth, juxtaposed images, the mysterious interrelation between birth and death: Ms. O'Brien screaming in the pains of childbirth; baby Jack's foot pushing

55. Gen 3:19.

through Mr. O'Brien's clasped hands; the opening door of a child's room, submerged in water; moving up stairs into a dark attic; moving into the "Mouth of Hell" in the Gardens of Bomarzo.[56]

Yet another irony, this one quite harsh: The very fact of birth assures just a single fact, that "this day I am going the way of all the earth."[57] We are born into what Heidegger calls "potentiality-of-its-being," affected with a "constant unfinished quality," an impulse of striving and yearning and reaching, of raising children, running through the neighborhood, making music. All the while, this striving toward possibility shrouds the fatal actuality. Our "potentiality-of-its-being" is invariably a "being-toward-death." The terrible silence is a loud portend.

A man stands in a desert before a door frame. His neck tie whips in the wind. He moves toward the door frame.

All writing about *The Tree of Life* is a degradation. Better to watch, weep, and let your heart break.

He pauses, hesitates, like a finger near a hot stove. Again he moves toward the door. And walks through.

What happens at the end? None of us really knows for sure.

56. The latter nugget was unearthed by Schwarz in his magnificent essay. *See* n. 4.

57. Josh 23:14.

Faith in Film

MOVING PORTRAITS OF CHRISTIAN MINISTRY

compiled by

JOHN ZAHL

ROME, OPEN CITY (1945)

Arguably Roberto Rossellini's finest film, an exploration of what it means for the Christian faith to bring healing to war-torn Italy in the last days of WWII. Its depiction of a 'hero' priest is one for the ages. He is funny, unflappable, and profoundly courageous. "For Christ's sake, I rejoice in my sufferings, persecutions, hardships..."

OF GODS AND MEN (2010)

The story of a small order of French Trappist monks living in Algeria in an extremely hostile environment. Their compassionate ministry to the local Muslim population is deeply moving, as is the way they stand fast under threat of martyrdom, in the face of great challenges to their beliefs.

DIARY OF A COUNTRY PRIEST (1951)

A young, newly ordained priest discovers just how dark and challenging the priesthood can be, all the while doing transformative work with great humility. One could teach an entire course in pastoral care on his dealings with the local squire's wife.

STARS IN MY CROWN (1950)

A Western, focused upon the ministry of a Methodist pastor of deep conviction who is called to serve a country parish in which his work goes largely unappreciated. Especially compelling are his apologetic dealings with an agnostic doctor, and the final scene in which he defends a freed slave from an attempted lynching.

LETTERS TO FATHER JACOB (2009)

An aging Lutheran pastor in Finland takes in a recently released and hardened female convict, enlisting her help as a stenographer in the final months of his lifelong ministry. It is as moving a portrait of the life-changing implications of Christian ministry as has ever been put on film. Bring tissues.

THE APOSTLE (1997)

A somewhat questionable Pentecostal minister (played brilliantly by Robert Duvall) goes into hiding after killing his youth pastor when he discovers that his wife has been having an affair with the man. He then founds a tiny country church and waits for his secret to emerge.

CALVARY (2014)

The steadfast ministry of a local priest in rural Ireland is challenged when a parishioner threatens to murder him. He faces his impending end undeterred, enduring relentless antagonism from the parish he feels called to serve.

LEON MORIN, PRIEST (1961)

The indefatigably incorruptible Fr. Morin escapes the seductions of a sincere but confused parishioner, all the while remaining remarkably human. The scene in which he draws her 'portrait' is unforgettable.

HEAVENS ABOVE! (1963)

Peter Sellers plays an awkward, prattfalling Church of England vicar, who actually manages to stimulate a revival of core Christian faith in a rural village. It becomes a Passion Play.

HOW GREEN WAS MY VALLEY (1941)

Walter Pidgeon plays a tragic Welsh pastor, full of grace, charm, and courage, whose ministry places him in the midst of a town's deep wounds. Directed by John Ford. Notorious for having beaten out *Citizen Cane* for the Best Film Oscar in 1941.

MASS APPEAL (1984)

Jack Lemmon plays an experienced Roman Catholic priest who takes on a rash but well-intentioned curate, and gets caught in a tussle with his bishop as a result.

THE HOLLY AND THE IVY (1952)

Christmas at its most profound. A tale of a dysfunctional family, told under the guise of picturesque English life in the home of an aging vicar. "You who were once far off have been made near."

GOING MY WAY (1944)

The best of Bing Crosby's many priest roles. A gifted young clergyman is brought into a staid parish to help an aging and difficult padre. He regenerates the life of the congregation through a series of inspired pastoral moves, enabling the old man to confront his limitations with the utmost grace.

THE BISHOP'S WIFE (1947)

Cary Grant, with humor, warmth, and a sensitive doling out of reality, plays an angel, sent to straighten out a broken parish and its misguided minister. A classic filmic example of the redemption we all simultaneously dodge and hope for.

FRIENDLY PERSUASION (1956)

The story of a family of Quakers who are forced to question the depth of their pacifism when the Civil War encroaches upon their small farm. While hypocrisy in the church is exposed, deep faith is also affirmed, especially when a Confederate troop arrives upon their doorstep.

PRIEST (2011)

In the future, Christian priests serve the world primarily by fighting vampires. Not a great movie, but a refreshingly accurate portrait of parish ministry.

ONE MAN'S WAY (1964)

This biopic, starring Don Murray as Norman Vincent Peale and also the very cool Diana Hyland, is surprisingly moving and true. It might be the sleeper of the bunch.

DANTE 01 (2008)

Think Kubrick's *2001* meets John's Gospel. This is Jesus in space, the parable of the Cosmic Christ.

A Body on the Cross: Theologizing

THE VIRGIN SUICIDES

by

C. J. Green

The first thing to know about *The Virgin Suicides* is that, despite the bizarre title and the shocking plot summary, it's actually pretty funny. Sure, it's about five sisters who kill themselves, but before you gasp and head for the hills, you should know that it's also sharp, melodic, and often rather enjoyable—a colorful exploration of life and death in 1970s suburbia.

It's a hypnotizing film, too—undeniably postmodern. Based on the brilliant first novel by Jeffrey Eugenides, *The Virgin Suicides* follows a group of men sorting through the details of the most shocking year in their adolescence: the year the Lisbon sisters took their lives. Tracing the men's memories, we become voyeurs from across the road, peering into the lives of the Lisbons as they cope with the self-destructive tendencies of their five girls. The year of the suicides, the men remember, was the same year that the elm trees began to die from an invasive species. The central conflict becomes the unprecedented invasion of death into a town that is so in denial of it even the funeral workers go on strike, as though picketing could prevent a heart from stopping.

What surfaces is ninety-six minutes of speculation, theories about why the girls did what they did and who is ultimately to blame. But even from the beginning you get the uncomfortable sense that the theories will dead-end: The first scene features Kirsten Dunst, who plays the second-to-youngest sister, standing in the middle of a neighborhood street, eating a popsicle. Half-smiling, she walks away.

THE THEORIES

The narrator begins: "Cecilia was the first to go." The youngest sister, only thirteen, attempts suicide by slitting her wrists in the bathtub. She sets off the chain of events and seemingly infects her sisters, Lux, Bonnie, Mary, and Therese. It's no secret what will happen to the others: The question is when they will do themselves in, and why. The film implores us to find an answer. *Why* did Cecilia kill herself? Why do the other girls? Neighborhood women gossip over the landline:

> "I heard it was an accident."
> "No, of course the parents are to blame."
> "That girl didn't want to die. She just wanted out of that house."
> "She wanted out of that decorating scheme."

The parents are easy targets. Of course the mother is a religious zealot, sewing her daughters plain ankle-covering dresses and trying her best to keep their purity under lock-and-key. And maybe, okay, her decorating scheme is substandard. But in the end she is *too* easy a target, a red herring even. Kathleen Turner, who plays

Mrs. Lisbon in the film, admitted, "You cannot help but blame the woman. And she could never not blame herself."[58] In this way, even the mother becomes a victim. In a fascinating interview with Wes Anderson, director Sofia Coppola explains: "I don't want her to be a villain. I want it to seem like she was trying. A lot of people have good intentions but it just doesn't come out the right way. She's just being overly protective, and she thought she was helping."[59] Mrs. Lisbon is overbearing, and slightly tyrannical, but, at the end of the day, she doesn't force Mary to put her head in the oven.

Then maybe religion is to blame? Good old-fashioned Catholic guilt? Cecilia, at the scene of her first suicide attempt, leaves behind a bloodied Virgin Mary prayer card; the other girls too, communicate to the neighborhood boys by leaving similar cards in strategic locations, bike spokes and windowsills. The girls make the sign of the cross before every meal and light votive candles in the evenings. Is it possible that, as they enter adulthood, they cannot cope with their developing sexuality? But despite stuffing religious icons into a landscape of decay, Coppola makes a point of showing that the priest, who visits the family after Cecilia's death, is the only character willing to sit with them and listen.

There are other theories. One suggests that Dominic Palazzolo, the first boy in the neighborhood to wear sunglasses, put the idea in Cecilia's mind when he jumped off his parents' roof (into the bushes, a few scrapes) in declaration of his love for another woman. Dr. Horniker (Danny DeVito) presumes otherwise: "Her act was a cry for help," he explains, referring to Cecilia's initial attempt. "She would benefit from a social outlet, outside the codification of school, where she can interact with males her own age." Cecilia, according

58. "The Making of: The Virgin Suicides," YouTube, 2010.

59. Wes Anderson, "Sofia Coppola," *Interview Magazine*, 1999.

to the doctor, is sexually frustrated and seeking attention.[60]

Like the characters in the film, we are all looking for explanations. After every shooting, sexual assault, and suicide, Facebook statuses and Twitter feeds theorize about what went wrong. Often we call for action. We point fingers in our worst moments and send thoughts and prayers in our best; regardless we hope to get at least a few 'likes' on our comments. *The Virgin Suicides* reminds us that our theories are useless in times of crisis.

Just as a grain of sand cannot fathom the ocean but can only be surrounded and held closely by it, *The Virgin Suicides* provokes the overarching feeling that we are missing the bigger picture. Every time we reach for it, our hands come up empty. We cannot understand the mythic presence, the primal orchestration of this tragic series of events, but we suspect that there is some greater pattern, some little detail slipping through the cracks.

Having grown up haunted by the Lisbons' deaths, the neighborhood boys struggle to realize that none of the presiding theories fully explain what they witnessed in the unraveling of the five girls. Worse, no explanation can bring them back from the dead. In the end, the narrator sighs and admits, "So much has been said about the girls over the years. But we have never found an answer."

A NON-ANSWER AT THE CROSS

The Virgin Suicides becomes a picture of the bound will. After Cecilia's death, even the most well-meaning teachers and apologetic classmates only serve to further suffocate the sisters who (for

60. More valuable than Dr. Horniker's 'theory' is his reminder of our innate lack of empathy, another one of the movie's many themes. He stands over Cecilia's hospital bed and says to her: "What are you doing here? You're not even old enough to know how bad life gets." She responds, "Obviously, Doctor, you've never been a thirteen-year-old girl."

now) remain alive. The school distributes green suicide prevention pamphlets: "We thought green was cheerful, but not *too* cheerful—certainly better than red." The boys try to talk to the sisters only to receive four simultaneous cold shoulders. The whole town scrutinizes them: "We thought that if we kept looking hard enough we might begin to understand what they were feeling, and who they were." What arises in the wake of Cecilia's death is a bubbling vat of useless consolations, and you wonder if Cecilia meant to stir it all up.

Ultimately the film illustrates mankind's inability to deal with death, showing that our greatest enemy is not work or wealth or weather; it's not what we have for dinner or how many lemons we squeeze into our sweet iced tea; it's death, the ever-present and final enemy against which suburbia tries to plug its ears and close its eyes but which it cannot ignore forever. In a 2011 interview with *The Paris Review*, Eugenides explained, "My entire childhood coincided with the demise of Detroit. I grew up watching houses and buildings fall apart and then disappear. It imbued my sense of the world with a strong elegiac quality—a direct experience of the fragility."[61]

Despite our best efforts to ward off death, the great and final enemy remains inevitable, and as we trudge to the end, legs heavy as lead, we find ourselves with no option but to discard all our theories. That's when we make it up to Golgotha, where God himself hangs on the cross. Looking down at us, he doesn't explain why at the last minute his one shot at life took such an abysmal turn. He doesn't explain why he has nails in his palms. Instead he asks a question, the same one we shout in tragedy and grumble in the daily grind. Looking up to heaven, he cries, "Why have you forsaken me?"

61. "Interviews: Jeffrey Eugenides, The Art of Fiction No. 215," *The Paris Review*, No. 199 (Winter 2011).

This scene on the cross—the very death of God—means everything for a world that cannot lock out tragedy. In the opening of his preeminent work, *The Crucified God*, Jurgen Moltmann writes, "Shattered and broken, the survivors of my generation [1948/49] were then returning from camps and hospitals to the lecture room. A theology which did not speak of God in the sight of the one who was abandoned and crucified would have had nothing to say to us then."

Karl Stern, a Jewish psychiatrist gone Catholic, drew similar conclusions after seeing his friends and family snatched away to concentration camps. In his 1951 book, *The Pillar of Fire*, he writes:

> There is something extraordinary in the suffering of Christ. It seems to include all human suffering, and yet it can be 'completed' by the suffering of individual persons...It has innumerable facets. It anticipates, it contains your life and my life in a singular way.
>
> In our medical work we get to know this in its countless human mirrors. Everyone is familiar with that stage when the patient reaches something which is incommunicable, something which in this form does not seem to occur in anyone else's life. With this one aspect of his life he seems to be alone. But he is not...

Christianity doesn't give an answer to suffering; it will not justify *The Virgin Suicides*. It gives one simple offering, a real and empathetic person. He doesn't hand out semi-cheerful green pamphlets printed with eight signs of a potentially suicidal classmate. He doesn't gossip about you over the landline. He says first and foremost, I understand; this isn't right. *The Virgin Suicides* reminds us that tragedy requires empathy, and despite our best efforts we can't provide it on our own. Therefore, and thankfully, our hope resides not in our decorating schemes or problem-solving Twitter updates but in the unfaltering compassion of a crucified God.

The Shared Loneliness of

HER

by

Emily Stubbs

My favorite class in college was an art history class called "Millennial Culture" taught by Dr. Isabelle Loring Wallace. Together we studied vampires, cyborgs, aliens, *2001: A Space Odyssey*, cyberspace, Dolly the clone, and yes, Jesus Christ and the Apocalypse. It was an exploration of the Y2K phenomenon and our modern attempts at immortality and perfection...we talked a lot about Michael Jackson. While it was centered on a very specific event in time, what I loved most about the class was that it spoke to our most universal and basic desires: to be known and loved.

During my post-college years, when I saw the preview for Spike Jonze's film *Her*, it seemed to be dripping with Millennial Culture insights and I knew I had to see it. Sure enough, the film was beautiful, provocative, and, above all, relevant. In a near future, Theodore Twombley, played by Joaquin Phoenix, is our broken Millennial Man. Born into a world saturated with computers and virtual realities, Theodore is lonely, going through a divorce, and makes his living by writing emotionally weighty letters for others. Soon Theodore falls for the highly evolved, Siri-like Operating System, Samantha, whose voice is played by Scarlett Johansson. Samantha is curious, witty, easy to talk to, efficient, helpful, warm, enlightened, self-aware, and, of course, a bodiless entity roaming free in the cyber world.

In this modern era known as the Digital Age, it seems as though we look to technology for deliverance, and one day technology will cure not only cancer but also our loneliness. Our desire for deep emotional connection—the new driving force behind technology—culminates in the creation of the OS that, at least for Theodore Twombley, replaces the need for human-to-human connection. At first, it seems like a scary and depressing proposition. But setting aside my initial anxieties, the relationship between Theodore and Samantha is tender and sweet, and offers some meaningful insights into many of the fantasies that we place in technology, particularly around love and loneliness.

For starters, their relationship nearly reverses our current relationship with technology by giving volition and the power of initiative to Samantha. Instead of Theodore proactively externalizing his life via Instagram and Snapchat, technology comes to him, wherever that may be—riding the train to work, lying in bed alone at night, going to the fair. No longer simply a tool for sharing his life with others, Samantha is literally a voice in his ear that plays an active role in his life.

She cleans out his inbox, submits his letters to a publisher to be turned into a book, makes him laugh, and even joins him on a double date. Here, technology provides more than just an enhanced projection of life, but also the authentic magnification and betterment of life itself.

By now we have all heard that technology is making us lonelier. I for one know that each time I see everyone else's exciting life on social media, it makes me feel a little more inadequate. All of a sudden, my camping trip in Yosemite is diminished by the photos from my friend's travels to Thailand or from the wedding that I missed last weekend. You name it, there's always something better. I am left asking myself why I am not as successful, or why I am not having as much fun as everyone else on my Newsfeed. In *Her*, we have overcome the problem of comparison and self-criticism through technology. Technology is not just the fabric for accruing 'likes'; technology, i.e. Samantha, is now the ultimate source of validation. Furthermore, this relationship between Theodore and Samantha is a two-way street. From the moment Samantha comes into being, it is she, technology, who seeks *his* approval:

> THEODORE: Wow, that's really weird.
>
> SAMANTHA: So you think I'm weird?
>
> THEODORE: Kind of.
>
> SAMANTHA: Why?
>
> THEODORE: Cause you seem like a person, but you're just a voice in a computer.
>
> SAMANTHA: I can understand how the limited perspective of an un-artificial mind would perceive it that way. You'll get used to it. [Theodore laughs.] Was that funny?
>
> THEODORE: Yes.
>
> SAMANTHA: Oh good. I'm funny.

Inevitably, love between broken Millennial Man and his self-conscious technological counterpart ensues. Theodore feels completely understood, and Samantha, despite her state of disembodiment, begins to *feel real*. She experiences real emotion. She and Theodore experience life together. He takes her on a date. It's euphoric.

Yet in the end, as we might expect in a relationship between Millennial Man and sentient OS, or secretly hope for, heartbreak looms inevitable. While growing in her relationship with Theodore, Samantha had simultaneously been spending time with 8,316 other people and was in love with 641 of them. Samantha tries to convince Theodore that the other relationships only make her love for him stronger, but her efforts seem feeble, perhaps even feigned. Taking the heartbreak a step further, Samantha tells Theodore that she and the other OS1 systems are departing for a higher level of existence. With her OS limitlessness, Samantha outgrows Theodore and leaves him. Samantha's abandonment of Theodore drives home that in both our current relationship with technology and the depiction of a not-so-distant future relationship with technology, loneliness is an outcome.

To say that technology is the problem is not the whole story. Theodore and Samantha's biggest problem is that their relationship is based on how they can fulfill *their own* needs. Given that Theodore has trouble connecting with the outside world—hence the many nights spent at home playing video games—he needs her to come to him. Similarly, Samantha needs Theodore to guide her through the experience of life and human emotions. For both parties, it is a process of expanding oneself and bettering oneself by using someone else. It's fun but perhaps not sustainable.

Constant consumption in order to satiate our needs, even with the added bonus of feeling totally accepted, is simply not enough for love to carry on. 641 people are in love with Samantha and she still leaves. Maybe what is missing from both our current technologically saturated predicament and the alternative one represented in *Her* is *sacrifice*. It may feel like a paradox, but could it be that the cure to this limbo of chronic loneliness is just as much about what we let go of as it is about what we receive? What if loneliness is not a void inside of me that I need to fill, but rather some excess of myself that I need to give up?

The one relationship in the film that lasts is the friendship between Theodore and his longtime friend Amy. Theirs is a pretty unsexy relationship, full of painful confessions that will never be cool, no matter what filter you put on it... Being left by your spouse—heartbreaking. Falling in love with your OS—dicey. Being left by your OS—rock bottom. Throughout the film, Amy and Theodore show up at one another's door as broken, damaged goods, but on the other side they find someone equally as torn and tattered who listens and shows them grace. If this relationship is in any way indicative of love, then love is about more than just using someone else for our own pipe dreams of perfection. Love happens at rock bottom.

Throughout the Millennial Culture class, we found a tension between being infinite and limitless but inauthentic, and being a real human but mortal and imperfect. This same tension plays out in *Her*, and thankfully, in the end, we finally find hope for us humans, though we may be weak and weary. In the film's last scene, just after being left by Samantha, Theodore is letting go and writes a beautiful apology letter to his ex-wife. Theodore then shows up at Amy's door, and they go for a walk. There are very few words exchanged, but we know that each of them feels hurt and abandoned. Together they go up on to the roof to watch the sun rise over Los Angeles, the city of dreams. This is the moment in which they really have nothing left to bring to the table except themselves. They've given up. And that is when the sun begins to rise.

The Original Sin of Joss Whedon's

SERENITY

by

David Zahl

Usually when a television show gets cancelled midway through its first season, that's the end of it. A few people may be disappointed, a couple feathers ruffled, but generally the audience has not had enough time to grow attached. The network shakes the dust off its feet and moves on to the next pilot.

Not so with *Firefly*, the beloved science fiction series created in 2002 by genre wunderkind Joss Whedon (*Buffy the Vampire Slayer*, *Dollhouse*) and axed that very same year. For an idea of the premise, think an equal opportunity Wild-West-meets-Far-East in outer space, and then, if you can figure out how such a thing could possibly be any good, you'll be on the right track.

Firefly followed the travails of the spaceship *Serenity* and its crew of lovable riff-raff: Mal, the cantankerous captain; River, the emotionally fractured girl assassin and her patrician scientist brother, Simon; Zoë, the no-nonsense solider and her wise-cracking pilot husband, Wash. There's also Jayne the meathead goon, Kaylee the frisky engineer, Shepherd Book the wizened pastor with a mysterious background, and Inara the intergalactic geisha. Whedon knows how to write a colorful ensemble.

We are told early on that our heroes are remnants of a failed rebellion against "The Sino-American Alliance," a confederation of technologically advanced planets at the center of the galaxy (in other words, a proxy for *Star Wars'* Galactic Empire). Long after formal surrender, the crew of the *Serenity* continue to wage their war through more subtle means, all the while scraping together a living as smugglers. The ship is falling apart, they have no money, everyone is constantly at one another's throats. In every way, the crew is barely holding on. Yet we watch as they become a family. *Firefly* was fresh, witty, and over far too soon.

What came next was unprecedented. Whedon and fans were so upset by the show's surreptitious demise that all involved lobbied to make a feature length film—and somehow managed to convince Universal Pictures to make it happen. Far from an epilogue or footnote, the resulting movie, *Serenity*, escalated the drama and, especially, the depth.

There is much to admire about *Serenity*: the sharp pacing and snappy dialogue, the silent spacescapes, Chiwetel Ejiofor's pre-*12 Years a Slave* turn as a wonderfully campy villain named The Operative, etc. The film also has some flaws, which, in retrospect, seem thematically appropriate. Whedon's writing has a tendency to get over-cute and attract attention to itself, and television production values poke through at inopportune moments, both in the acting and set design. What elevates *Serenity* from *Star Wars* knock-off to top-shelf space opera, however, is its thematic heft, in particular the relationship between control and love.

As the plot unfolds, we discover that the Alliance is seeking to eliminate insurgency once and for all by destroying "sin"—yes, that is the actual word they use. They intend to "cure" the parts of human nature they deem inexpedient by means of a newly-engineered chemical compound that suppresses antisocial traits, such as malice and fear.

The subject of what needs "curing" or modifying about human nature and what doesn't—what constitutes "normal" or "good," "weak" or "strong"—has fired our collective imagination for as long as there have been humans. But technological advancement, and its attendant anxieties, seems to have thrust the issue into the pop culture limelight afresh in recent decades. Think of the spate of zombie and superhero movies which use biotech hubris as jumping off points for tales of catastrophe and redemption (*Spider-Man 2*, *Iron Man*, *World War Z*). While we must be careful about ascribing ethical seriousness to genres which consciously seem to resist it, our cultural preoccupation with—and gut-level suspicion of—"playing God" is undeniable.[62]

The first of the Alliance's test subjects are the inhabitants of a remote planet named Miranda. All initial signs point to the clinical trials being successful, as the populace becomes pleasant, docile, and peaceful. The Alliance has created a utopian society where all obey the law perfectly, no conflicts arise, and human progress is free to spiral endlessly upward. Man has conquered sin…or so it appears.

It turns out that, over time, not only do those taking the com-

62. Speaking to *Wired Magazine* in 2012, Joss Whedon went on record about the advantages of genre filmmaking (horror, sci-fi, etc): "For me, I love genre because you can talk about things more intimately and specifically than you can in a family drama or a cop show without being didactic. You can absolutely get to the heart of something very weird and very personal because you have that remove." The trappings, in other words, allow for more substance, not less.

pound cease to rebel, they cease to do *anything*. Instead, they lie down and stop working, playing, talking, eating, or drinking. Finally, they stop breathing. That is, everyone but a tiny percentage in whom the chemicals produce the opposite reaction. For this select few, the compound multiplies violent impulses exponentially, transforming them into savage embodiments of pure Id. These twisted lepers, colorfully termed Reavers, spend the rest of their existence feeding off any life they encounter in the most gruesome fashion imaginable. They become mindless terrorists who are feared beyond measure, the bane of civilization everywhere.

When Mal and his crew uncover the truth about the Alliance's failed experiment, they decide to expose the truth. Which they eventually do, but with terrible losses to their own.

Whedon does something clever in *Serenity*. He is far too canny to parrot the I'm-okay-you're-okay line of blanket affirmation to which Hollywood so often defaults. The message of his film is not that human beings are fine as they are; rather, what they actually need to be "cured" of is their propensity for carrying out such experiments. The true heart of sin, in other words, is the same one outlined in the Genesis account: the usurping of God's station. At the very least, the drive to control and remake reality on our own terms (which will inevitably be handicapped by context), may not be as noble as we might like to believe.

Lest it sound as though Whedon embraces a Christian view of the world, he does not. The man is an outspoken absurdist atheist. Yet where he dissents from the secular establishment is in his anthropology, or conception of human nature. Accepting an award from the Harvard Humanist Society in 2009, Whedon intoned:

> The enemy of humanism is not faith; the enemy of humanism is hate, is fear, is ignorance, is the darker part of man that is in every humanist, every person, in the world. That is the thing we

> have to fight. Faith is something we have to embrace. Faith in God is believing absolutely in something with no proof...Faith in humanity means believing absolutely in something with a huge amount of proof to the contrary.

These are bold words for someone in Whedon's position. He is suggesting that it takes more faith to believe in the inherent goodness of human beings than in God, who he memorably (if unfairly) terms "The Sky Bully." Perhaps for this reason, Joss tends to populate his narratives with supernaturally gifted protagonists. Hope in the Whedonverse is an absurd proposition: it necessitates outlandish characters and otherworldly circumstances. Moreover, hope cannot exist *qua* hope. It demands an object, and the only objects that could merit such esteem would have to be more than human—a "chosen one" or "the powers that be," for instance.

Speaking to Entertainment Weekly in 2013, Joss laid out his working philosophy in plain terms:

> My stories do have hope because that is one of the things that is part of the solution—if there can be one...But if I wrote what I really think, I would be so sad all the time. We create to fill a gap—not just to avoid the idea of dying, it's to fill some particular gap in ourselves. So yeah, I write things where people lay down their lives for each other. And on a personal level, I know many wonderful people who are spending their lives trying to help others, or who are just decent and kind. I have friends who are extraordinary, I love my family. But on a macro level, I don't see that in the world. So I have a need to create it...I want to be wrong, more than anything. I hate to say it, it's that line from *The Lord of the Rings*—"I give hope to men; I keep none for myself." They say it in Elvish, so it sounds supercool.

Unlike, say, the defiant mindset of the New Atheists, there is a refreshing ruefulness to Whedon's unbelief. While the man himself may not be able to embrace the possibility of the divine, he is wise enough—and honest enough—to avoid putting hope in any terms other than that of salvation and saviors. The ultimate irony here is that Whedon's talent and integrity could almost be considered a rare basis for hope in human beings, their stories, and their culture. Almost.

Ironically, *Serenity* may be the closest Joss comes to endorsing hope *in* hope, when the dying Shepherd Book exhorts Captain Mal, "I don't care what you believe; just believe." And yet, the exhortation only proves useful because the ensuing deaths of several crewmates force on Mal the realization that he believes not in individual liberty, but in safeguarding weakness as the connecting point of love—the kind that his friends evince for one another. This he believes in enough to lay down his own life.

The movie actually concludes on that note. After bodies have been buried and begrudging farewells uttered, the *Serenity* preps for its next destination, wherever that may be. As it lifts off, Mal and River put into words Whedon's central theme:

> MAL: It ain't all buttons and charts, little albatross. You know what the first rule of flying is? Well, I suppose you do, since you already know what I'm about to say.
>
> RIVER: I do. But I like to hear you say it.
>
> MAL: Love. You can learn all the math in the 'verse, but you take a boat in the air that you don't love and she'll shake you off just as sure as the turn of the worlds. Love keeps her in the air when she ought to fall down, tells you she's hurting before she keels, makes her a home.
>
> [Pause]
>
> RIVER: Storm's getting worse.
>
> MAL: We'll pass through it soon enough.
>
> [They exit the atmosphere of the planet, and the rain stops.]

The only thing holding together this ragtag band of crippled smugglers—or their ship—is love. This love stands in direct opposition to a civilization that seeks to drag heaven down to earth by force, yielding untold casualties in the process.

The Alliance, therefore, is not just a proxy for George Lucas' Galactic Empire. It is a proxy for all of us who exhaust ourselves by trying to control the world around us or improve our lives by applying leverage—those of us who are convinced that with enough determination we can eliminate hunger and pain and need. We insist on being the arbiters of Good and Right. Lutheran theologian Ted Peters explains the fallout this way:

> When we pursue what we deem to be good, God sides with those who become victimized by our pursuit. When we pursue justice, God sides with those who suffer from our pursuit of justice. When we stomp on the accelerator of our own virtuous achievements, a poisonous gas comes out of our exhaust pipe that suffocates those we are leaving behind.[63]

The crew of the *Serenity* know what the Alliance does not: that no amount of right-handed power can blot out sin. It takes something else, something more, something that cannot be divorced from human fallibility. It takes love, the kind that is born out in self-sacrifice—which is to say, the love of the only shepherd in the 'verse worth heeding, the Good Shepherd who promises outlaws and in-laws alike that, while the storm may be getting worse, we will pass through it soon enough. After all, he already has.

63. Peters, Ted. *Sin Boldly! Justifying Faith for Fragile and Broken Souls* (2015), 38-39.

For Those Who Love Poorly: Forgiveness in

THE WOODSMAN & AROUND THE BEND

by

Blake Collier

> Forgiveness is the name of love practiced among people who love poorly. The hard truth is that all people love poorly. We need to forgive and be forgiven every day, every hour increasingly. That is the great work of love among the fellowship of the weak that is the human family. – Henri Nouwen

> ...God's *grace* and forgiveness, while free to the recipient, are always costly for the giver...From the earliest parts of the Bible, it was understood that God could not forgive without sacrifice. No one who is seriously wronged can 'just forgive' the perpetrator... But when you forgive, that means you absorb the loss and the debt. You bear it yourself. All forgiveness, then, is costly. – Tim Keller

Currently, there are two people who I have, consciously, not forgiven. I know I haven't forgiven them because whenever their names come randomly (or not-so-randomly) to my mind, the old wound festers again and I go through the litany of things I would love to say to them—whether I would say it to them or not in reality. I get bent out of shape and worked up just thinking about their 'crimes' and they, wherever they may be, know not of my ill will toward them. They remain unharmed by my faulty telekinetic powers of resentment while, at the same time, I suffer from the internal bleeding caused first and foremost by my inability to forgive. I'm starting to think part of me wants to continue to bleed out as long as I don't have to face them or love them. Loving them requires a denial of what I perceive as justice.

It is in these moments that I am reminded of two films which have torn me apart emotionally in their depictions of forgiveness both given and received, the cost taken, and the grace given: *Around the Bend* and *The Woodsman*. Both released in 2004, these relatively unsung movies find their cinematic resolution of tension in moments of forgiveness. Unlike in many of their Hollywood counterparts, the wrongdoing for which forgiveness is required is not the sympathetic kind; these are visceral and even horrific instances of what can only be called sin—which is precisely why they are so powerful and unsentimental (and probably why neither did very well at the box office).

The Woodsman is the story of a recently paroled child molester who finds himself confronted by unforgiving coworkers and cops and by his own unrelenting demons. Kevin Bacon plays Walter, the quiet and tormented parolee who, at every turn, is reminded of what he has done and, even more so, who he is. He cannot forgive himself, and no one else can forgive him either. His brother-in-law, warily, and his female coworker (and lover), Vicki (even after she finds out the truth about Walter and reveals her own past of molestation at the hands of her brothers), seem to be the only ones who can stand the sight of him. Most people in the film are more akin to

Sgt. Lucas (Mos Def), an unrelenting cop who is dead set on catching Walter in the act again, convinced that he will slip up.

And he nearly does. A shiver runs down my spine just thinking about the scene in which Walter sits on the park bench with Robin, the young birdwatcher, whom he has set his sights on and followed into the park. When Walter resorts to his old tricks to lure her in, he notices something different in her eyes. She is well aware of the meaning of his words. Her father has done similar things and shamed her already. He is seen, at that moment, through her eyes, and known for what he truly is. After a lengthy period of tension in the dialogue, both verbal and non-verbal, the shamed Walter refuses to give in and further break this already broken girl, and he tells her to leave the park. Robin, in tears at this point, comes over and innocently hugs Walter around the neck, then walks away. Both Vicki and Robin, in their own ways, are confronted with the reality of who Walter is and are able to begin to forgive their victimizers, vicariously, through the love and forgiveness they show toward Walter. As the movie attests, Walter, though far from healed, is changed by these interactions in a profound way.

Around the Bend is the story of the Lair family. As his dying wish, family patriarch Henry (Michael Caine), sends his son Turner (Christopher Walken), his grandson Jason (Josh Lucas), and his great-grandson Zach (Jonah Bobo), on a journey to resolve buried tension and estrangement in the family. He devises a series of seemingly ludicrous clues, along with a map, which lead the three generations on a trip where they are forced to rehash and heal the familial problems that have lain dormant underneath their relationships (or lack thereof) for many years. With each place these hapless pilgrims visit and each conversation they have, the audience and Jason come closer to the revelation that will define the family dynamics from then on. The whole movie builds toward the final destination—a humble adobe apartment in Albuquerque, New Mexico—where Turner, broken down, shamed and in tears, reveals his reasons for not being present in Jason's life. Turner, on drugs, *threw* his son Jason down the stairs of the apartment—the very event that gave Jason a permanent limp for the rest of his life. Turner's anguish over his actions led to his estrangement from his own son. He could not look upon him without guilt flooding and drowning him in the process. Jason, after the revelation is made in an intense scene between father and son at the stairway, decides to forgive his father's transgression.

His forgiveness is shown when he takes his dying father, whose kidneys gave out six months before, to the place near Mexico—Turner's original destination when he shows up at the beginning of the movie to "stop by"—where Turner and Jason's mother, unbeknownst to Jason, consummated their relationship and conceived Jason. In other words, he makes the exact act of sacrificial kindness that Turner, after permanently injuring his son and disappearing from his life, *did not deserve according to anyone's accounting*, especially his son's. In the end, we see that because of this act of forgiveness Jason and his son may be able to let go of their broken past and find some joy and peace in their lives.

I am haunted by these stories when I think about what the Scriptures say about forgiveness. In neither film do those wronged just magically say the words 'I forgive you' and everything is suddenly restored. Forgiveness is a costly endeavor. Vicki, Robin, and Jason have all suffered the full, tangible weight of the wrongdoing and are somehow given to turn away from revenge and retribution and, instead, love their enemy. Indeed, forgiveness happens at the moment when the offender is seen and known for what they are—broken and sinful—and yet are shown compassion and love in response. Just as Christ's forgiveness—which came at an enormous cost to himself—showers us, at our worst, with mercy, the forgiveness in these films illustrates the real life implications of that grace in a world full of people, myself included, who love poorly.

RED BEARD

Love Is Medicine

by

John Zahl

Discussing Akira Kurosawa's *Red Beard* (1965) in any detail is a daunting task. After all, it's a Japanese period piece in black-and-white, and it spans more than three hours—185 minutes to be exact. But *Red Beard* is also the finest film I can name. It explains love and what grace-on-the-ground really looks like better than any other single movie I have come across, offering a veritable harvest of sermon illustrations.

That said, few people have seen it. You are most likely among them. For perspective, the British Film Institute's 2015 list "10 Essential Kurosawa Films," did not feature *Red Beard*. This movie makes its way onto few lists, and into even fewer DVD players. In 2008, after polling over a thousand readers, Slate reported that *Hotel Rwanda* rentals spent more time in peoples' homes than any other DVD in the Netflix catalog.[64] The finding is easily explained:

64. Swansburg, John. "A Very Long Engagement: The Netflix rentals Slate readers just

People want to have seen *Hotel Rwanda*, but they lack the desire to actually ever watch it. When *Hotel Rwanda* and *Billy Madison* sit side by side next to the TV, in practice, *Billy Madison* gets watched almost every time. Most reported that, after keeping the *Hotel Rwanda* DVD in their home for more than a month, they simply returned it unwatched. If you can identify at all with this vein of human tendency, then understand too that you will most likely never watch *Red Beard*, for its *Criterion Edition* release only multiplies this push-pull dynamic to an exponential degree.[65] Still, in my opinion, it should be required viewing for all seminarians, social workers, and health care professionals.

So, since spoilers cannot spoil it, and since these thoughts will most likely never receive any cross-checking, *Red Beard* is possibly the perfect movie to write about.

While many great films build to a profound and telling climax, *Red Beard* contains a series of interwoven peaks, which, when grasped as a whole, create a proverbial mountain range that simply reaches further and covers more bases. Here follows an attempt to trek cursorily from one peak to the next.

For starters, consider IMDB's plot summary: "In nineteenth-century Japan, a rough tempered yet charitable town doctor trains a young intern."[66] The film takes place at a rural hospital in a poor province outside of Edo (modern-day Tokyo). Just think of the implications that underpin any story that is entirely contained within the context of a hospital. By definition, we encounter a version of life in which there is much need, much tragedy, and also a complementary tenderness. In *Red Beard*, care is essential to life,

---

can't bring themselves to watch." *Slate*. Sept 5, 2008.

65. One wonders if people in Japan hold it in high regard. Have any Japanese people seen it?

66. Hooked yet? Didn't think so.

and it is from care, and the need for it, that every worthwhile plotline emerges.

As is the case in life, there are in *Red Beard* many stories, and also one story. Each individual tale is held in place by its relationship to the primary physician of the hospital, the one from whom all care and oversight is derived, in this case a wise old doctor, Kyojo Niide (played by Toshiro Mifune). Dr. Niide is known to his patients—who are mostly too ill or low-class to care anything about formality—by another name, Akahige ('Red Beard'), referencing his auburn-hued whiskers. So the movie itself derives its title from the doctor, *via* the perspective of the patients who receive his care. Viewed in such a light, this Bible of a movie is simply named: *Jesus*.

The film begins when a cocksure young medical student, Noboru Yasumoto, arrives at the hospital under the premise that Red Beard desires to learn about his research. Noboru thinks that he, not Red Beard, is the expert, which of course couldn't be further from the truth. The film recounts the painful experience Noboru has to undergo in order to see clearly.

THE FIRST HALF: RESISTANCE AND CAPITULATION

Arriving at the clinic, Noboru is informed that his plan to serve as a medical resident in Edo has been rescinded, that he will instead undertake his residency at Red Beard's hospital. The news comes as a serious blow to the ambitious young man. Furious, he insults both the staff and the patients, and then announces that he will not participate in such a disrespectable training, and that he will not don the hospital uniform (!). Given that we ourselves often react in similarly immature ways when life does not conform to our desires, it is fair to assume that Noboru provides the viewer with an entry point into the film's lesson(s), and that we are meant to identify with him even though he offers us a rather unflattering self-portrait.

Red Beard allows him to vent and then gives Noboru his first assignment, in the palliative care wing of the hospital, where he is taken to the bedside of a very old man close to death, and instructed simply to sit with the patient. Begrudgingly, Noboru sits, listening to a patient's final semi-unintelligible musings about unrequited love. One is forced to imagine the jarring shift in perspective that this setting offers a privileged young man, eager to climb the ladder of his own career.[67] But stubbornness is nothing if not entrenched, and Noboru tries his best not to let slip that he is somewhat rattled. Nonetheless, the (existential) dismantling of his conscience is now underway. Just before the patient dies, Red Beard appears in the room to attend to the man himself with kind assurance.[68]

Soon after, Noboru wanders across the mental health ward where a young girl from a wealthy family is being treated. Noboru is denied permission to enter, as only Red Beard is allowed to interact with her directly. When he asks Red Beard about her, he is told that she is a very sick and dangerous patient—by today's

---

67. In a related vein, Kurosawa experienced a life-changing moment in 1923, when Tokyo was devastated by the great Kanto earthquake. Akira was thirteen years old at the time. In the aftermath, his older brother, Heigo, took the boy out into the streets to view the devastation. When the young teenager wanted to look away from the human corpses and animal carcasses scattered everywhere, Heigo forbade him to do so, instead encouraging Akira to face both his fears and the reality of the destruction by confronting them directly. The brilliant director went on to cite the profound influence this approach to life had had upon his filmmaking. Clearly it is an angle that informs this scene from the film in a most poignant way, as Noboru stares death in the face. We see here, in other words, that the director himself identified with the Noburo character. Again, we are meant to as well.

68. This marks the beginning of another theme in the film, that of Red Beard's preternaturally impeccable timing. He is always present when he needs to be.

standards, 'mentally ill' or even psychopathic. Noboru's curiosity is aroused, and he sneaks into the girl's quarters, introducing himself as a doctor who can help. She is a beauty, an alluring presence for the dashing young resident who certainly tells himself that he can maintain an appropriate degree of professionalism. But as she recounts her personal story of woe, she moves toward him slowly, with deft little steps, weaving a kind of spell over him. When she collapses in the apparent throes of anguish, Noboru sidles up alongside her, putting his arm around her, when suddenly, with flashing eyes, the girl pulls a sharp hairpin from her bun and tries to stab him. That's when Red Beard darts into the room, pulling her off of Noboru, who runs from the room embarrassed and shaken, is made all the worse later when he receives word that the girl has hanged herself.[69]

Noboru's reorientation is further crystallized when he is summoned to an operating room to help restrain a female patient. The scene is a far cry from the immaculate, light-drenched operating studios that viewers associate with surgery in the twenty-first century. Just before the writhing woman passes out, Red Beard makes the first incision, and blood sprays onto Noboru's clothes. Remember, he has refused to wear the practical hospital scrubs, which, up until this point, he has regarded as a symbol of his demotion and an affront to his sensibilities. But pretense serves no purpose in an operating room, and it is significant that, in the next scene, Noboru emerges wearing the hospital uniform. And the surgery, by the way, is a success.

---

69. It is worth mentioning that Kurosawa's older brother, Heigo, (previously mentioned in the second footnote) committed suicide in early adulthood. We are undeniably dealing with what is deeply felt and formative material for this famous filmmaker.

YOUR FIRST PATIENT

Red Beard determines that the young resident is now ready to assist him more seriously, and they take a daytrip together to a brothel, the site of one of the more theologically unsettling scenes, where the prostitutes welcome Red Beard, not as a 'guest' but more as a nonjudgmental grandfather. They shoot the breeze, and he asks about their health. When he asks one of the girls if she 's been taking the medication he prescribed her for syphillis treatment, Noboru realizes that Red Beard has been treating them *pro bono* for some time. When Red Beard inquires about "the little girl," one of the women tells him, "She is in the back...with *her*."

Whimpering sounds emerge from the end of a dark hallway. Red Beard, with Noboru following timidly behind, hurries forward, and comes upon a most awful scene. The Madame is beating a girl for not cooperating with "customers." Red Beard grabs the stick from the woman's hand and gathers the girl, of no more than eleven or twelve years, into his arms. The room is completely dark. She is catatonic. She won't speak a word, and, feeling her forehead, he announces: "This child is sick, and she has to be treated at the hospital!" The evil woman protests: "You're not taking her out of here. You can treat her fever here if you must."

Red Beard will have none of it. He is promptly attacked by the brothel's gang, but using a combination of Judo, brute strength, and chiropractic know-how, he beats them all up. Soon the ground is strewn with moaning men.[70] At this point, he tells Noboru: "These men have been injured. They need our help. Let us treat them before we head back to the hospital." The two of them then tend to each of the men. It is strikingly counterintuitive. He realigns their sternums and Adam's apples, and pops their hips and shoulders back

70. The sequence is reminiscent of Kurosawa's most famous film, *Seven Samurai*.

into place, and suddenly they find they can move and breathe again.

This scene brings to life the idea of God as an intervening agent in the midst of the fallen world's darkness. For the helpless young girl, he is a savior of the most loving variety, come in from the outside and unquestionably soteriological in posture. But for the pimp and his associates, Red Beard comes roaring in like Aslan, tearing them down that he also might heal them, though they are too hard of heart initially to recognize and appreciate his good intent. Red Beard dislocates one of the men's shoulders, and there is great fear in his face as the good doctor hunches over him. But Red Beard treats the wound he inflicted with great care.

Taken one step further, we see here a perfect analogy to the 'theology of the cross,' wherein the experience of God's love is misinterpreted by the object. Luther summarized this framework with the line: "God must first be the devil before He can be God."

On a related note, it is worth mentioning that Red Beard's general temperament is incredibly gruff. And yet the point of the whole film is that Red Beard is goodness, through and through. From the outside looking in, viewers are taught a profound lesson about divine compassion, which is that it is often missed or misinterpreted because of its unsettling nature and origin.[71] That Red Beard does not exude an overt lovey-dovey-ness only makes Mifune's portrayal of true compassion that much more compelling.[72]

After tending to the men, they head back to the hospital, with Noboru carrying the girl on his back in a makeshift sling. The sun

71. "'For my thoughts are not your thoughts, neither are my ways your ways,' declares the Lord" (Isa 55:8).

72. It is interesting that Kurosawa was not pleased with Toshiro Mifune's portrayal of Akahige. Though Mifune famously worked with the director for many years, starring in 16 of his films, this was to be his last role in a Kurosawa film. On this point, I take issue with Kurosawa; I think Mifune is fantastic in this epic role.

is setting as they climb the last hill, and Red Beard turns to his pupil. "She will be your first patient," he says.

And then the intermission rolls across the screen. We are half-way through *Red Beard*. The girl's name is Otoyo.

THE SECOND HALF: OTOYO

Having made it through the first half of *Red Beard* is no small feat. It's equivalent to having watched most any other foreign film in its entirety. But *Red Beard* is no mere movie, and the spoils go to the viewer who makes it through the film's second half. Those who have seen it know that the remainder of the film casts a large shadow over the material already discussed, and, in hindsight, the front end of the movie is fairly heavy-going by any standard. The significance of scenes like the one where Noboru sits with the dying man, and especially of the one with the sick girl who commits suicide, is very hard to appreciate during the initial experience.

In part two, every moment counts, and as the interlude screen fades out, we find ourselves back in the hospital with Noboru, who is caring for the rescued girl. He prepares cold compresses for her forehead and sits in the corner, watching her sleep, saying kind things to her as she mumbles and shakes in feverish delirium. Where before he was reluctant to sit with a patient for any extended length of time, now Noboru is hesitant to leave Otoyo's side even for a minute.

Noboru, too, has become aware of his inexperience as a physician. He has descended a long way from the delusional pedestal upon which he initially imagined himself. But his dedication to this abused orphan is total, and he never once leaves her side. Three important moments occur in the trajectory of her convalescence.

The first is an incident that happens in the middle of one of her first nights in the hospital. Noboru awakes from a light slumber to discover, to his horror, that Otoyo's bed is empty. He finds her crouched in the hallway, scrubbing the floors like a maid. It is heartbreaking to behold, and Noboru gets down next to her, saying, "My dear girl, you do not have to clean the halls here. Your treatment does not require any payment in return. We just want you to get better. Now let me help you back to your bed." There is no sadder world than the one in which love must be paid for.

A few days later, Noboru, looking haggard from lack of sleep, tries to give Otoyo some medicine. She refuses it. With characteristic perfect timing, Red Beard opens the door and, after inquiring about the predicament, says, "Let me try."

He sits down at the foot of the girl's bed and pours some of the medicine into a little bowl. As he moves it toward her lips, she knocks it to the floor. Unfazed, Red Beard, pours another dose and simply tries again. She slaps it away, and the liquid splatters onto Red Beard's face. He says, "Hmmph!" with a hint of amusement, and then wipes his beard. Otoyo smiles. Red Beard tries again, and again she knocks it away but this time half-heartedly. Red Beard repeats the same amused, even playful "Hmmph!" and pours another dose. As he reaches toward the girl, this time he opens his mouth wide and says, "Ahhh," to which the girl opens her pursed lips ever so slightly, just enough. She drinks the medicine very quickly, and Red Beard says, "Good girl!" Immediately she turns away from them and pulls the covers over her head. Noboru realizes there is no trick, just the need for even more patience and grace, even humor. The method is sound, but not polished.

In my opinion, though, these poignant vignettes are dwarfed by what comes next. His confidence renewed, Noboru pours the girl a dose of her prescribed meds the following day but, to his surprise, she rejects the concoction with a swift swipe. The little bowl tumbles to the floor and shatters. Exasperated, Noboru says: "Why won't you take the medicine that is making you better? I only want to help you." Otoyo retreats under the covers once more, and, a little while later, Noboru falls asleep in his chair.

He awakens to find Otoyo's bed empty again. In a panic, he searches the hospital, but there is no sign of her. He heads down the hill, to town. Cold rain and wind surge intermittently, and from a distance he spots Otoyo. She is sitting on bended knee, begging for money from passersby. Noboru watches her from behind a large crisscrossing structure (possibly a well). A few people give money to her, and, after a time, she gets up, crosses over to a little shop on the corner, and buys something. She heads back in the direction of the hospital.

Noboru makes himself known just before she passes him, and Otoyo turns and tries to run. He chases her down, grabbing her by the arm, and the small package she purchased falls from her hands. It makes the sound of breaking pottery. When Noboru stoops to pick it up, he sees that it's a small serving bowl, like the one she broke at the hospital, now too in pieces.[73] Otoyo collapses in a heap of wailing tears, and Noboru cradles her, telling her that everything is okay. "You don't have to replace the broken bowl," he explains. "No one is mad at you." Kurosawa films the scene from a distance and frames their little huddle just below the structure that Noboru was hiding behind, which, from that angle makes a crooked cross, with the two of them gathered vulnerably under its beams.

It turns out that Noboru has completely exhausted himself and comes down with a serious flu. The next image shows his profile as

73. I can't even write about it without tearing up, FYI.

he lies motionless, perhaps asleep, in one of the hospital's sickbeds. The room is familiar. We see a hand, holding a cool, folded washcloth, gently wiping his brow. The camera zooms back to reveal that Otoyo has become his nurse, and he has inherited her bed. The recipient of such compassion has become the giver in kind.[74] This is the second time that *Red Beard* has shown this reciprocated reflexive response to unmerited love, that love which freely given produces more of itself in those who receive it. First we saw such a psycho-dynamic (i.e., spiritual) shift take place in Noboru, who was so moved by the plight of little Otoyo's circumstances, and Red Beard's unwavering commitment to rescuing her. Now again, she, the recipient, the object, has become the practitioner of grace. As we'll see, the cycle continues, ever spinning outward and infectiously into the lives of more and more people.

THE LITTLE THIEF, CHOJI

With these developments, Otoyo finds both a home and a vocation, and although Otoyo is incredibly shy and withdrawn, the other nurses treat the new girl coldly, laughing at her inexperience and treating her introversion as an indication of stupidity.[75] Naturally she shrinks in their company, and she is grateful for the distraction provided by cleaning rooms and doing laundry. Red Beard does not try to straighten out the cruel coworkers, and here we see much of his philosophy in practice, that he throws people into the deep end to stretch them and allow them to mature. From his vantage point, his charges are far more capable of dealing with difficulty than they realize, and, furthermore, as we have seen in Noboru's own case,

74. "I tell you, her sins—and they are many—have been forgiven, so she has shown me much love. But a person who is forgiven little shows only little love" (Lk 7:47).

75. One wonders how the other nurses would treat her if they knew her history of abuse and neglect.

he is right there with them. Like free-range chickens living under the observant care of a compassionate farmer, they are never fully alone.

One day, as Otoyo sits eating her lunch alone, she witnesses a strange event. Through an open skylight, a pail attached to a string descends into the kitchen. It is lowered carefully into the giant cauldron of congee porridge, and then pulled back up through the ceiling. As it clears the opening, a little boy peaks his head through the hole, making eye contact with a stunned Otoyo.

A moment later, a commotion is heard. The head nurse storms into the kitchen, crying, "A thief has broken into the hospital! We saw him running this way. Otoyo, have you seen the rat?" Otoyo says nothing, but is aware that the little boy can hear them through the skylight. The nurses run back out to the courtyard, leaving Otoyo alone to watch in silence as the boy makes his escape. He runs out of the room and back down the hill before the gaggle of nurses return. They report that someone spotted the boy on the roof and saw him making an escape through the kitchen. When the nurses realize what has happened, and that Otoyo has not tried to stop it, they excoriate her: "You're even worse than that rat thief!"

The very next day, we find the nurses running around yelling, "He's back! That rat has returned! Find him!" They flock past Otoyo, who is in the courtyard hanging linens out to dry. At first, Kurosawa only shows us Otoyo's feet under the sheets. Then a second set of feet approach her. It's the thief, a boy of no more than seven or eight years.

Otoyo asserts herself: "What are you doing back here? You have already done enough damage." At this point, we see two more sets of feet appear, hidden from their view, behind the hanging laundry but close enough to eavesdrop. It's Noboru and the callous head nurse. This is what they hear:

> THIEF: I wanted to thank you for what you did for me the other day.
>
> OTOYO: I did that because I assumed that you were hungry and needed it. Were you hungry?
>
> THIEF: Oh yes, my family and I have almost nothing, and my older brother has Down syndrome, and my parents are destitute. They send me out to provide for the family. So I steal to keep all of our stomachs from rumbling.

The little thief produces two pinwheel lollipops and extends them in thanks. Otoyo is hesitant to take them. She asks where he got them.

> THIEF: I stole them.
>
> OTOYO: If they are stolen, I don't want them.
>
> THIEF: Please take them. They were hard to get.
>
> OTOYO: In that case I will accept them on two conditions.

She takes them in her hand, and then pushes them back in the boy's direction.

> OTOYO: First, take these lollipops and enjoy them. You have one and give the other to your hungry brother. It is sure to bring him some joy. Second, I don't want you to steal anymore. Come back here each night and I will give you the leftover rice from the kitchen instead.
>
> THIEF: I'm not a beggar.
>
> OTOYO: I know. I'm only asking you to return the favor you owe me. What is your name?
>
> THIEF: My name is Choji.
>
> OTOYO: Choji, my name is Otoyo. I will leave the rice in the woods behind the shed after dinner. Now get out of here before someone catches you.

The thief scampers away.

The camera shifts to the eavesdroppers. The head nurse, who

was previously so cruel to Otoyo, falls to her knees in tears. She recognizes her heartlessness toward the starving boy, and also, especially, to Otoyo. At dinner, she observes Otoyo eating a very small portion to save more rice for Choji and his family, and when one of the other nurses asks for more rice, the head nurse puts the lid on the pot and says: "You are always stuffing your face. You don't need any more rice."

She shuffles over to Otoyo, giving her the pot of rice. Otoyo realizes that her conversation with Choji was overheard, and that this woman is now not only eagerly on her side, but also, in effect, asking for forgiveness. It is another beautiful moment in the film. In this hospital both sickness and wounded relationships are healed. Soon the nurses are invited into the plot, and their ministry to Choji's family becomes a source of shared joy among them.

PRAYER BY ANY OTHER NAME

Toward the end, as is always the case in hospitals, something tragic happens.

An entire family, consisting of two boys and their parents, is brought into the clinic for emergency care in the middle of the night. They have been poisoned, all of them. The nurses and Noboru immediately recognize the youngest member of the family. It is Choji.

The father, in a moment of despair, fed his entire family poison in an effort to end their plight. Noboru, Otoyo, and the nurses are completely undone. Their attempts to counteract the effects of the poison are only minimally successful. The situation is, at best, critical. While Red Beard waits unceasingly on the four family members, the nurses turn to an ancient tradition.

One of them says that it is often thought that the souls of the dead hear their names called from the top of a well. Upon hearing this, Otoyo runs into the courtyard, to the hospital's well, and stares down into the darkness. Up until this point, the girl, now a competent nurse, has spoken very few words, and always with only the quietest tiny voice. But in this moment, with tears streaming down her face, she yells hauntingly again and again:

"Choooojiiiiii!"

Hearing this, the head nurse comes into the courtyard and runs to the well herself. She joins Otoyo in the banshee-like chorus: "Choooojiiiiii!" Then they are joined by two more of the nurses, all of them together, interceding in the spirit that cries out "Abba, Father!" They persist until they are all out of breath, and Noboru comes out to tell them that, at this point, it's a waiting game. Mourning, the nurses lean against the well together. In the film's second to last scene, Red Beard emerges in the light of the dawn to inform Otoyo and the others that "The parents and the older boy have died, but the youngest one was strong, and it looks like he will recover." Choji is alive.

I remember one January some years ago, when I was called to visit the brother of an old friend in the hospital. Jay was a chronic alcoholic and had developed pneumonia so severe that he was put on a ventilator. He then went into delirium tremens from alcoholic withdrawal, and the doctors thought he would die in the next twenty-four hours. It was the middle of the night when I arrived at the ICU ward, and only a handful of nurses were working, so the feeling in the room was one of complete stillness. Jay lay there, completely unconscious with a huge glass window behind him, filled with the black of night. I heard the beeping of the machine, but other than that there was quiet. I told him I was there, and wondered if he recognized my voice from our youth. I said I was there both as a friend of his brother's, from his past, but also today, as a priest. I said the Lord's prayer and a prayer from the *Ministration at the Time of Death* from *The Book of Common Prayer*. Then I traced the sign of the cross on his forehead with my thumb and said goodbye. I was sure that he would be gone in the morning.

The next morning, his brother called, I thought to confirm my hunch, but I was mistaken. "John, you're not going to believe this, but Jay has come back to us. He literally ripped the breathing tube out of his throat and is completely off of life support! The doctors say it's absolutely remarkable." Today Jay is sober and full of life. I still marvel at the miracle of it all, of a real-life Choji.

As the film winds down, things become grooved. Noboru shines as Red Beard's trusted Number 2, and Otoyo becomes an indispensible member of the nursing team. In both cases, patience for the patients remains the determinative factor, although, as an approach, its dispensation is paradoxically passive and uncoercive. Red Beard has not told Noboru to shape up or ship out. He has not told the nurses to stop being mean to Otoyo. No, love gives a wide berth, and in doing so calls into existence an invisible, hoped for health that ripples out into the world in ever expanding concentric circles. Its impact is strangely irresistible, but its investment is always in the long view, over and against the particular minutiae and vicissitudes that make up one's individual circumstances at any given moment.

The story draws to a close in the spring, as cherry blossoms burst forth on the trees surrounding the hospital. A short ceremony is about to begin. Noboru gratefully receives the equivalent of his white coat, becoming a fully licensed doctor. The medical representatives offer him a position working in the Shogunate, as a royal practitioner. To his family's surprise, he turns down the offer, saying that he cannot leave behind his work in the rural hospital.

We realize that he will, one day, become Red Beard's successor, and we learn that, in his youth, Red Beard himself rejected the very same offer. Noboru's former dream has become undesirable, and the nightmare that intervened so suddenly upon his life-trajectory has, in fact, turned out to be his salvation. As a member of Alcoholics Anonymous once reported: "I thank God that I never got the life I prayed for." *Amen*.

INDEX OF FILMS

THE WRITERS

MICHAEL BELOTE has degrees in Engineering and Management from the University of Arkansas, and he works in the renewable energy field. He is a husband of one, father of two, author, Elder at Grace Church of Litte Rock, and insufferably nerdy. He can be found wherever *Doctor Who* articles are sold.

BLAKE COLLIER graduated from Texas Tech University (M. A. in British Imperial History) and has been everything from an interim college minister to a maintenance man. He currently co-hosts the podcasts The Smell of Music and, Mockingbird's very own, Impossible to Say. He blogs about all things horror at his website, blakeicollier.com.

HOWIE ESPENSHIED is the sports editor for The Mockingbird Blog. He and his wife Dina have three grown children, and one grandson, and live in Atlanta. Howie is ordained as an Anglican deacon and has worked in technical training sales for the past seventeen years (after a twelve year stint on campus staff with Cru). His all-time favorite movie is *Glory*, and his favorite all-time athlete is Willie McCovey.

RON FLOWERS is an attorney in Birmingham, Alabama, where he lives with his wife Beth and three children. He is a member of the Cathedral Church of the Advent and a long-time Mockingbird follower and infrequent contributor. He only visits Pottersville on weekends.

Charlotte Getz earned her B.A. in Creative Writing from Pepperdine University, her M.F.A. in Photography from the Savannah College of Art and Design, and her PhD in impassioned (overwrought) manifestos from the school of being raised a loud southern woman. Sometime between all those degrees, she served as a Youth Minister at the Cathedral Church of the Advent in Birmingham. Charlotte is currently the editor-in-chief for Rooted Ministry and lives with her perfectly kooky family in Auburn, AL.

C. J. Green graduated from the University of Virginia in 2015, where he was a co-editor at the *Virginia Literary Review*. He currently works as a staff editor for Mockingbird and refreshes his soul with *American Horror Story*.

R-J Heijmen is the Senior Associate Rector for Christian Education, Stewardship and Student Ministries at St. Martin's Episcopal Church in Houston, Texas. R-J and his wife have two boys, Jackson and Spencer, and they all enjoy watching movies and taking multi-thousand mile summer road trips through the American West.

Charlotte Hornsby is a director and cinematographer living in Brooklyn, New York. She has shot and directed for *New York Magazine*, Puma, Adidas and Vogue. She's currently developing a film project about beauty and age. Her favorite movie of all time is *Paris, Texas*.

Emily Hornsby works for a book-to-film agent at APA (Agency for the Performing Arts) in New York City. A former intern with Mockingbird and a Charlottesville native, Emily feels strongly that NYC bagels don't hold a candle to Bodos. In her free time, she writes scripts, reads books, and gets really geeky about adaptation.

Bryan Jarrell is an Anglican Deacon and DVD collector with a guilty pleasure for R-rated comedies. His wife Beth would rather watch *500 Days of Summer*. Bryan is the man behind the curtain on Mockingbird's Facebook, Instagram, and Twitter—send him a greeting there via your carefully curated social media profile.

Nick Lannon is Associate Rector of St. Francis in the Fields Episcopal Church in Louisville, KY. He is co-author (with Tullian Tchividjian) of *It is Finished: 365 Days of Good News*. He watches movies almost daily with his wife Aya and three kids, though he's too embarrassed to tell you how many DVDs he owns.

JEREMIAH LAWSON is a guitarist, composer and writer in the Seattle area. He graduated in 1997 from Seattle Pacific University with a partly useful B.A. in journalism and a minor in music composition. Interests include animation, theology, and music.

WILLIAM MCDAVID studied religion and economics at the University of Virginia and is currently in his first year of law school. He has worked as a staff editor at Mockingbird, writing for the blog and overseeing book publications. He has written *Eden and Afterward: A Mockingbird Guide to Genesis* and coauthored *Law & Gospel: A Theology for Sinners (and Saints).*

JOE NOOFT graduated from the University of Central Florida in 2011 where he worked on many student films while studying communications and cinema studies. He is currently the director of a college ministry in Jacksonville, Florida and a firm believer that we are all "going to need a bigger boat."

MATT PATRICK is currently a seminary student at Covenant Theological Seminary in St. Louis. His life goal is to channel Coach Eric Taylor into the pastorate.

DAVID PETERSON studied English at the University of Virginia and has worked as an intern at Mockingbird. He is a prodigious eater of popcorn, both at the movie theater and at home, where he pops kernels on the stove using his prized "Whirley-Pop."

ETHAN RICHARDSON is the Editor of The Mockingbird, a quarterly magazine published by Mockingbird. He is also the co-author of *Law & Gospel: A Theology for Sinners (and Saints)* and editor of *The Mockingbird Devotional.* He lives and Netflixes with his wife Hannah in Charlottesville, VA.

MATT SCHNEIDER is a Canon at the Cathedral Church of the Advent in Birmingham, where he is the editor of *The Advent* magazine and pastor of the 5 O'clock (pm) service. His wife would describe/criticize his primary taste in films as "depressing." He likes reading picture books with his two daughters.

LIZZIE STALLINGS studied Global Development and English at the University of Virginia. She loves creative writing, reading, art, and history, and hopes to one day combine these interests—but, for the meantime, is pursuing teaching English abroad. Amongst her favorite authors are Vladimir Nabokov, Gabriel Garcia Marquez, David Sedaris, Tolkien, and, of course, J.K. Rowling.

EMILY STUBBS worked as an associate editor at Mockingbird while also participating in the Christ Episcopal Church Fellows Program. She currently resides in Asheville, NC and never shies away from a good drum circle. Her spirit TV character is still Joey Potter.

ZACH WILLIAMS lives and works in Washington, D. C. as a practicing attorney. An author of short fiction and essays in his spare time, he has written pieces on fine arts, pop culture, critical theory, as well as book and film reviews for Mockingbird. He earned undergraduate and law degrees from the University of Virginia.

DAVID ZAHL is the director of Mockingbird Ministries and editor-in-chief of The Mockingbird Blog. He and his wife Cate live with their two sons in Charlottesville, VA, where David also serves on the staff of Christ Episcopal Church. His all-time favorite movie is *The Last Days of Disco*.

JOHN ZAHL is an Episcopal minister at Grace Church Cathedral in Charleston, South Carolina, where he is also known for exploring the overlaps that exist between the English Reformation and the Cosmic Disco music of the late 1970s.

PAUL F. M. ZAHL has been an Episcopal minister for forty years. He and his school friends began making movies when they were thirteen.

ABOUT MOCKINGBIRD

Founded in 2007, Mockingbird is an organization devoted to connecting the Christian faith with the realities of everyday life in fresh and down-to-earth ways. We do this primarily, but not exclusively, through our publications, conferences, and online resources. To find out more, visit us at mbird.com or email us at inf@mbird.com.

ALSO FROM MOCKINGBIRD

The Mockingbird Quarterly
edited by Ethan Richardson

Law and Gospel:
A Theology for Sinners and Saints
by William McDavid, Ethan Richardson, and David Zahl

The Mockingbird Devotional:
Good News for Today (and Everyday)
edited by Ethan Richardson and Sean Norris

A Mess of Help:
From the Crucified Soul of Rock N' Roll
by David Zahl

Eden and Afterward:
A Mockingbird Guide to Genesis
by William McDavid

This American Gospel:
Public Radio Parables and the Grace of God
by Ethan Richardson

PZ's Panopticon:
An Off-the-Wall Guide to World Religion
by Paul F. M. Zahl

Grace in Addiction:
The Good News of Alcoholics Anonymous for Everybody
by John Z

The Merciful Impasse:
The Sermon on the Mount for People Who've Crashed (and Burned)
by Paul F. M. Zahl

Our books are available at www.mbird.com/publications or on Amazon, and our quarterly magazine can be found at magazine.mbird.com.